IMAGES
of America

PUEBLO

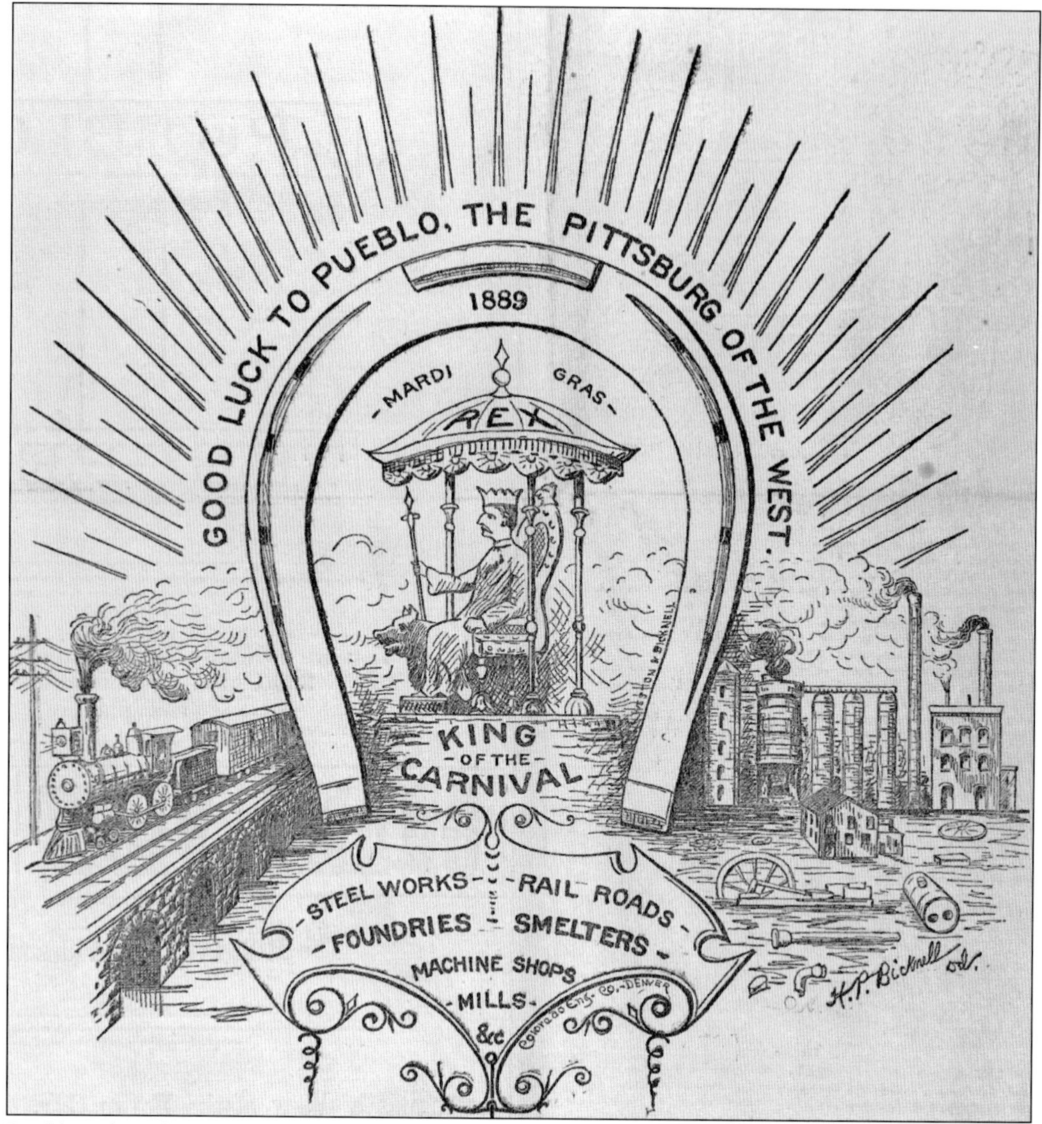

Pueblo ushered in the Gilded Age in 1889, when the January 1 edition of the *Pueblo Chieftain* proudly declared Pueblo as "the most prosperous town on earth!" The Board of Trade of Southern Colorado prospectus reported that real estate values in Pueblo had doubled in the previous year and were forecast to double again in 1889. The etching shown here was published on February 27, 1889, and depicts Pueblo's grandeur with the growth of the railroads, steelworks, and smelters. It also documents the Mardi Gras celebration. (*Pueblo Chieftain*, drawing by H.P. Becknell.)

On the Cover: A crowd arrived on foot, on bicycles, and in carriages to see the newest models of automobiles in 1915. This gathering occurred in front of the Star Journal Building and the Vail Hotel at Grand and Union Avenues. The Vail Hotel was only four years old; it was built in 1910–1911 by John E. Vail, founder of the Star Journal Publishing Company. In 1978, the Vail Hotel was listed in the National Register of Historic Places. (Special Collections Department of the Pueblo City-County Library District, PH-P-360-03-001.)

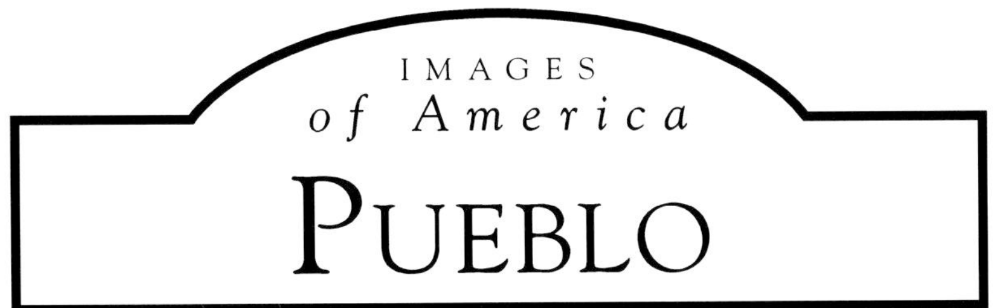

Charlene Garcia Simms, Maria Sanchez Tucker,
Jeffrey DeHerrera, and the Pueblo City-County Library

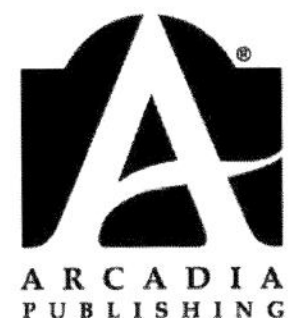

ISBN 978-1-4671-2414-0

Published by Arcadia Publishing
Charleston, South Carolina

Printed in the United States of America

Library of Congress Control Number: 2016953534

For all general information, please contact Arcadia Publishing:
Telephone 843-853-2070
Fax 843-853-0044
E-mail sales@arcadiapublishing.com
For customer service and orders:
Toll-Free 1-888-313-2665

Visit us on the Internet at www.arcadiapublishing.com

To my husband, Edward Terrones Simms, the journey continues
(CGS)

To my mom, Angelina Sanchez, my inspiration
(MST)

To my inquisitors, Deatrice, Violet, and Maverick,
who want to know everything about everything
(JD)

To all the people who passed through Pueblo and
added to its diverse and interesting history

Contents

Acknowledgments

The history of Pueblo is important to the entire state of Colorado. In 1874, Pueblo almost became the territorial capital, with a vote passing in the territorial house but not in the senate. Its rich history is comprised of stories and events related to people from all ethnicities and walks of life who made it possible to tell a fascinating story. We hope we have captured a glimpse into the struggles and triumphs that have made Pueblo the diverse and thriving community it is today.

We are grateful to the following people and groups who donated, collected, and preserved the images and history included in this book in order for us to share and capture the true heartbeat of Pueblo's past: Bob Simonich, historian; John Korber, historian; George Williams, historian; Pueblo County Historical Society; librarians assigned to the Special Collections Department (previously known as Genealogy and Western Research) of the Pueblo City-County Library District (PCCLD), who collected and preserved thousands of historical photographs and records over the last 100 years; the *Pueblo Chieftain* and its journalists and photographers who captured many stories and images that will live forever; and all the authors who wrote books and articles about Pueblo.

We thank Jon Walker, executive director of the PCCLD, who saw the importance of undertaking this project; Tammi Moe, archivist librarian, who made sure all images were of the highest quality for reproduction and gave us sound advice on other matters; beta readers Heraldo Acosta, PhD, Jane Carlsen, Bob Craig, Ken Gardner, Megan Hedberg, Deborah Martinez-Martinez, PhD, David Sandoval, PhD, Mike Thomason, and Jeff Tucker; and our special collections support staff—Tabitha Davis, Jose Ortega, Megan Petersen, and Crystal Talley. Special thanks go to George Williams, who wrote the introduction.

All images, unless otherwise noted, are from the Special Collections Department at the PCCLD, including *Pueblo Chieftain* articles. An identification number follows each image. This is not a comprehensive history. If you have more interest in Pueblo's history, please visit the PCCLD special collections department or the PCCLD website (pueblolibrary.org), which contains more digital images and more detailed history.

INTRODUCTION

The histories of the Pueblo area and those who have lived in or visited the area since prehistoric times are extensive and diverse. Fortunately, many of these histories have been recorded in text and on drawings, glass negatives, and film. Researchers have also been willing to expend a great amount of time and effort to clarify or expand the known information and investigate possible other histories.

Private citizens throughout the city and county of Pueblo and various governmental institutions have demonstrated their dedication to preserving the overall history of the Pueblo area for more than 13 decades. This has been accomplished in many ways, including but not limited to the following:

- Cooperative efforts of all types
- The formation of numerous privately funded/operated societies, associations, and organizations—which often maintain a museum or office—to preserve and add to the records of a specific part of Pueblo's history, such as archaeology, ethnicity/genealogy, preservation/identification of historic buildings, industry, mental health, etc.
- Supporting the efforts of tax-supported functions and the establishment of historic preservation commissions
- Churches providing space and sponsoring/conducting activities to preserve and share the histories of Pueblo's many ethnic and religious groups
- The publicly and privately funded publication of information about a historic subject or event

Throughout the years, Pueblo's public library has been the major depository and source for historical information of all types, and the members of its excellent staff have been and remain a source of great assistance.

We who have an interest in preserving and sharing the history of the Pueblo area sincerely appreciate the efforts of the Robert Hoag Rawlings Public Library Special Collections Department staff and everyone else who contributed to the research and production involved in creating this unique historical record.

These efforts have provided an impressive collection of historic images with informative captions that persons of all ages can learn from and enjoy and refer to countless times in the future.

—George R. Williams for the Pueblo County Historical Society

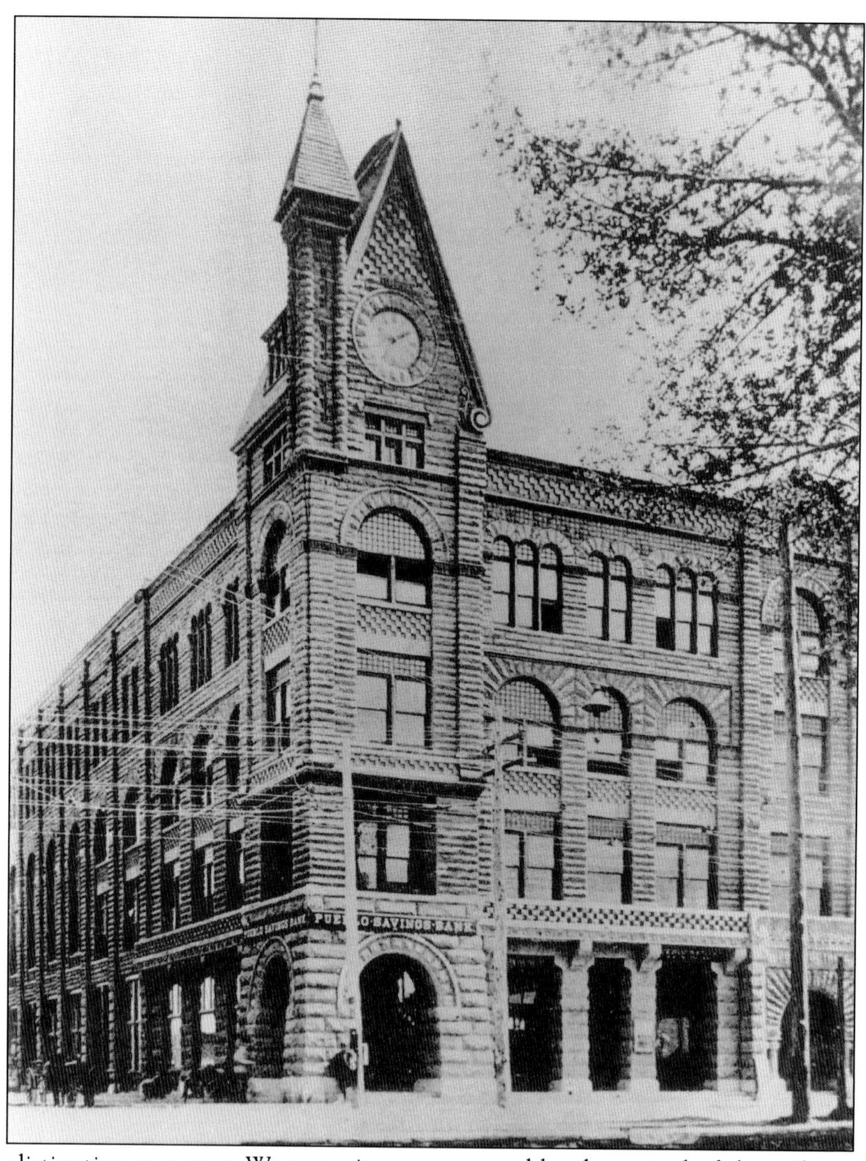

Pueblo's distinction as a great Western city was actuated by the arrival of the railway in 1872; Pueblo was finally integrated into the system of travel and trade that led to the disappearance of the American frontier. Business enterprise was the most distinguishing characteristic of Pueblo during these formative years, and capital investment weighed heavily on the future of the region. Attracting productive citizens, creating revenue streams, and increasing property values were the priorities of investors. An 1891 volume of the *Colorado Journal of Industry* states: "The material wealth of Pueblo increased daily in the latter years of the nineteenth century, giving rise to one of the most important manufacturing and commercial centers of the west. As an advertisement of the resources, progress, prosperity, and prospects the Board of Trade was born; fostered by the most substantial business men of Pueblo." American business tycoon Andrew McClelland financed the iconic building (pictured), which emphasized wealth and stability. The Board of Trade of Southern Colorado's inaugural event—an honorary reception and banquet for the Colorado congressional delegation—took place at the Grand Hotel in 1891. This caption was written by Tammi Moe, archivist librarian. (PH-P-38-03_001.)

One

Early History

Many diverse groups have influenced the history and growth of Pueblo. The first inhabitants of the region were Native Americans who traversed the foothills and camped at the confluence of the Arkansas River and Fountain Creek. The first European nation to fly a flag in the area was Spain, which retained control from the 1600s until 1821. French fur-trappers were in the area by 1763.

In 1779, New Mexico governor Juan Bautista de Anza led a campaign into southern Colorado to remove the Comanche, who were portrayed as treacherous to travelers and villages while protecting their own interests. When the United States negotiated the Louisiana Purchase with France in 1803, the American government remained in a dispute with Spain about the southern border of the United States. This dispute was resolved with the Adams-Onis Treaty of 1819, which designated the Arkansas River as the international boundary between the United States and Spain.

Mexico gained its independence from Spain in 1821, and Mexico's northern frontier opened for trading with the United States, which Spain had previously prohibited. El Pueblo Trading Post was established in 1842, and among its founders were Joseph Doyle and George Simpson. By 1848, the two-year Mexican-American War had ended with the signing of the Treaty of Guadalupe Hidalgo, and Mexico ceded half of its land to the United States. This moved the border south from the Arkansas River to the Rio Grande in south Texas.

Only a few years later, in 1854, tragedy struck on Christmas Eve when a party of Utes and some Jicarilla Apaches attacked the occupants of El Pueblo. This conflict resulted in the deaths of 12 New Mexicans and four Utes who waged the attack. The event discouraged new settlements in the surrounding area, and El Pueblo trading post was abandoned.

The gold rush of 1858 brought many people to Colorado. Some of these people settled in the Pueblo area and established Fountain City east of Fountain Creek. The city of Pueblo was established across the creek from Fountain City during the winter of 1859–1860.

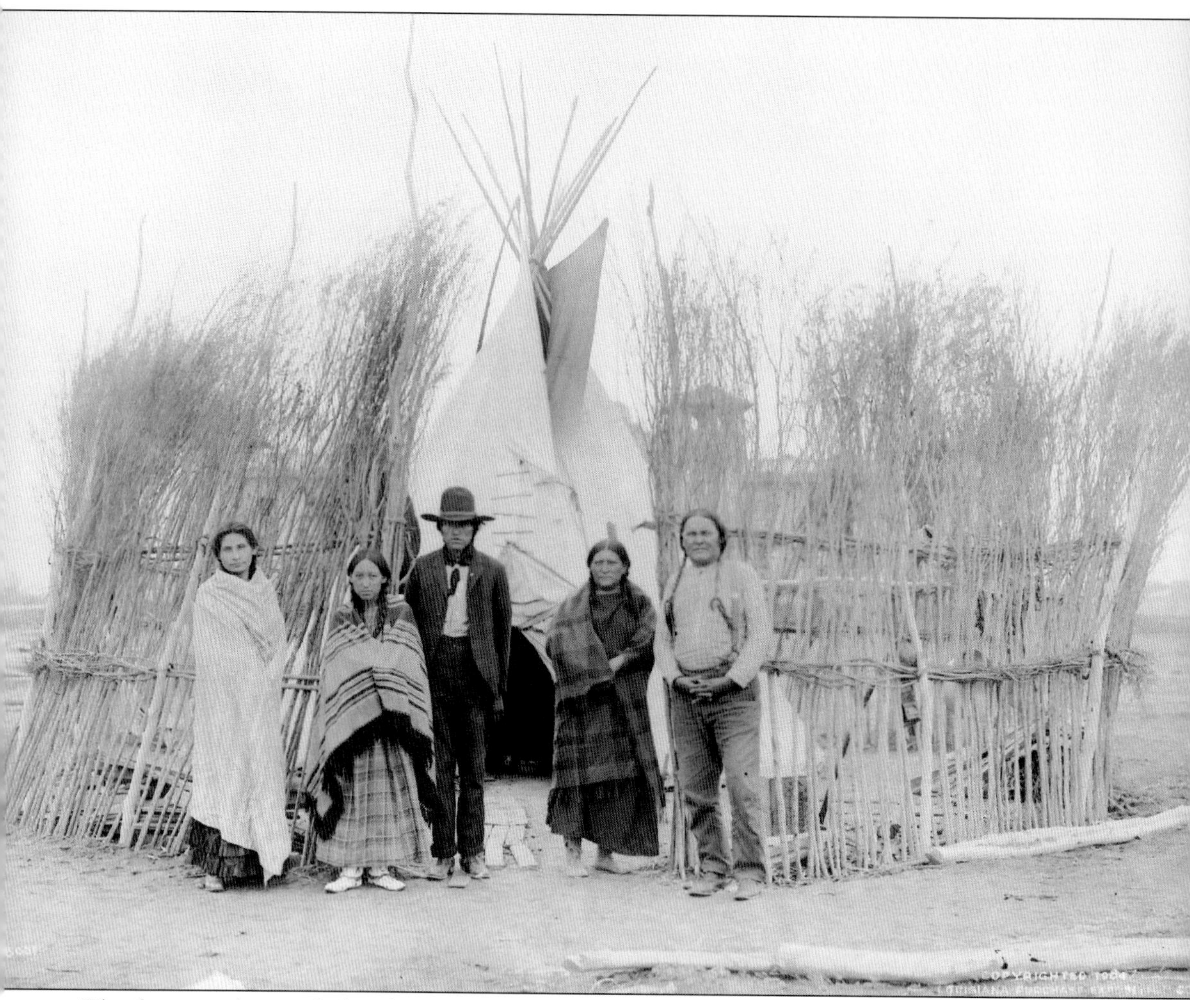

The first people to inhabit the area of Pueblo were Native American groups whose livelihood depended on the land. Tribes in the area included Apache, Arapaho, Cheyenne, Comanche, Kiowa, Pawnee, and Ute, all of whom traded with one another. When the Spanish introduced horses to North America, this allowed the Indians to travel greater distances. They also traded with the Spanish and, later, with the Americans. Arapaho Indians, pictured here in an unidentified location, knew Pueblo's eastern landscape very well, and when Fountain City was founded, the settlers traded with them for several necessities. In time, the cultures clashed, and conflict ensued over the land and its resources. It took many treaties to finally bring peace, first with the Spanish and then with the Americans, which resulted in the Native American tribes losing many of their traditions, land, and lives. (Library of Congress LC-USZ62-132398.)

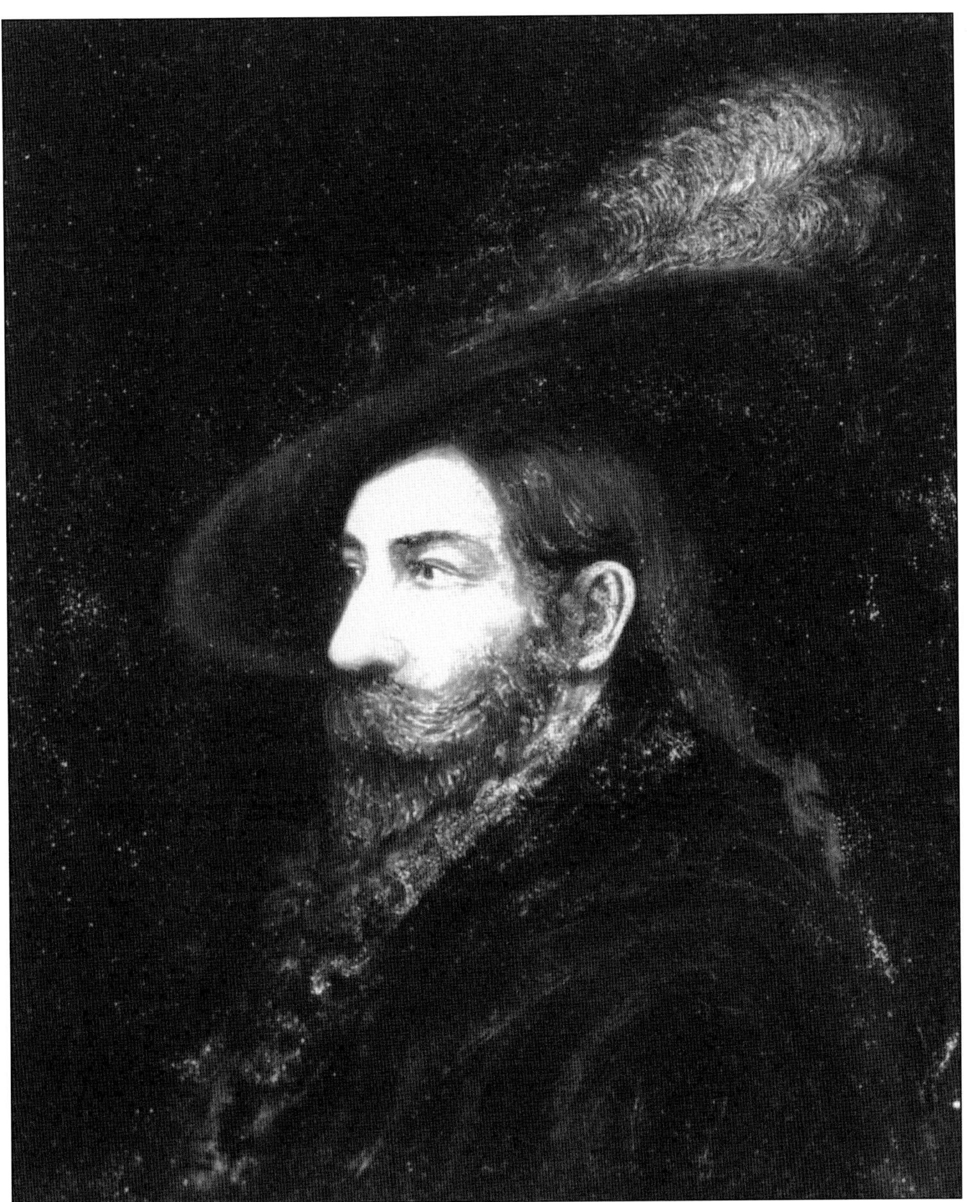

In September 1779, Juan Bautista de Anza, governor of New Mexico, led a military force that included Utes and Apaches along the western edge of the Sangre de Cristo Mountains into the headwaters of Fountain Creek. They encountered the Comanches led by Chief Cuerno Verde (Green Horn) and commenced a running battle, continuing south past the Arkansas River to the base of the mountain named for Cuerno Verde. On September 3, a decisive battle ensued in which Anza's troops killed Chief Cuerno Verde and several of his men. For the next 10 years, Anza negotiated broad treaties for peace, one of which the Comanche signed in 1786. In July 1787, Anza organized a group of men from Taos, armed with tools, to help the Comanche establish a settlement on the Rio Nepeste (Arkansas River) near a spring called San Carlos de los Jupes. In less than a year, the Comanche abandoned the settlement because a woman died there and they saw it as an omen. (Palace of the Governors Photo Archives, New Mexico History Museum/ Department of Cultural Affairs.)

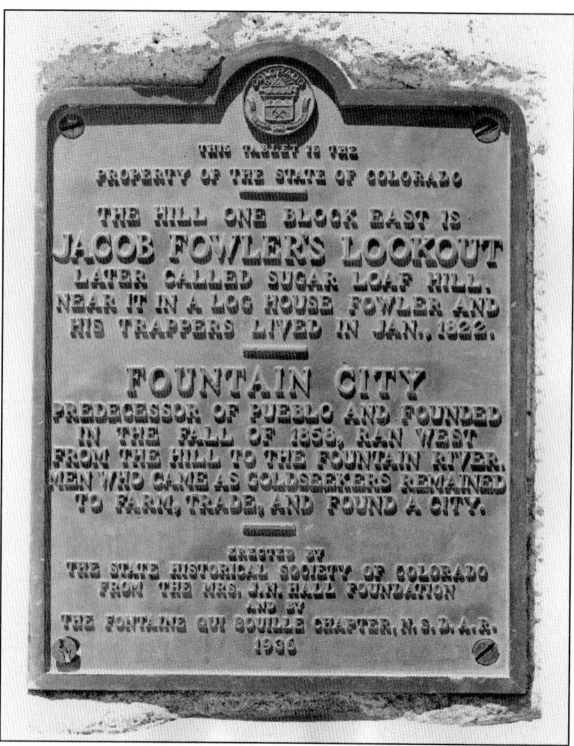

This historical marker explains that in 1822, explorer Jacob Fowler established a post—Jacob Fowler's Lookout—on a hilltop northeast of the confluence of the Arkansas River and Fountain Creek. The first structures at the site included a horse pen and a three-room house, both of which were used for about a month. These are the first structures positively identified as being in what became Fountain City and, later, Pueblo's Eastside neighborhood. (PH-P-318-06-003.)

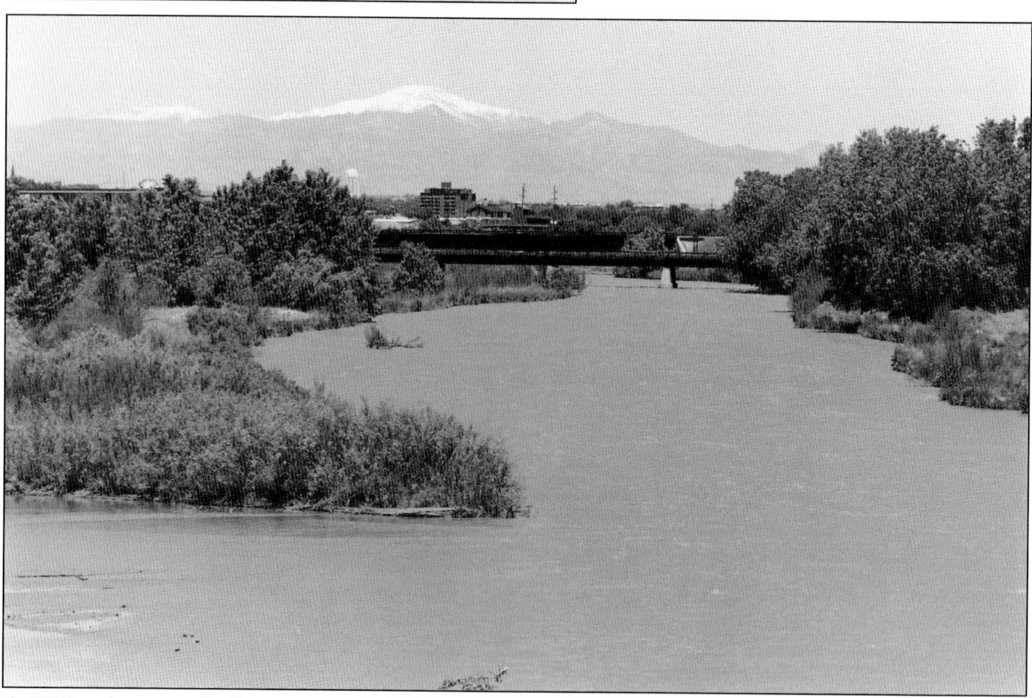

A 1970s photograph shows a view of Pikes Peak from the confluence of the Arkansas River and Fountain Creek. The Tabeguache Utes called the mountain "Tava," and the Spanish called it "El Capitan." Today, the mountain is named after Zebulon Pike, whose expedition explored the region between 1804 and 1806. (Pikes Peak Library District; photograph by Myron Wood.)

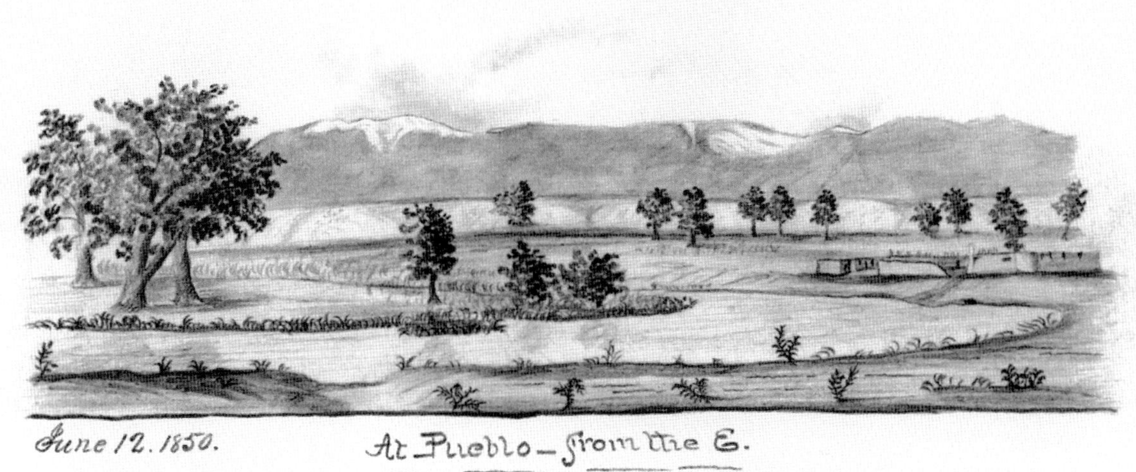

In 1842, El Pueblo Trading Post was built a few miles above the junction of the Rio Nepeste (present-day Arkansas River) and the Fontaine-qui-Bouille (present-day Fountain Creek). Several men pooled their money and formed partnerships to build the trading post. Some of these men were from the eastern United States and had arrived in Taos, New Mexico, years earlier where they became Mexican citizens, and many married New Mexican women. The fort was built by adobe masons from Taos who produced the handmade bricks, while others provided the carpentry. Women then finished the walls with a layer of soft adobe by spreading it with their palms, a Spanish process called *embarrar.* Author Janet Lecompte states that "without the women's presence, the places the men built would have been mere trading posts." The women had great influence in building, trading, hunting, and farming methods. For entertainment, they also held weekly dances called fandangos. This sketch was drawn by William Quesenbury on June 12, 1850, from a vantage point to the east of El Pueblo Trading Post, perhaps from a rise now known as Goat Hill. (Nebraska Historical Society.)

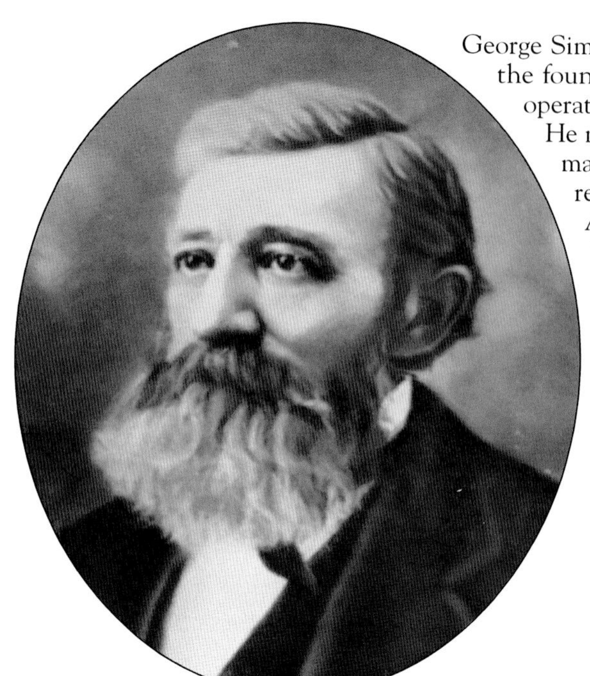

George Simpson, pictured here, is considered one of the founders of El Pueblo Trading Post. He later operated stores in Pueblo, Denver, and Trinidad. He married Juana Suaso, sister of Cruzita who married Joseph Doyle (pictured below). Early residents of El Pueblo were Robert Fisher, Alexander Barclay, Mathew Kinkead, Teresita Sandoval Suaso (mother of Juana and Cruzita), Francisco Conn, Joseph Mantz, Dick Wooton, and James P. Beckwourth. (PH-B-398-01_001.)

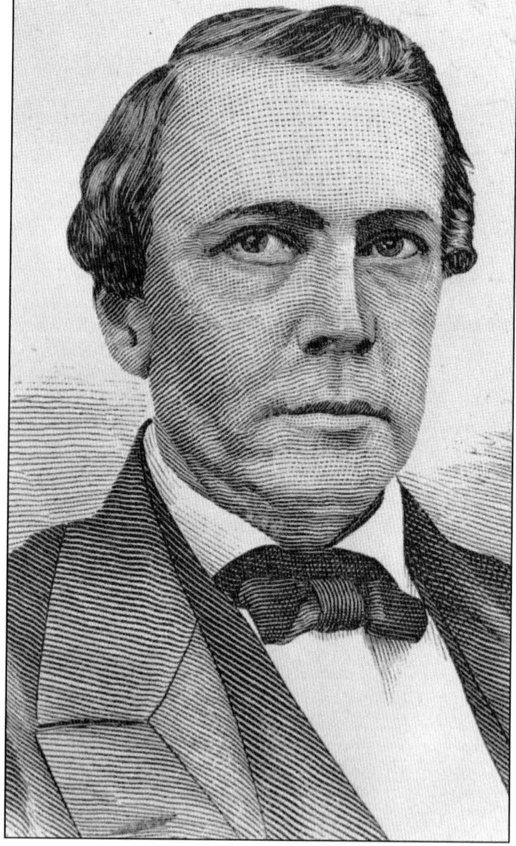

Joseph Doyle, one of the founders of El Pueblo and considered the richest man in Colorado Territory, became a territorial legislator. Doyle purchased two square miles of the St. Vrain/Vigil land grant in 1859, located in the Huerfano River valley, where his workers planted and harvested the best crops they could. On March 1, 1864, while attending a legislative session in Denver, he suffered a heart attack and died. (PH-B-127-01_001.)

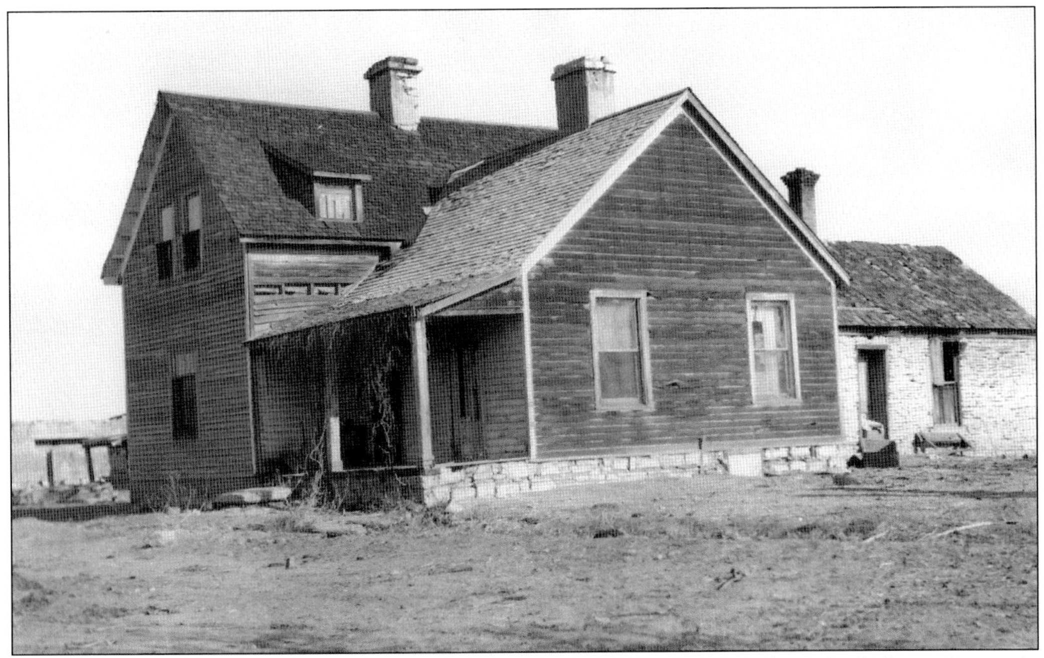

Pictured on the Doyle ranch is a two-story clapboard house that was furnished elegantly, made of lumber from the East, staffed with many servants, and painted white, which Doyle called Casa Blanca. There was also a large store, post office, schoolhouse, flour mill, a wagon and blacksmith shop, and houses for his employees. (PH-C-114-05.)

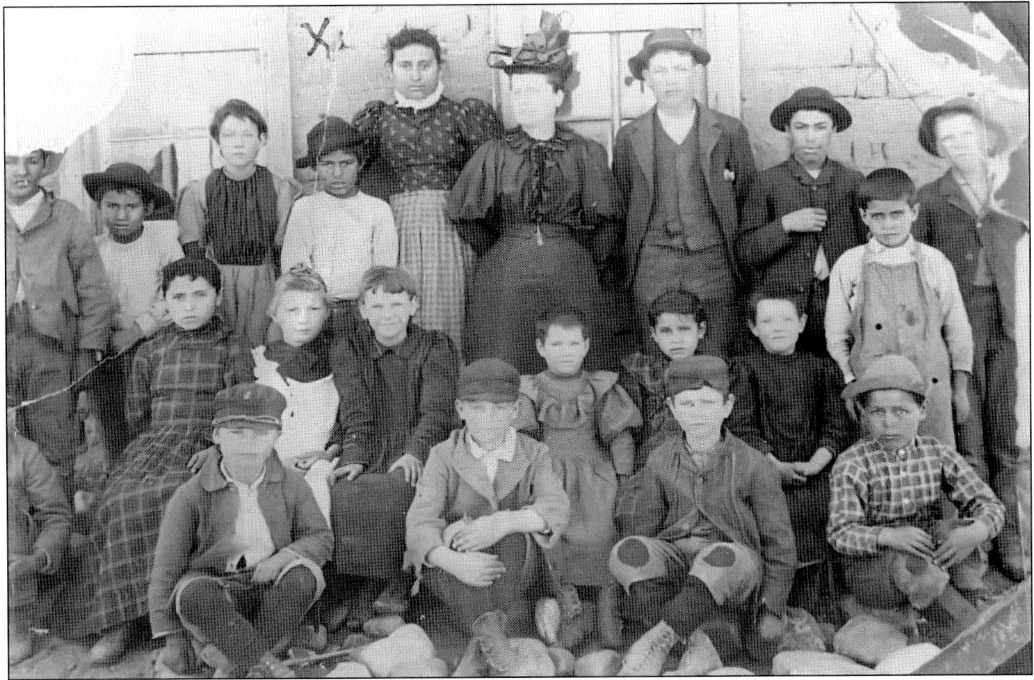

The school Doyle built was one of the oldest one-room schools in Colorado. Doyle had brought O.J. Goldrick, one of Colorado's first schoolteachers, to tutor his children. Pictured are unidentified teachers and children who attended Doyle School in the 1890s. (PH-C-114-04-001.)

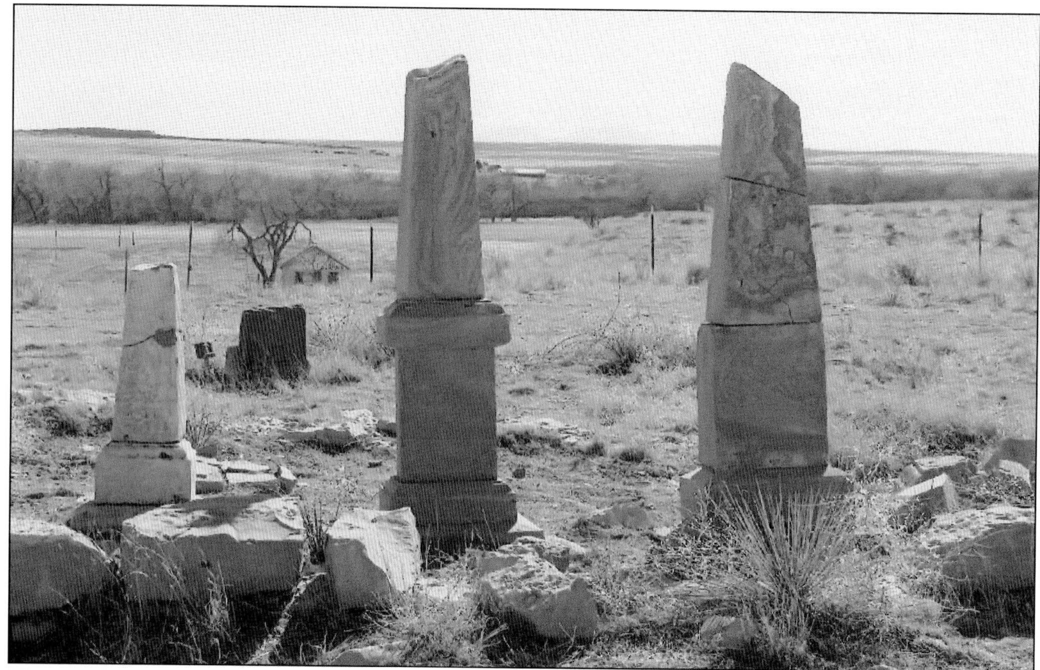

The Doyle Cemetery, shown here, is a family burial plot located southeast of Pueblo on a hill near the Doyle School. In 1987, Joseph Doyle's grave was vandalized by grave robbers. In 1993, the skeletal remains were reinterred with full observances and a 21-gun salute. The skull was never found. The cemetery is in a beautiful setting, and on a clear day the Spanish Peaks are visible. (Charlene Garcia Simms.)

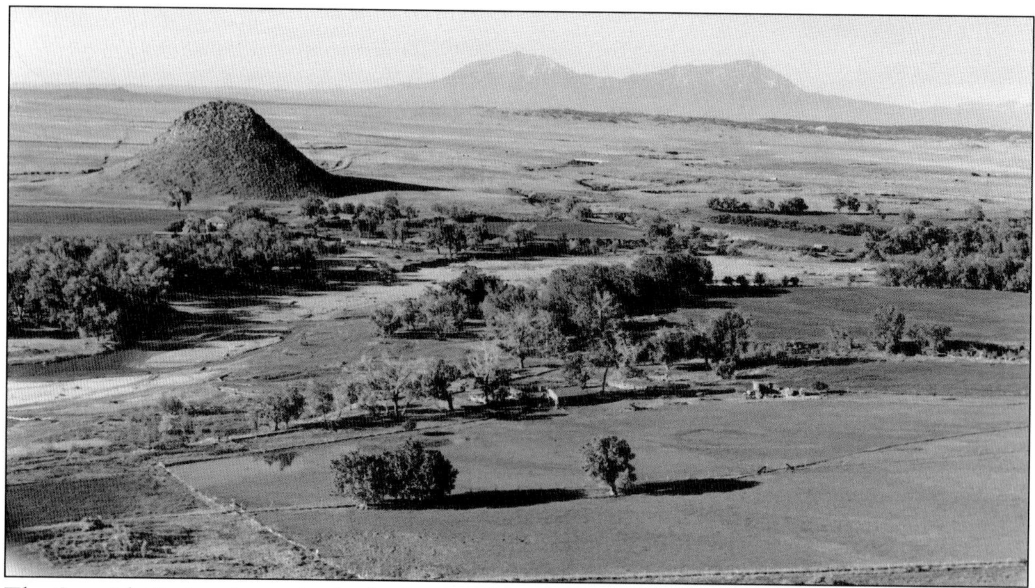

The Spanish Peaks, shown in the background, are among the most important landmarks south of Pueblo. The Ute Indians named them Huajatolla ("Wa-ha-toy-a"), meaning "Breasts of the Earth," a metaphor for sustenance from the Ute creation story. In 1821, the Santa Fe Trail was established with the peaks as guideposts for nearby wagon routes. Huerfano Butte stands alone to the left. (Pikes Peak Library District; photograph by Myron Wood.)

Explorer John C. Frémont made four expeditions into Colorado seeking a transcontinental railroad route. On his second expedition in 1844, Frémont recorded that on the banks of the Arkansas were a "number of mountaineers." Frémont stated they had married Spanish women in the valley of Taos, had collected together, and occupied themselves in farming, carrying on at the same time a "desultory Indian Trade." (PH-B-158-01.)

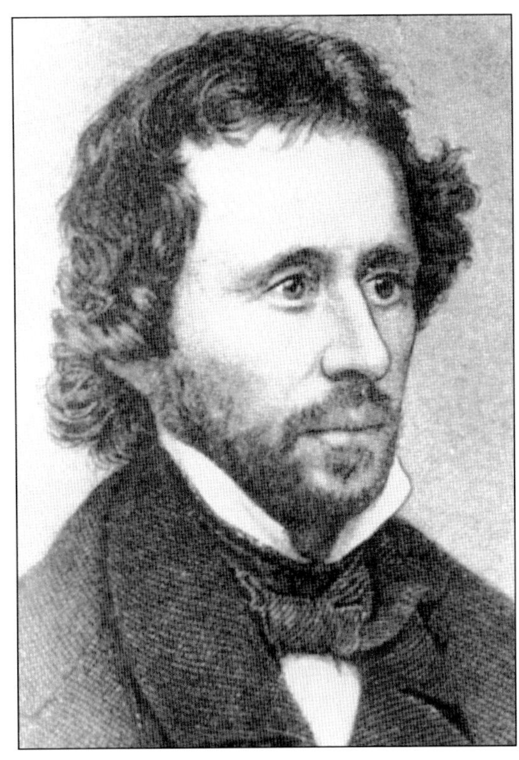

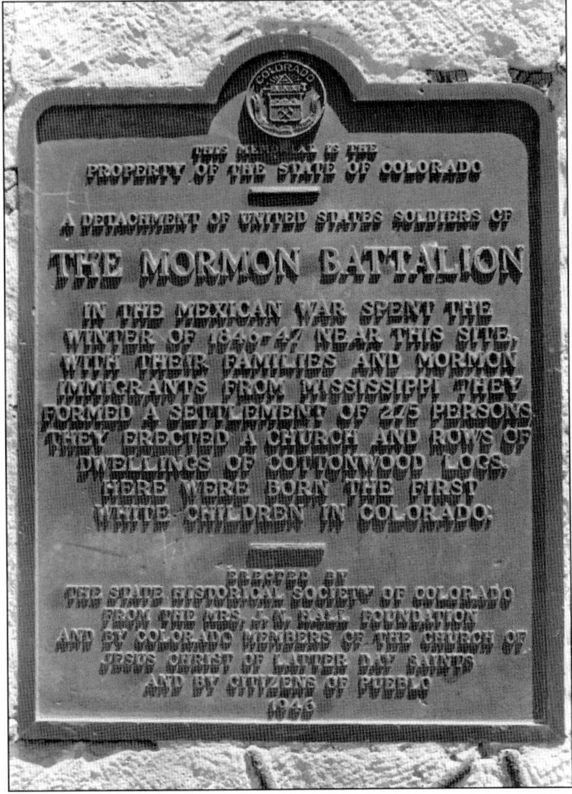

A historical marker relates that from August 1846 to May 1847, a group of Mormons, on their way to Utah, lived about half a mile from El Pueblo Trading Post. They were joined by invalid soldiers from the Mormon Battalion, initially formed to fight in the war with Mexico. The group learned irrigation practices from previous settlers along the Arkansas and later resumed their travels in the spring of 1847. (PH-P-322-02-001.)

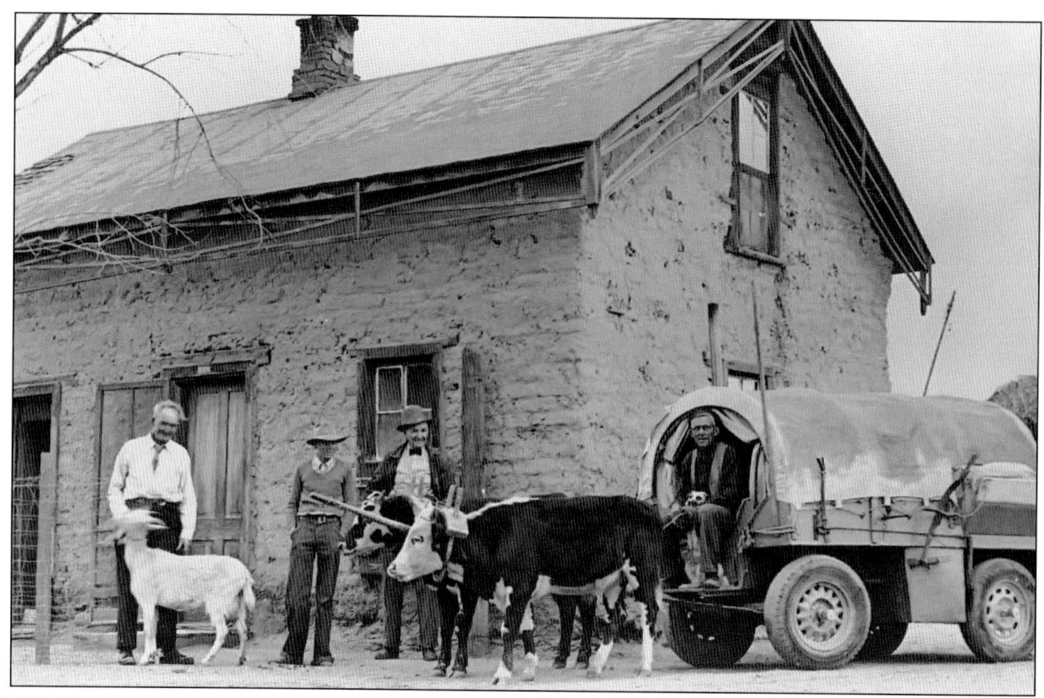

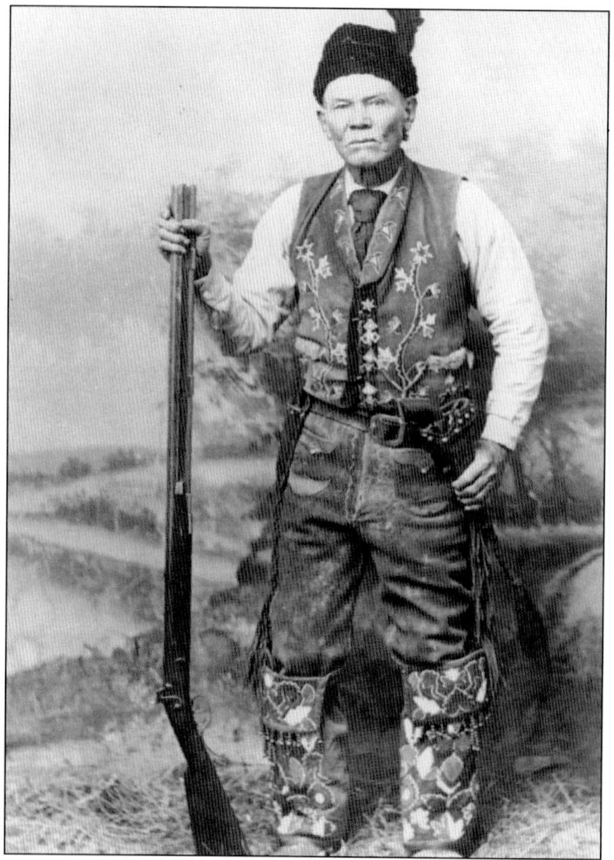

This house is believed to have been built in 1850 and was known as one of the oldest houses in Pueblo. The house was made of adobe, of which many of the first structures in Pueblo were built. Although one-story is more common for adobe structures, this is a two-story example. In the 1980s, the house was razed when Joplin Avenue was widened. (PH-P-506-02-001.)

Tom Tobin was born in Missouri around 1823, and traveled to Taos at 14 with his half brother Charles Autobees. A mountain man and scout, Tobin took part in several events around Pueblo. He is infamous for tracking the fugitive Espinoza brothers near the headwaters of the Cucharas River in the Sangre de Cristo Mountains southwest of Pueblo. (PH-B-446-02.)

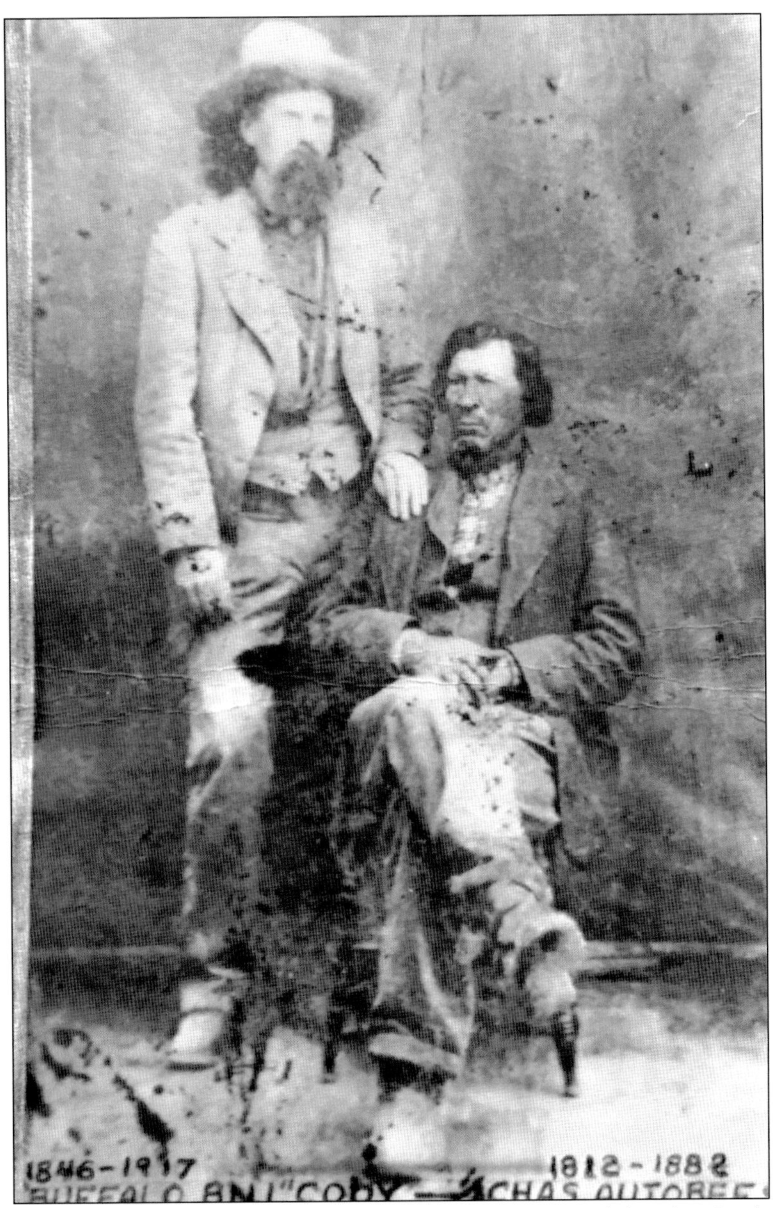

Charles Autobees came west from Missouri with the fur trade, and shortly after he arrived, he went to work for Simeon Turly in Arroyo Hondo, New Mexico, in 1836. Turly had a distillery notorious for producing "Taos Lightning," an alcohol sold throughout the region and illegally traded to the Indians. Autobees hauled the wheat alcohol to El Pueblo for Turly through the Taos Mountain Trail. On February 20, 1853, Autobees founded his settlement on the west bank of the Huerfano River, two miles south of its junction with the Arkansas and part of the Nolan Land Grant. Quickly channeling irrigation ditches, he and his companions soon had the bottomland producing garden vegetables. He married Serafina Avila from Taos. He also had an Arapaho wife named Sycamore. The Autobees family remained in the Pueblo area and contributed greatly to the community. Over time, the *s* was dropped from the surname, and Autobee is now used. Autobees is shown seated with William F. "Buffalo Bill" Cody. (Steve Cruz and Lillian Armijo Montez Collection.)

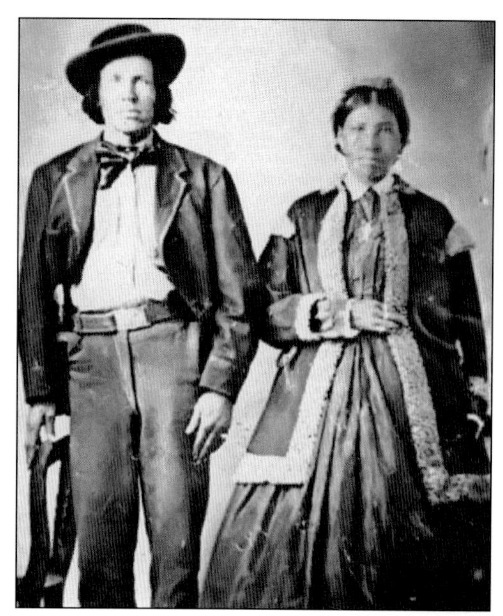

Mariano Autobees, son of Charles and Serafina, and his wife, Elena, are shown at left when they were first married. Below are Elena and her eldest son, Antonio. Elena was the daughter of Marcelino Baca and Tomasa, a Pawnee. About 1838, when Marcelino was on Pawnee lands near the Platte River, he was taken captive and threatened with death when Tomasa intervened and asked her father to spare his life. They eventually married, and Marcelino farmed and served as a guide for travelers. Marcelino moved to the mouth of Fountain Creek on the north side of the Arkansas in 1853. After the attack at El Pueblo in 1854, Baca moved his family to New Mexico. During the Civil War, he enlisted with the New Mexico Volunteers and was killed in 1862 fighting for the Union. (Left, Pioneer Museum Colorado Springs, Cragin Collection; below, Steve Cruz and Rachel Gallegos Collection.)

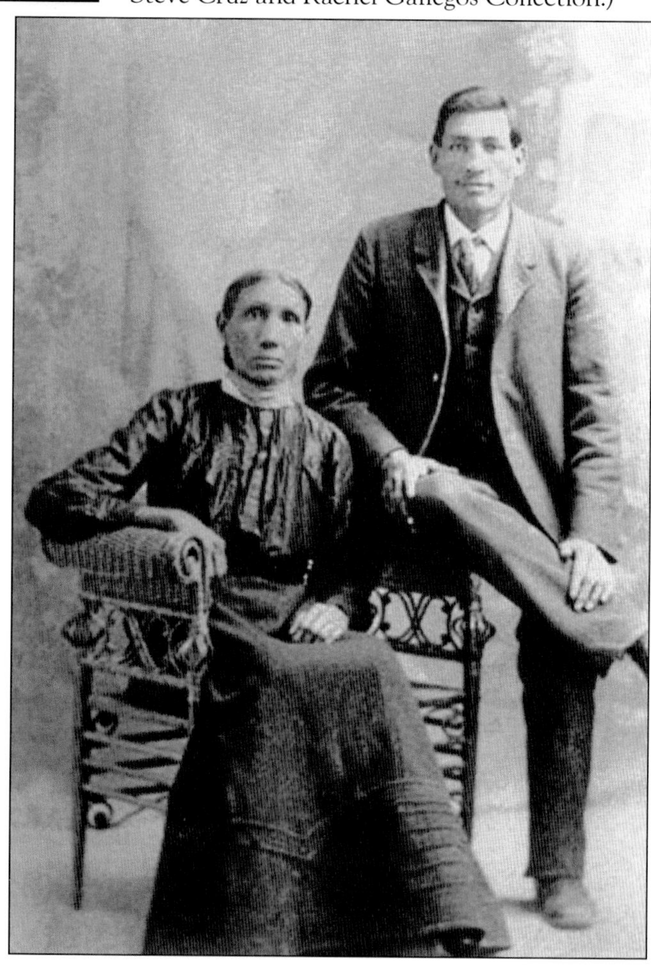

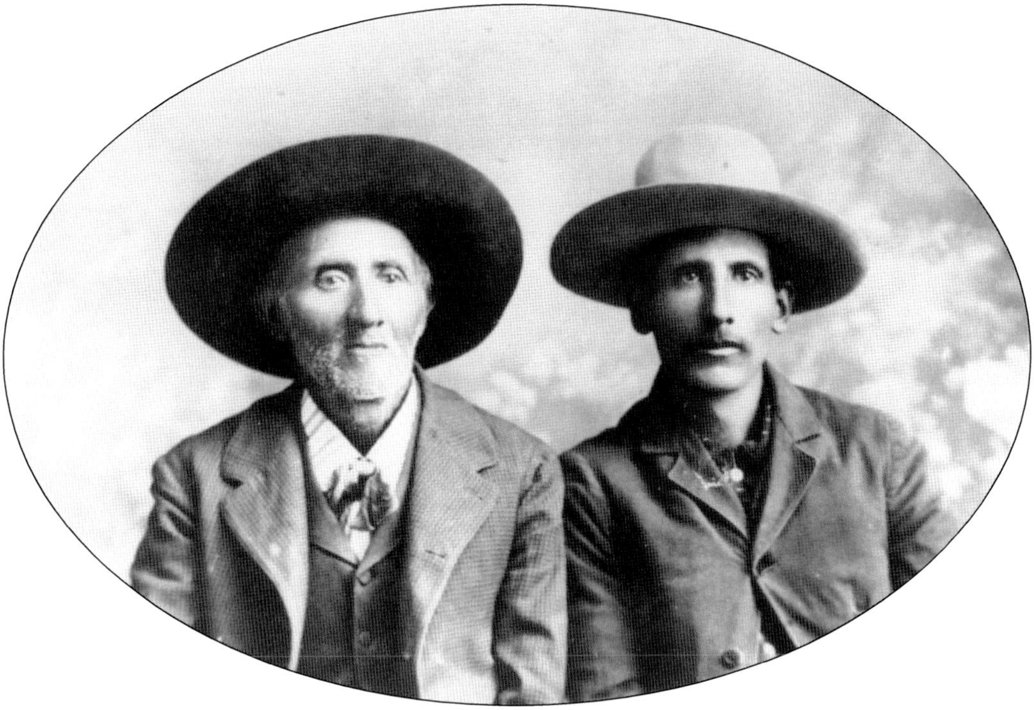

Jesus Vialpando (left), with one of his sons (right), was an early pioneer of Pueblo who migrated from New Mexico. Jesus was with the group of men who helped bury the dead after the attack on El Pueblo on Christmas Eve 1854. His descendants continue to live in the Avondale area just east of Pueblo. (Pioneer Museum, Colorado Springs, from the Cragin Collection, Accession No. S995.0109.0002.)

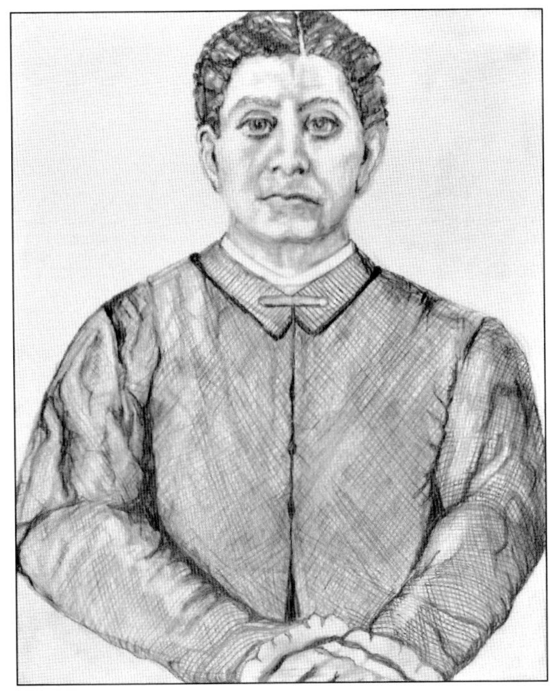

Archibald Metcalf, a trader from New York, arrived in Taos in the 1840s and married Maria Luz Trujillo (depicted here). They soon moved to Pueblo where she sometimes accompanied him on trading trips to Manitou Springs. While Metcalf traded blankets, needles, scissors, and other items for robes with the Ute, Cheyenne, and Arapaho, Luz made bread using the charged mineral waters of the springs as leavening. (Sketch by Tammi Moe, from a photograph provided by Ceferino Ahuero-Baca.)

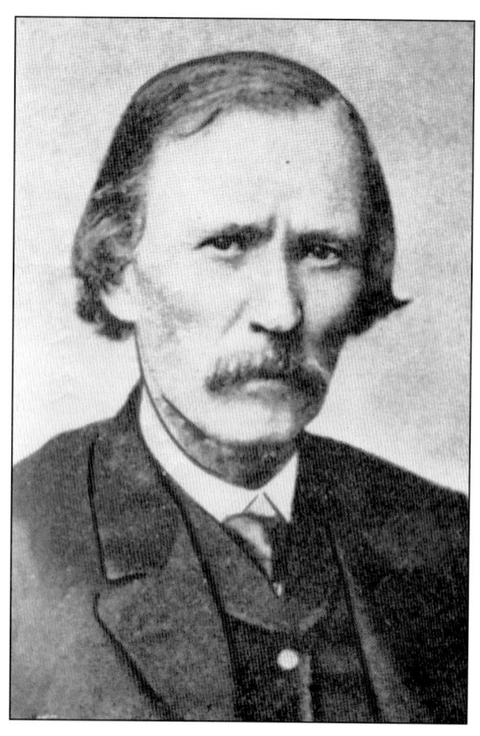

Christopher "Kit" Carson (pictured) was one of the best known frontiersmen turned military man and frequently served as a guide for John C. Frémont. Carson married Josefa Jaramillo, an heir to the Vigil/St. Vrain Land Grant, and they lived in Boggsville, located south of today's Las Animas and situated on part of the grant. Carson died on May 23, 1868, in Fort Lyon, when Pueblo County stretched all the way to the Kansas border. The text shows page four of his original will. Dr. Henry Tilton persuaded Carson to write his will only one week before his death. Carson was illiterate, so the will was written in the hand of Dr. Tilton but closes with Kit Carson's distinct signature of "C. Carson." The will was subsequently filed in the Pueblo County Courthouse where it was stored for several decades. In 1976, the will was officially presented to the Pueblo Regional Library, where it is stored in the Special Collections Department. (Left, PH-B-92-03; below, SC 0231.1.)

Tenthly. It is my will, that any moneys which may be due from Mr L. B. Maxwell for cattle sold to Mr Frank Pape, be paid to my administrator, the amount so received, to be used by him, for the support of my Children.

Lastly. I hereby appoint Mr Thomas O Boggs of Pueblo Co, Col. Ter. my administrator, to carry out the provisions of this, my last will and testament.

Signed this 15th day of May. One thousand eight hundred and sixty eight, in the presence of

J. A. Fitzgerald
H R Tilton

C. Carson

Recorded, Oct 6, 1868
M. G. Bradford
Probate Judge

Two

LAND, OPPORTUNITIES, AND INDUSTRIALIZATION

Pueblo attracted settlers for many reasons such as water, land, climate, proximity to mining resources, business opportunities, and simply dreams. In September 1858, a party traveling to the goldfields of Colorado from St. Louis arrived at the confluence of the Arkansas River and Fountain Creek. The travelers discovered the region could be more prosperous for them as merchants than as prospectors. They platted the town of Fountain City east of Fountain Creek that same year. Between 1859 and 1860, some of these settlers and others laid out the city of Pueblo west of Fountain Creek. Land patents became available, and land developers and industrialists arrived, turning Pueblo into a rapidly growing industrial city. In 1862, just one year after the Colorado Territory was created, Pueblo County was organized, becoming one of the original 17 counties.

In 1868, Annie Blake purchased the Northern Nolan Land Grant (not to be confused with the Southern Nolan Land Grant) from the Nolan heirs in Mora, New Mexico, for $10,000. Both grants were part of the Mexican land grants that Gov. Manuel Armijo issued in the 1840s. She sold one-third to Peter and Jacob Dotson for $5,000 and another third to Charles Goodnight for the same price. Later, they all sold parts of the land grant that bordered the Arkansas to Gen. William Palmer to develop a railroad line in South Pueblo.

The early city of Pueblo was consolidated from four towns: South Pueblo, Central Pueblo, Pueblo, and Bessemer. Its growth started humbly with agriculture and cattle, but steel became the main enterprise when General Palmer founded the Colorado Coal and Iron Company (CC&I) to expand the railroad and to eventually produce steel. Palmer also brought the Denver and Rio Grande Railroad to Pueblo in 1872. This opened the town to expanded commerce and transportation possibilities and made Pueblo a hub for several railroad companies. Additionally, Pueblo businesses capitalized on the steel production and constructed several smelters. Small and large entrepreneurs also recognized opportunity and opened up several supplemental businesses.

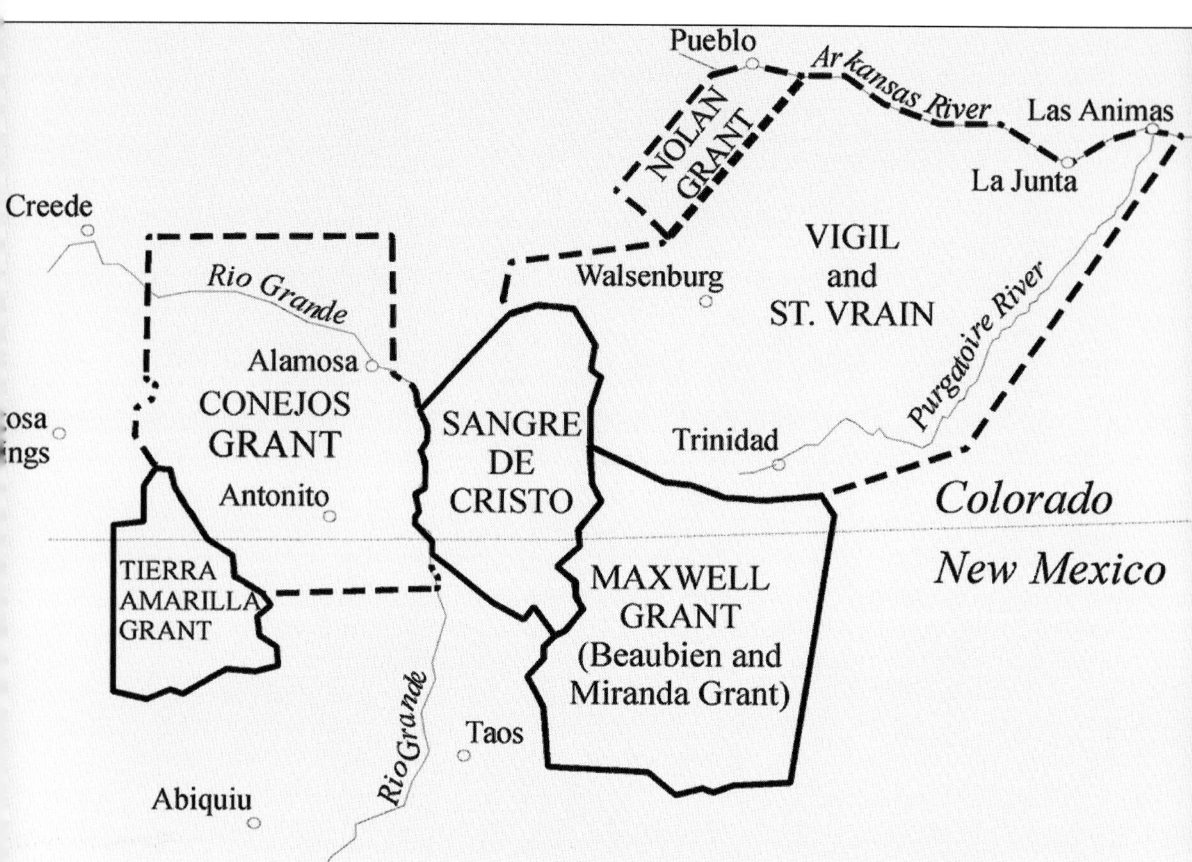

While southern Colorado and northern New Mexico were under Mexican rule (1821–1848), several land grants were issued by Governor Armijo. Mexico was trying to solidify its claim to its northern borderlands by encouraging more settlement on the frontier. The two land grants that affected Pueblo directly were the Nolan Land Grant and the Vigil/St. Vrain Land Grant. After this region became part of the United States at the end of the Mexican-American War, grantees still needed the United States Congress to review and confirm the grants before ownership could be determined. The broken lines enclosing both grants indicate the approximate boundaries of the original grants. The Nolan Land Grant was reduced from approximately 576,000 acres to more than 48,000 acres when approved by Congress in 1870. South Pueblo and the southwestern portion of Pueblo were part of the Nolan grant. The Vigil/St. Vrain Land Grant was reduced from approximately four million acres to 97,000 acres and extended from East Pueblo to Las Animas. (Ed Simms, El Escritorio Publishing.)

In 1862, President Lincoln appointed Allen A. Bradford (pictured) as one of the first justices of the Colorado Territorial Supreme Court, Third Judicial District. The people voted Judge Bradford to represent the territory of Colorado in the United States House of Representatives in 1865. Judge Bradford received three land patents in the east side of Pueblo between 1870 and 1872. His landholdings marked the beginning of speculative real estate investments. Judge Bradford's younger brother, Mark G. Bradford, came to Pueblo in 1860. He was a member of the first trustees and first school board in Pueblo. In 1892, a new school known as Capitol School (below) was erected at First Street and La Crosse Avenue in East Pueblo. The name was later changed to Bradford Elementary in honor of one of the Bradfords or perhaps both, a topic that is still debated. (Right, PH-B-54-02-001; below, PH-P-506-02-002.)

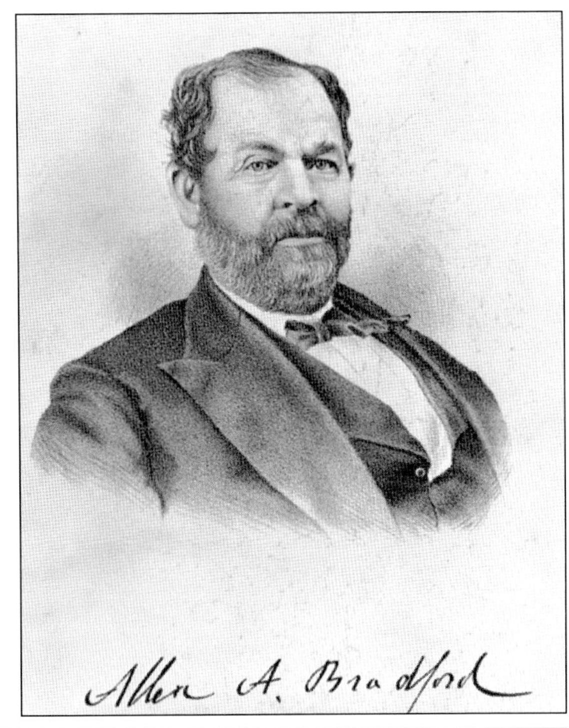

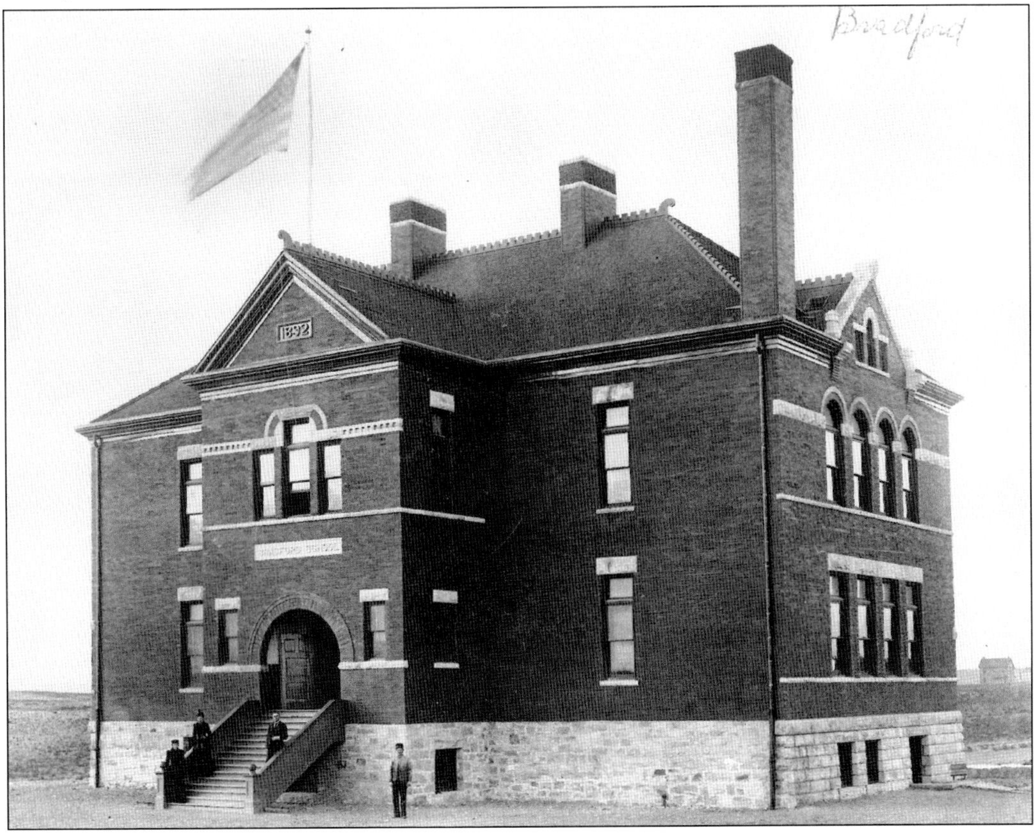

Annie Blake (shown with an unidentified granddaughter) was an extraordinary businesswoman and essential to Pueblo's development. She traveled to New Mexico to purchase the Northern Nolan Land Grant and realized a great profit when she sold two-thirds of the grant for the same amount she paid for it. (PH-B-45-02.)

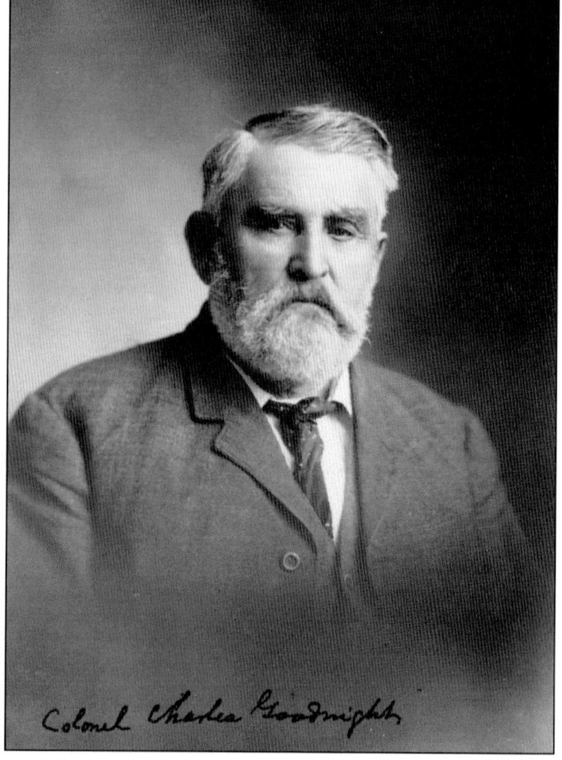

Annie Blake sold one-third of the Nolan Land Grant to cattleman Charles Goodnight for his Rock Canyon Ranch, located five miles west of South Pueblo, which Goodnight used for his cattle operations from 1869 to 1875. (PH-B-170-02-002.)

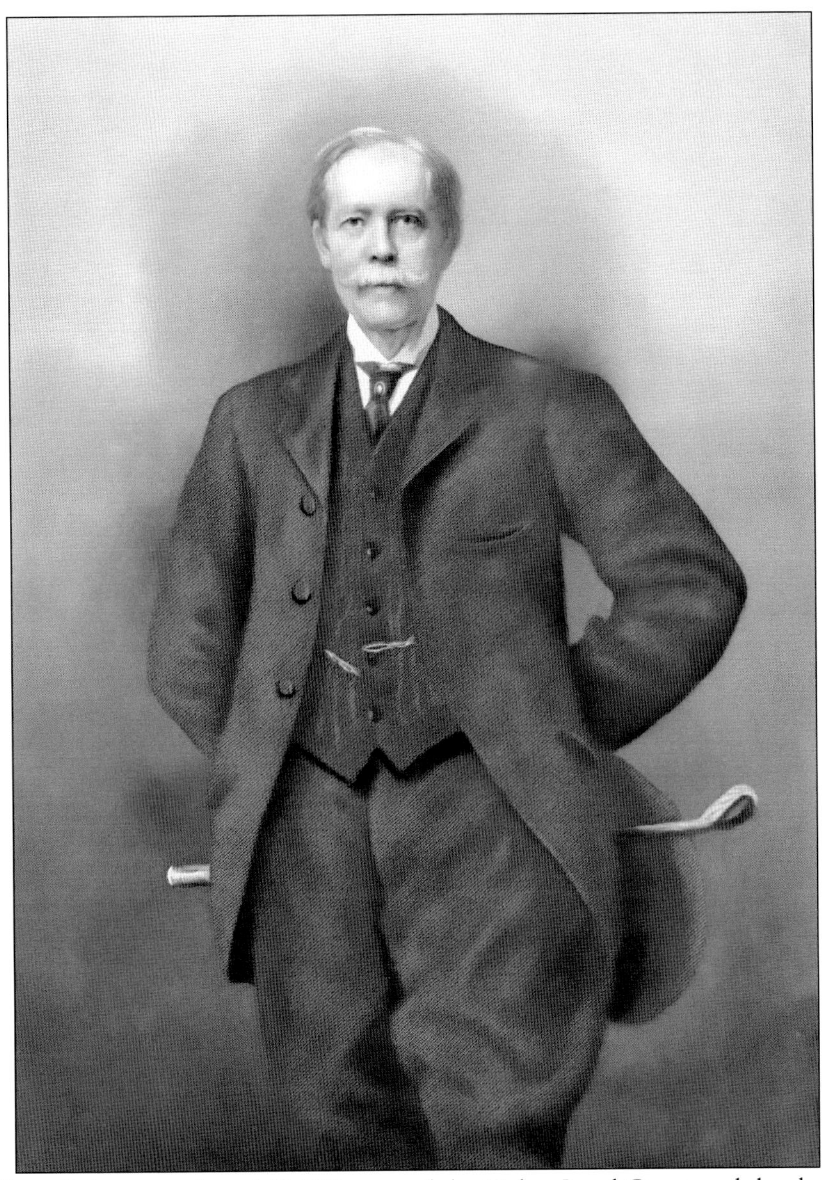

Gen. William Palmer purchased 48,000 acres of the Nolan Land Grant and developed South Pueblo, where he brought the Denver and Rio Grande Railroad to Pueblo in 1872. He envisioned rail access from the United States to Mexico and named the streets in South Pueblo after small towns in Mexico to emphasize a Mexican-American connection. While Palmer is known for the development of Colorado Springs, he was one of the most influential investors and developers of early Pueblo. Palmer also created the Central Colorado Improvement Company (CCIC), an important factor in the welfare of the railroad. Owned by the same men who owned the Denver and Rio Grande Railroad, the company was authorized to purchase, develop, and sell agricultural lands, mineral springs, coal and iron deposits, quarries, and water rights. This led to the opening of the Colorado Coal and Iron Company (CC&I), a predecessor company to the Colorado Fuel and Iron Company (CF&I), which made the production of steel the mainstay of Pueblo's economy for over a century. (Painting of Gen. William Palmer by unknown artist, from *Semi-Centennial History of the State of Colorado.*)

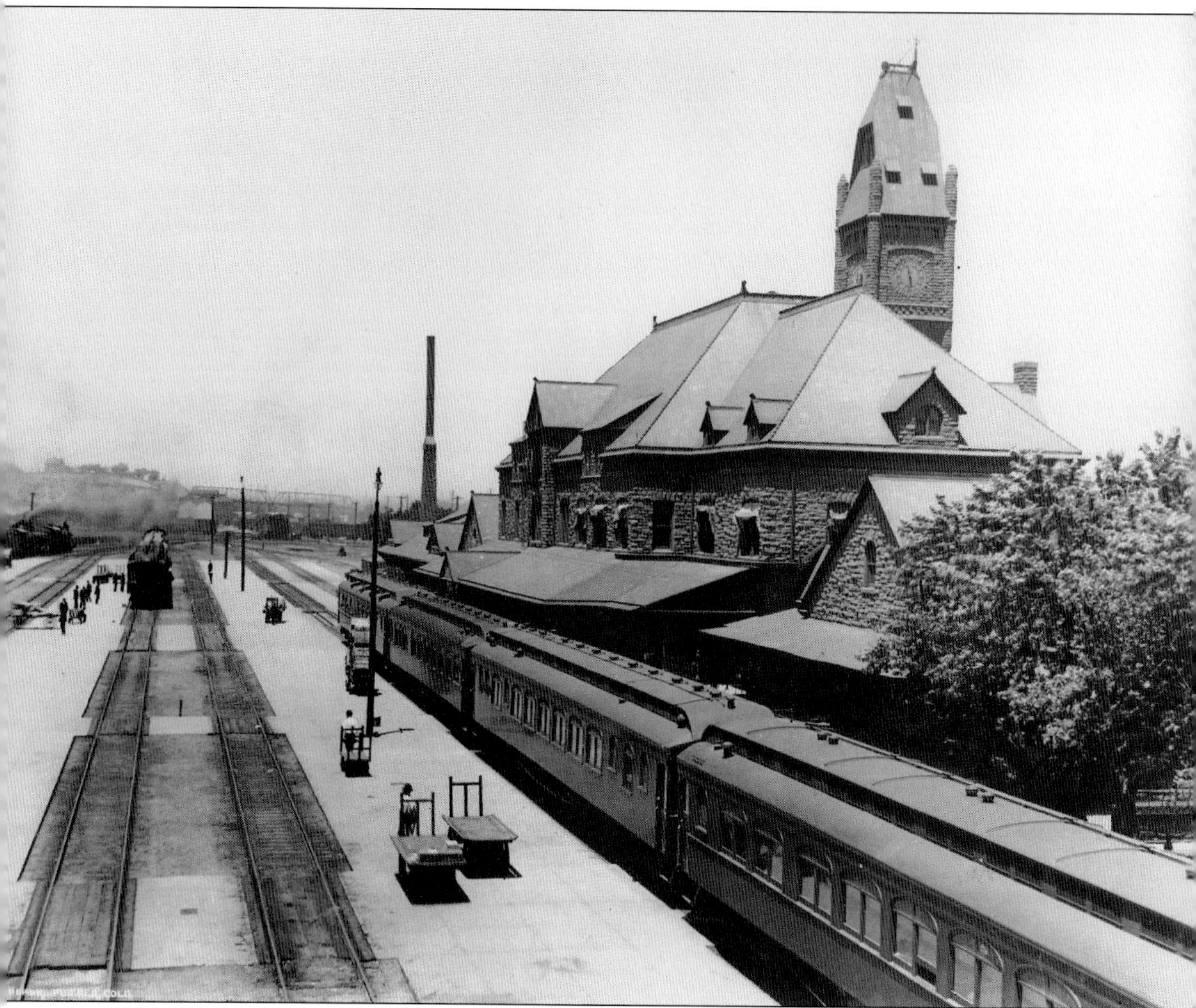

On July 2, 1872, at 1:00 p.m., the first train arrived in Pueblo carrying several dignitaries from Denver. The first depot was located slightly north of downtown. The Union Depot, shown in its permanent location on West B Street, was built in 1889–1890. The Denver and Rio Grande; Texas and Fort Worth; Chicago, Rock Island and Pacific; the Atchison, Topeka and Santa Fe; and the Missouri Pacific were the five original railroads served by the depot. At the height of operation, 55 trains moved through the depot daily, and the depot served approximately 160,000 passengers per year. Passenger service ended in 1971. The Union Depot was listed in the National Register of Historic Places in 1975. (PH-P-712-07.)

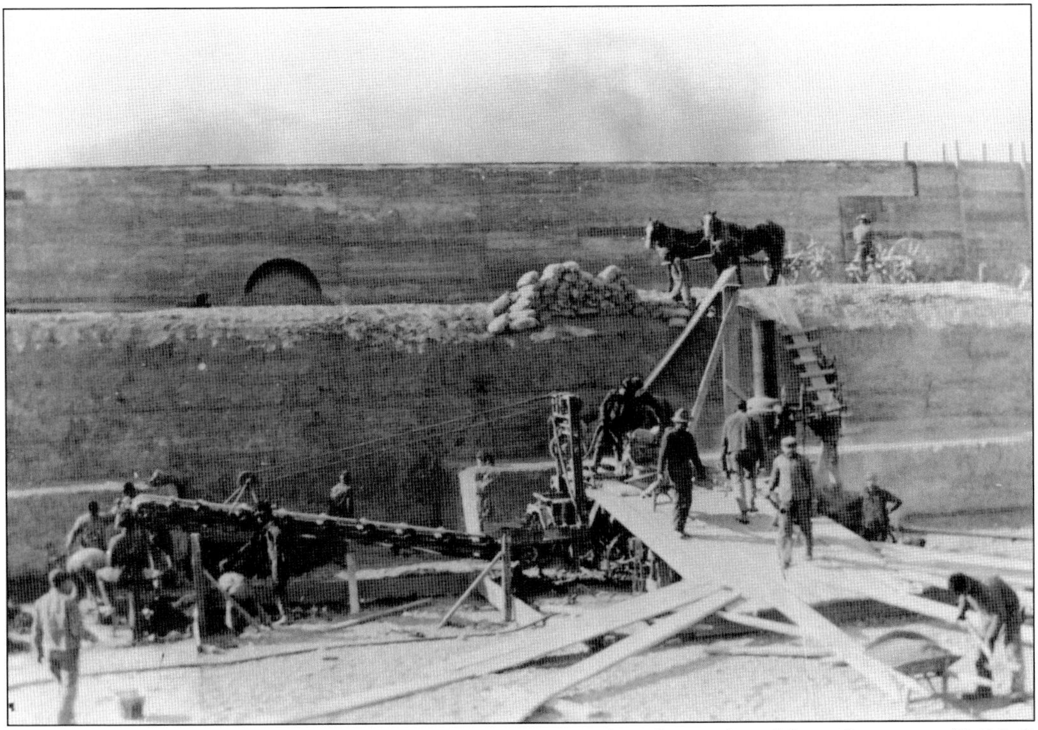

These two images show the early construction of the Colorado Coal and Iron Company (CC&I) steelworks, later known as Colorado Fuel and Iron Company (CF&I). Mules were used to help with the heavy work. CF&I was the first vertically integrated steel mill west of the Mississippi. Pueblo was the perfect location for steel and production because the region was rich in coal, iron ore, and other mineral resources. Industrialists foresaw a large profit, not only in steel production, but also in their real estate investments. CC&I settled on 1,260 acres of land just southeast of South Pueblo for its endeavor. Surveying the land began in February 1880, and a crew of eight men earning $3 per day began work on the mill's first blast furnace. The company eventually employed thousands of men and women as it expanded over the years. For nearly a century, CF&I was the largest employer in Colorado, with a maximum workforce of approximately 11,000. (Above, PH-P-244-06-001; below, PH-P-244-03-004.)

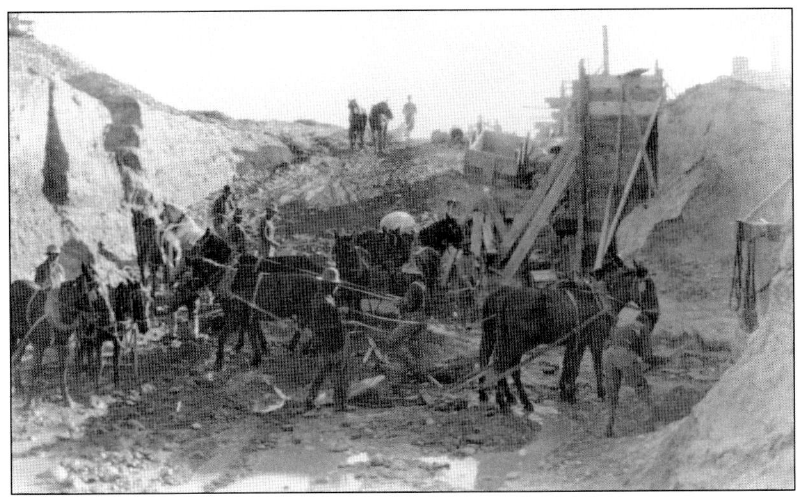

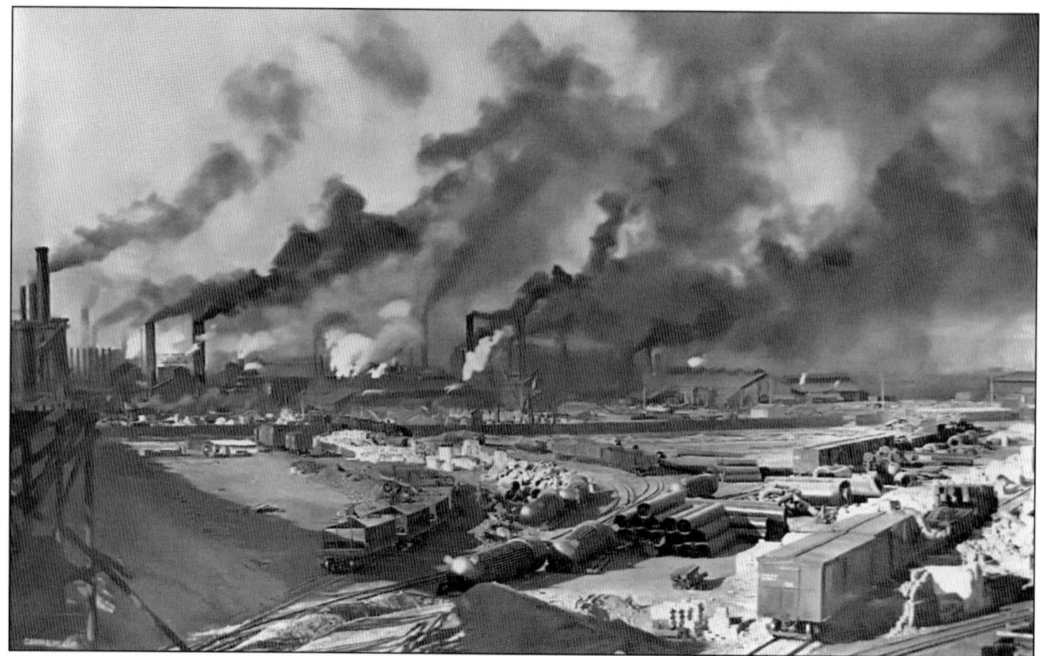

The first of two blast furnaces at CF&I was blown on September 5, 1881. Steel production, using the Bessemer steel process, started on April 12, 1882. Black skies signaled economic prosperity in the late 1800s and early 1900s, and in no place was this more evident than at CF&I. In this photograph, the profits are clearly visible as the smoke rises. (PH-P-227-20.)

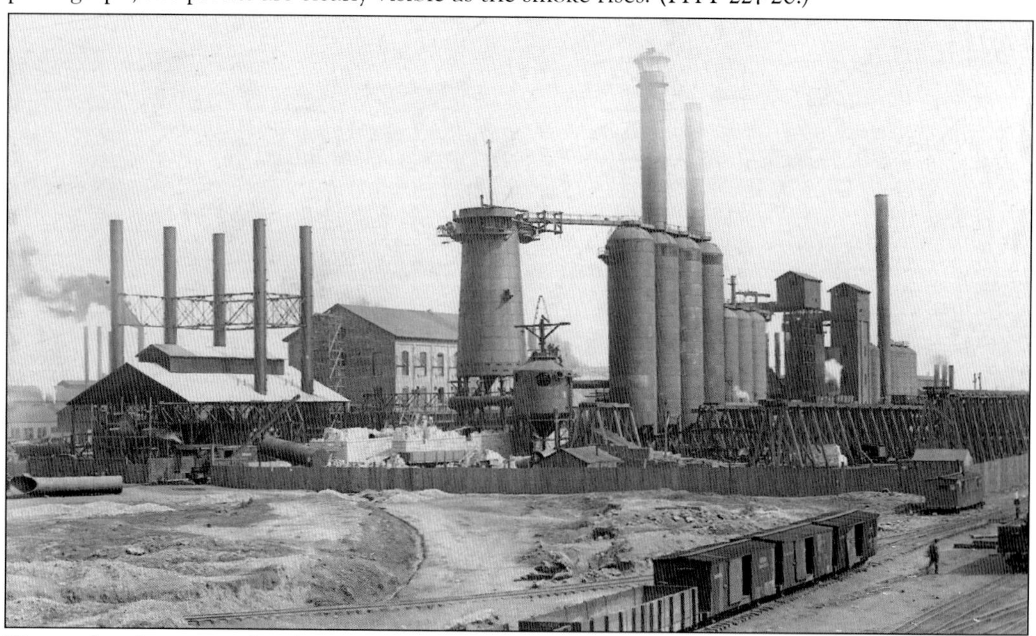

The steelworks operated under several changes in management and ownership. With the company on the verge of bankruptcy in 1903, George Jay Gould (who controlled the Denver and Rio Grande Railroad) and John D. Rockefeller (founder of Standard Oil Company) purchased a controlling interest in the company's stock. One of their goals was to modernize the mill. Gould only stayed four years. The Rockefellers disposed of their interest in the company in 1944. (PH-P-218-05.)

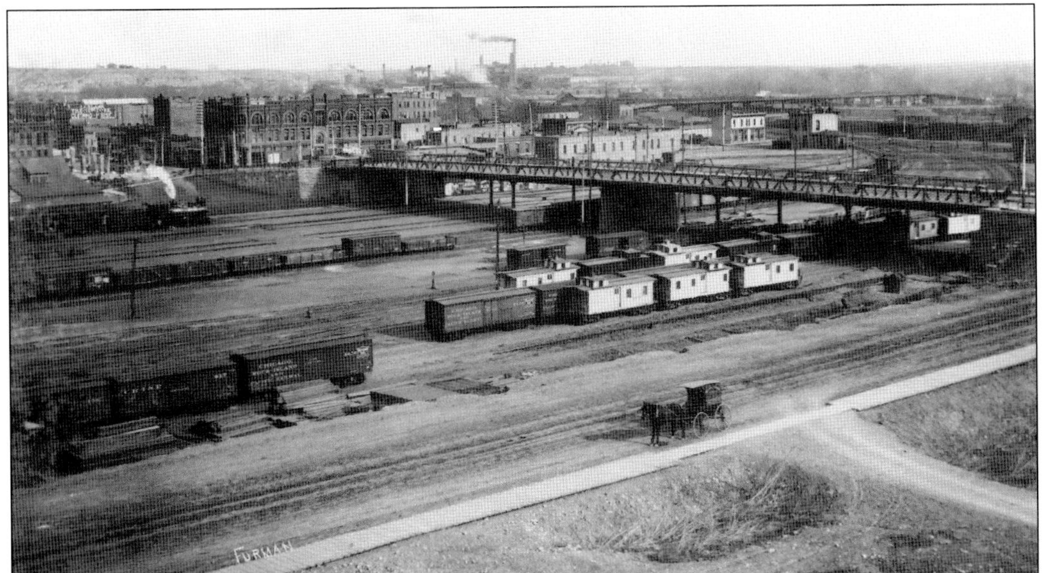

From a vantage point above the extensive rail yards in downtown Pueblo, the steel mill operation is visible. Pueblo was known as the "Pittsburgh of the West" for its large rail and steel mill commerce, as steel was produced and shipped by rail. Pueblo grew because of the railroads that serviced the smelters and steel mill. Pueblo became the largest steel manufacturer in the West. (PH-P-712-11.)

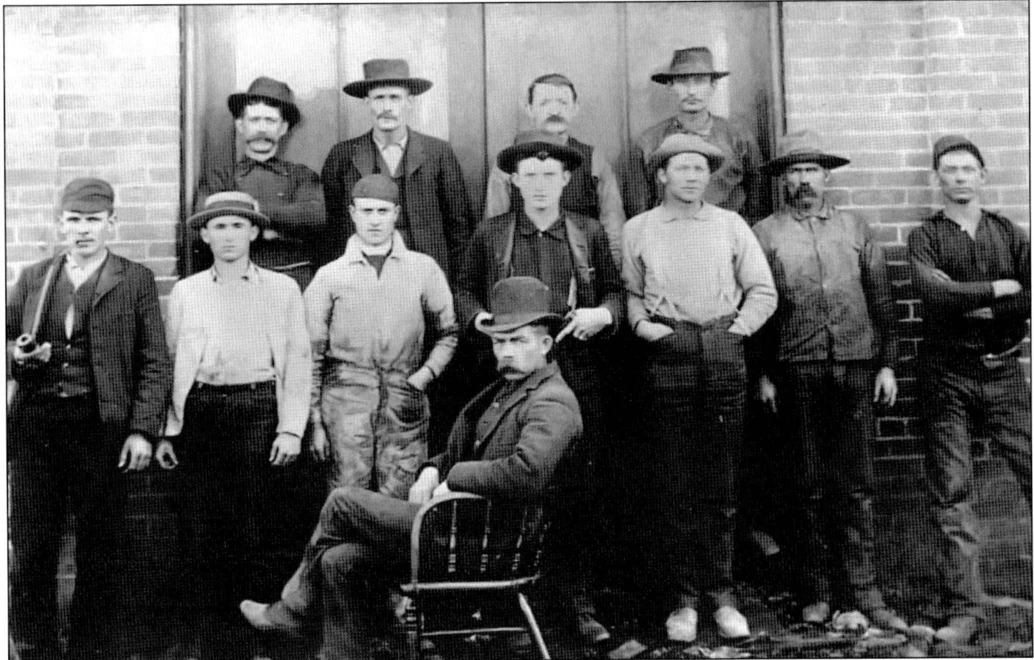

This group picture taken in 1880 represents a dozen nationalities of employees that handled the ores and steel in Pueblo's smelters and steel mill. Nationalities include Greek, Italian, Slovenian, Serbian, Croatian, German, Mexican, Irish, and others. Although no CF&I mines were located in Pueblo County, thousands of men passed through on their way south and west to the coal and mineral ore mines. (PH-P-225-05.)

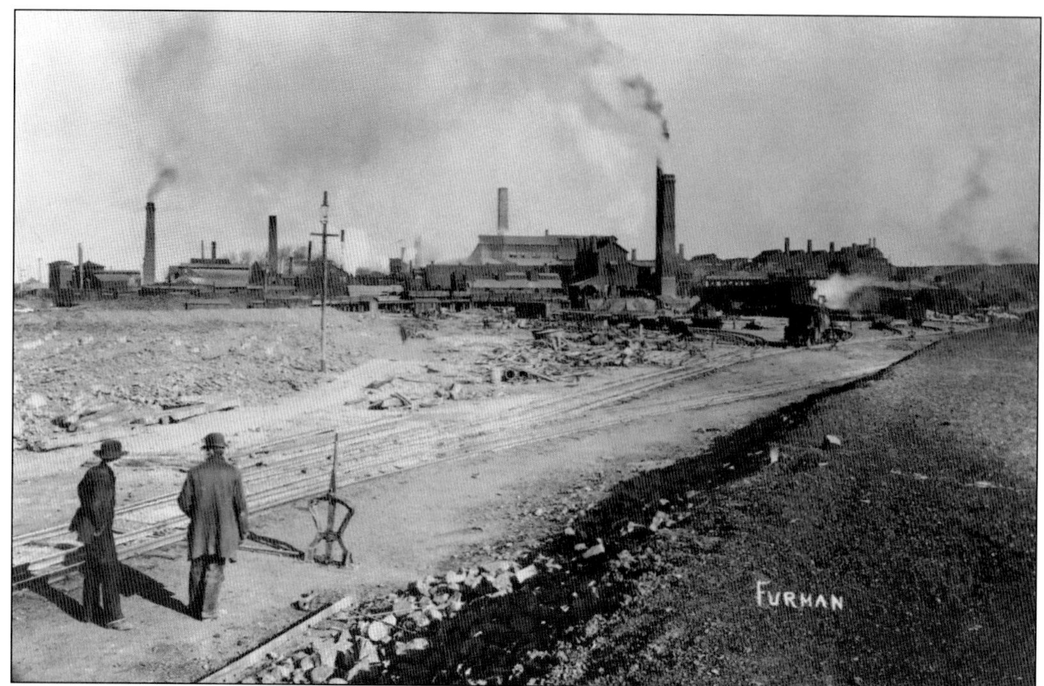

There were four smelters operating in Pueblo by the 1890s. The Pueblo Smelting and Refining Company, was built by Joseph G. Mather and Alfred W. Geist in 1878 and closed after the 1921 flood. The Colorado Smelting Company, started in 1883–1884, was located on Santa Fe Avenue and was known as the Eiler's plant. Anton Eiler was the general manager, and the plant operated until 1917. The Philadelphia Smelting and Refining Company was built in 1888 and was owned by the Guggenheim family. It was located adjacent to the CF&I mill and stopped operation in 1907. The zinc smelter, operated by the US Zinc Company, was located in an area known as Blende and was in operation from 1893 until 1921. Men from several European and Asian countries came to Pueblo to work in the smelters. (Above, PH-P-583-02-02; below, PH-P-583-02-01.)

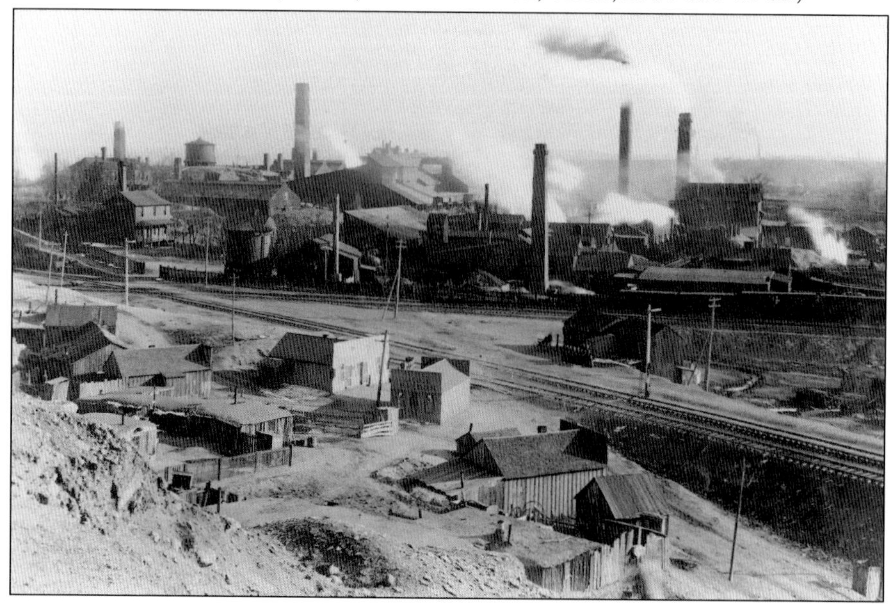

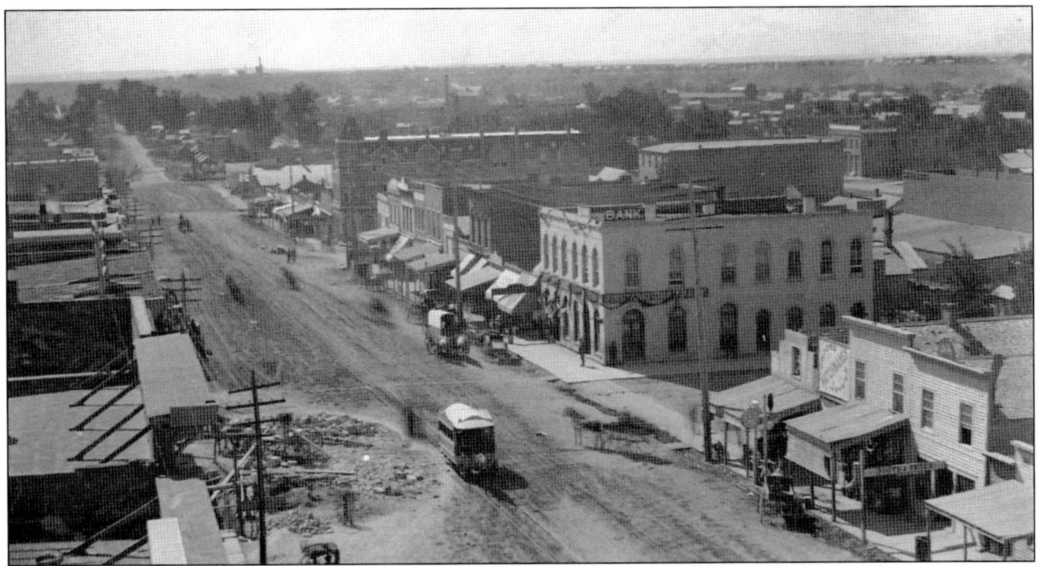

Pueblo's first main street was Santa Fe Avenue (pictured here in 1881), which runs north and south. In 1878, the Pueblo Street Railroad was organized, and soon horse-drawn streetcars were running between Santa Fe and Union Avenues. A trolley is seen on the road heading south. The white corner two-story building shown here is the First National Bank. (PH-P-683-08.)

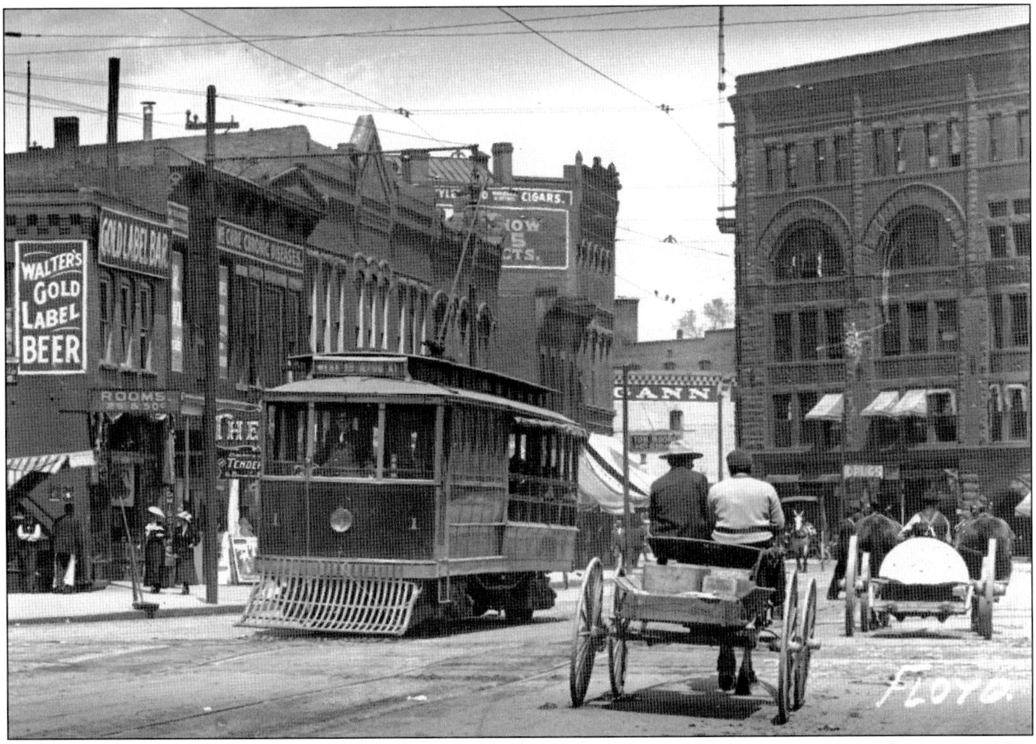

By 1890, more than 20 miles of streetcar lines in the city were electric, as seen by the cables overhead. An average of 20 trolleys ran daily through the city. For at least the next 30 years, the streetcar system would echo the roller coaster of the local economy, as evidenced by several different owners and managers. (PH-P-662-12-006.)

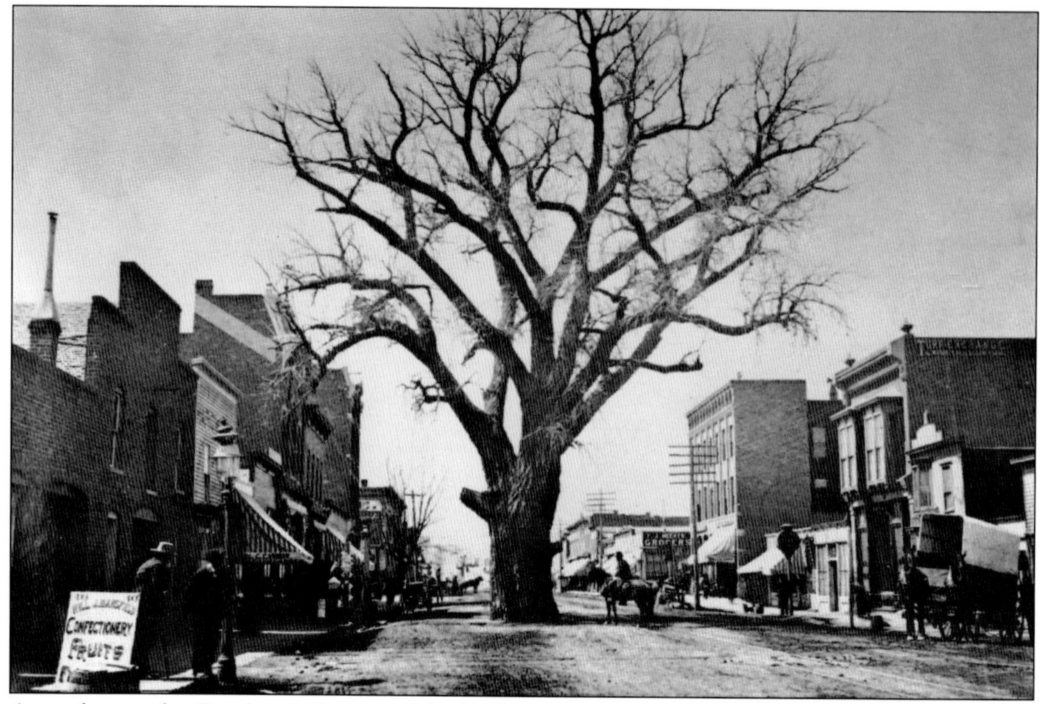

According to the October 1993 issue of the Pueblo County Historical Society's monthly magazine, *Pueblo Lore,* "Old Monarch cut down in South Pueblo on June 25, 1883, was 388 years old, had a circumference of 29 feet and was 88 feet tall." It eventually became known as the "hanging tree," and was located at present-day 218 South Union Avenue. It has not been validated that anyone was actually hanged from the tree. (PH-P-310-03_001.)

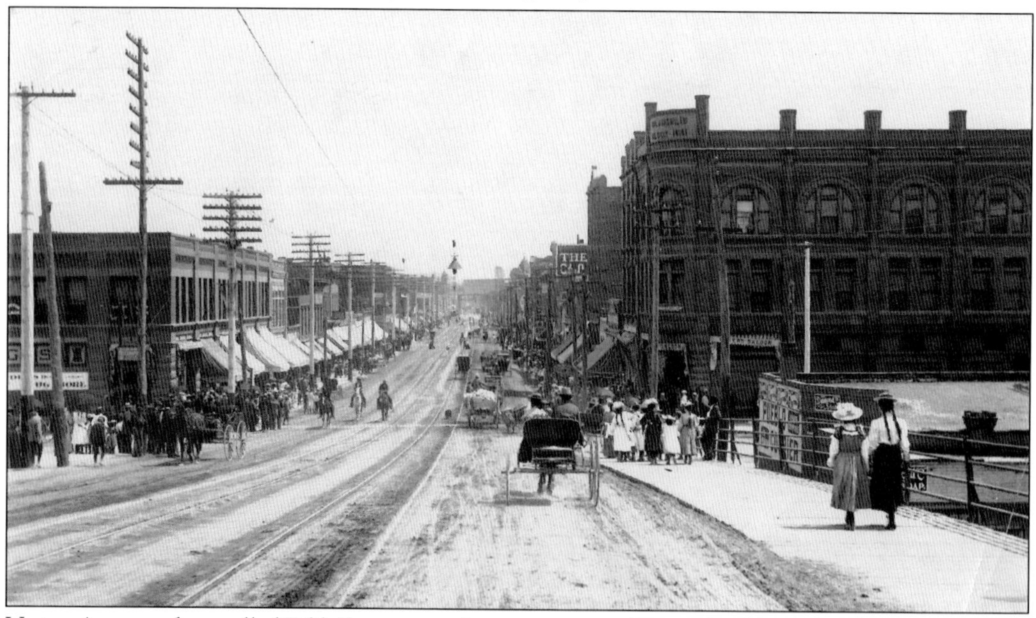

Union Avenue, then called Fifth Street, was the main street of South Pueblo. After the consolidation of the three towns in 1886, there was a building boom, especially along Union Avenue. Union Avenue is presumably named due to its location in the consolidated city. (PH-P-699-13_001.)

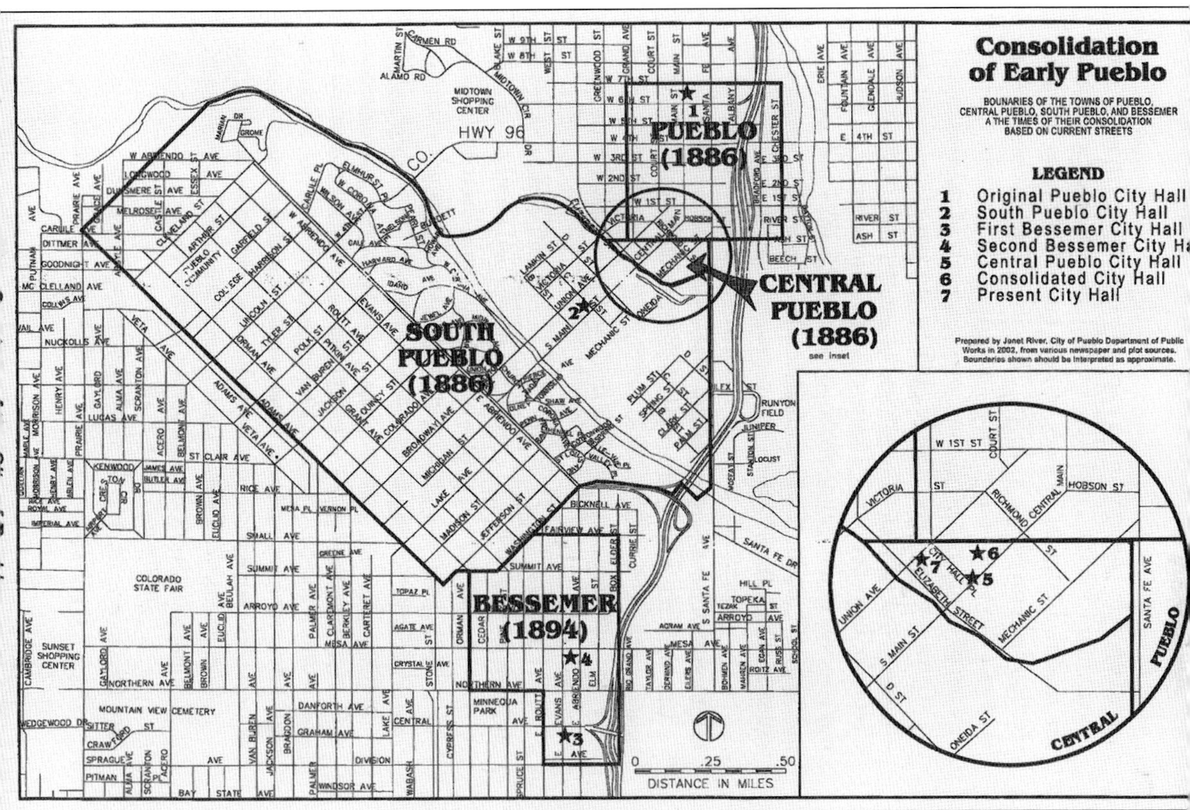

Shown here are the four towns that incorporated to form the early City of Pueblo. Pueblo incorporated in 1870, South Pueblo in 1873, and Central Pueblo in 1882. On March 9, 1886, a vote was taken to consolidate the three towns, with 1,381 voting for and 87 against. In the same year, the Town of Bessemer was incorporated to house steelworkers and businesses, and eventually it also consolidated into Pueblo in 1894. Before incorporation, South Pueblo was divided into three subdivisions: upper (Mesa Junction), middle (Bluffs/East and West Blocks) and lower (Union District). (City of Pueblo.)

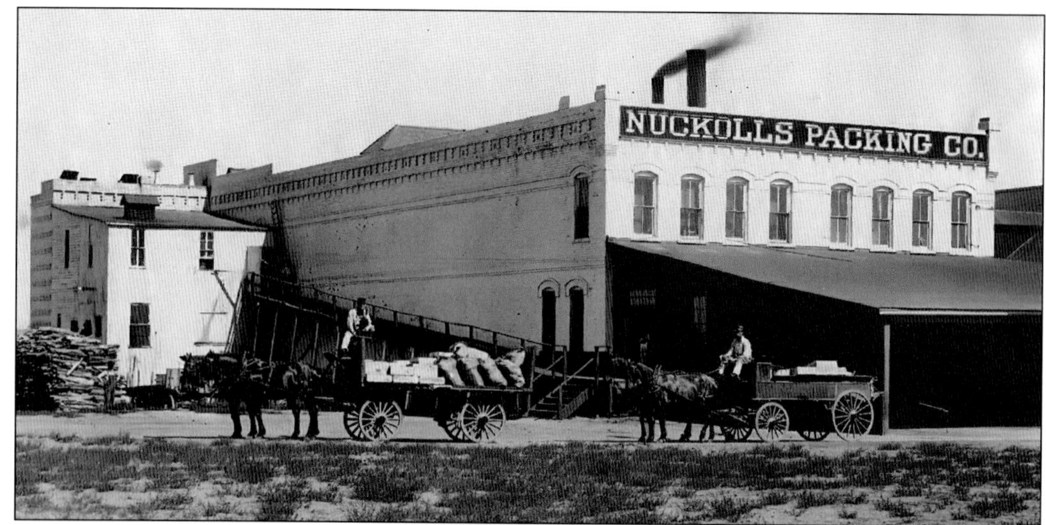

The Nuckolls family purchased the Nuckolls Packing Company in 1892, and it was incorporated on June 18, 1899. The capital stock was $100,000, and the company employed about 50 men. By 1935, the plant capacity had increased tremendously, and the workforce had increased to 500, making it the second-largest employer in Pueblo. The plant changed hands and was enlarged many times. In 1980, the company, then known as Alpha Beta Markets, closed permanently. (PH-P-114-01-001.)

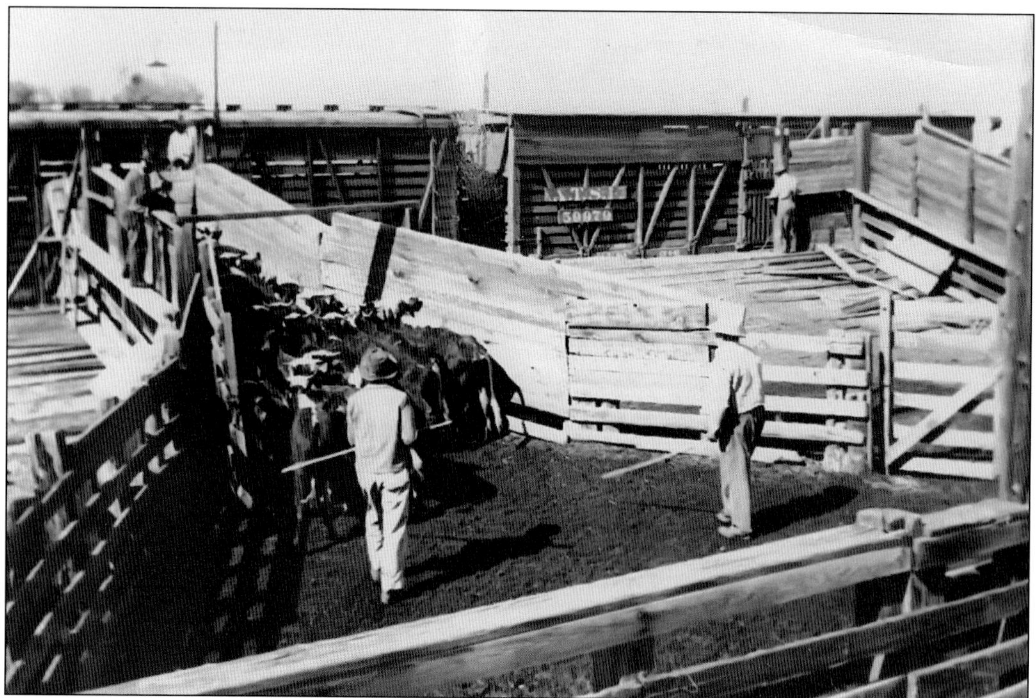

The stockyards, opened in 1902 at 1200 South La Crosse Avenue in East Pueblo, were owned by the Missouri Pacific Railroad. The main business was unloading, feeding, and resting of cattle, horses, and sheep because federal law only allowed livestock to be in a railroad car for a certain amount of time. Much of the stock arrived on the D&RGW or the AT&SF, and the animals were switched over to the Missouri Pacific Railroad for their final destination. (PH-P-147-02-001.)

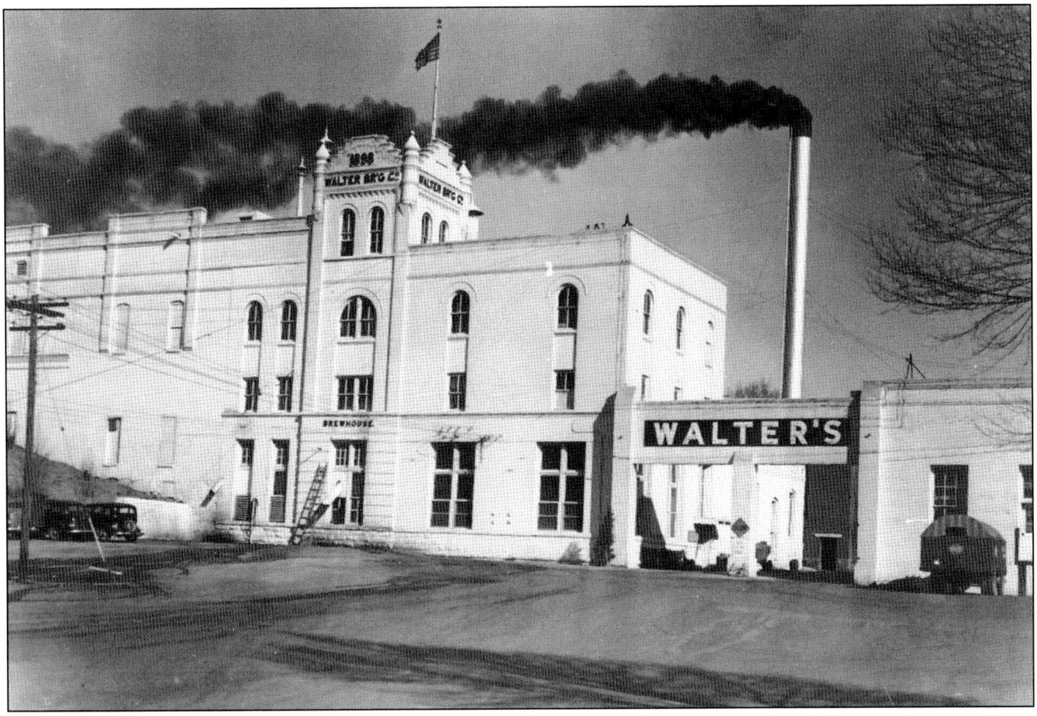

The Pueblo Brewery Company changed ownership several times until it fell into the hands of the Walter brothers in 1898. Walter's Beer then became the city's beer; letters on the bottle read "Pueblo Beer" as there was no label. The brewery bottled beer for 27 different brands and distributed to seven Western states. (PH-P-141-03-001.)

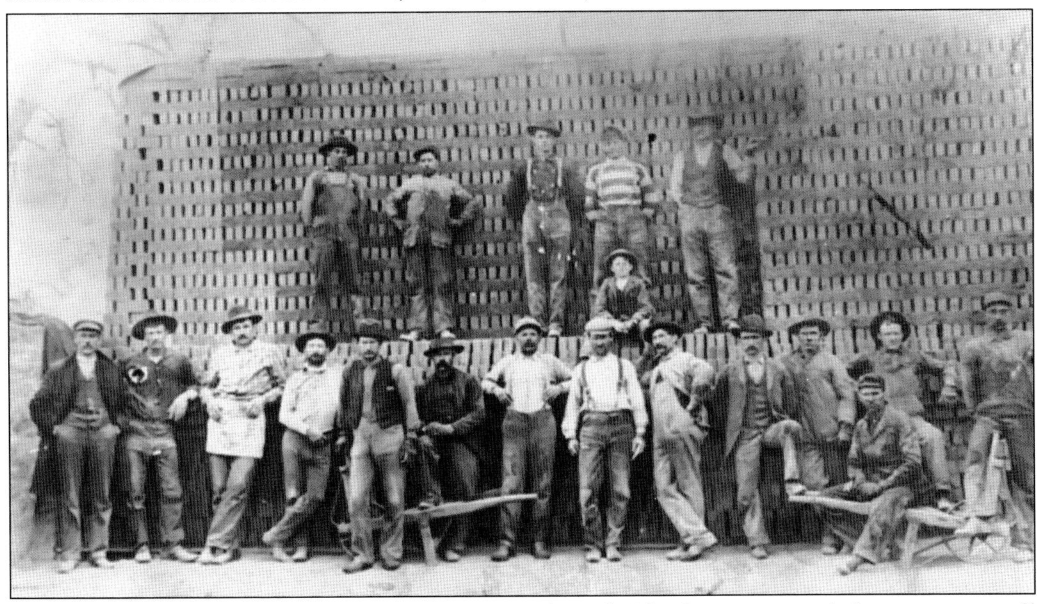

In 1902, Joseph Welte founded the Summit Brick and Tile Company, and the company still resides at its East Pueblo location as of this writing. Shown here is the Summit Brick and Tile Company crew standing on the company's product in 1907. The company has grown to export bricks internationally. (PH-P-138-02-002.)

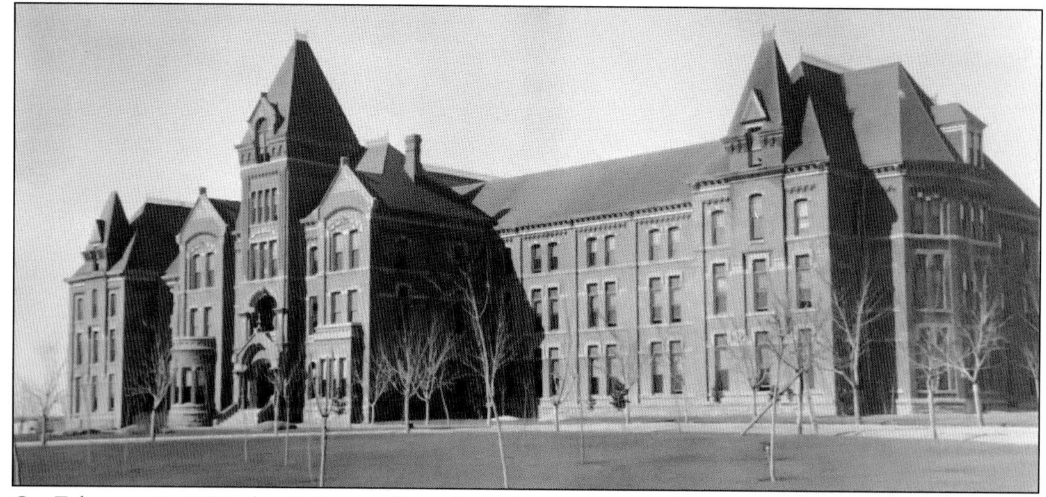

On February 8, 1879, the Colorado State Legislature approved an act establishing the Colorado Insane Asylum in Pueblo. It opened on October 23, 1879. First called the Colorado Insane Asylum, its name was later changed to the Colorado State Hospital; today, it is known as the Colorado Mental Health Institute. Initially, the hospital had two similar buildings—one for men and one for women. (PH-P-340-02.)

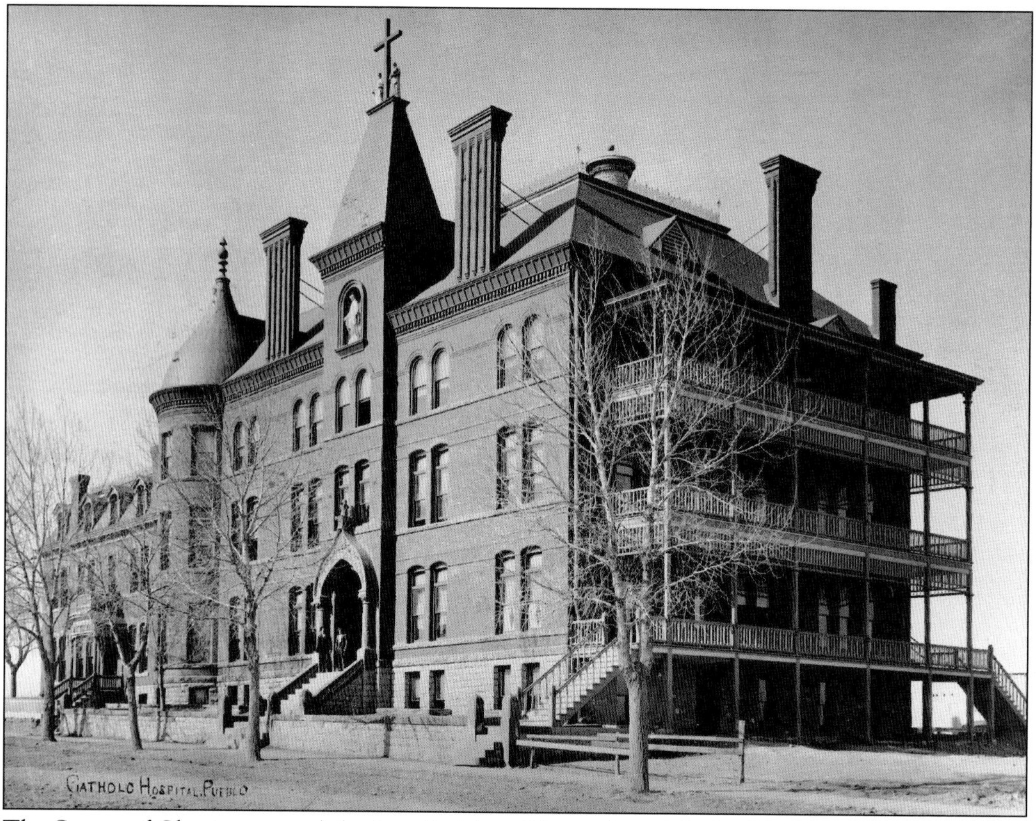

The Sisters of Charity opened the first St. Mary Hospital on July 31, 1882; it was located in the Grove neighborhood. Later, a building was acquired on Quincy and Grant Streets, and several additions were made. The north porches were used for tuberculosis patients. (PH-P-350-04.)

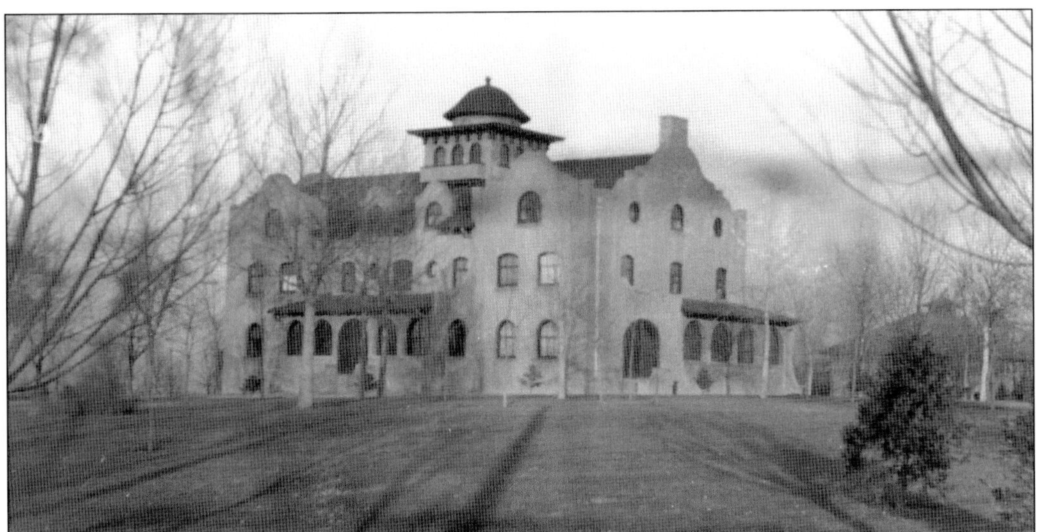

Minnequa Hospital officially opened on a 10-acre tract of land in August 1902. The 13 Mission-style buildings were designed to meet the health-care needs of the CF&I employees. It eventually became St. Mary-Corwin, named after Dr. Richard W. Corwin. (PH-P-349-03.)

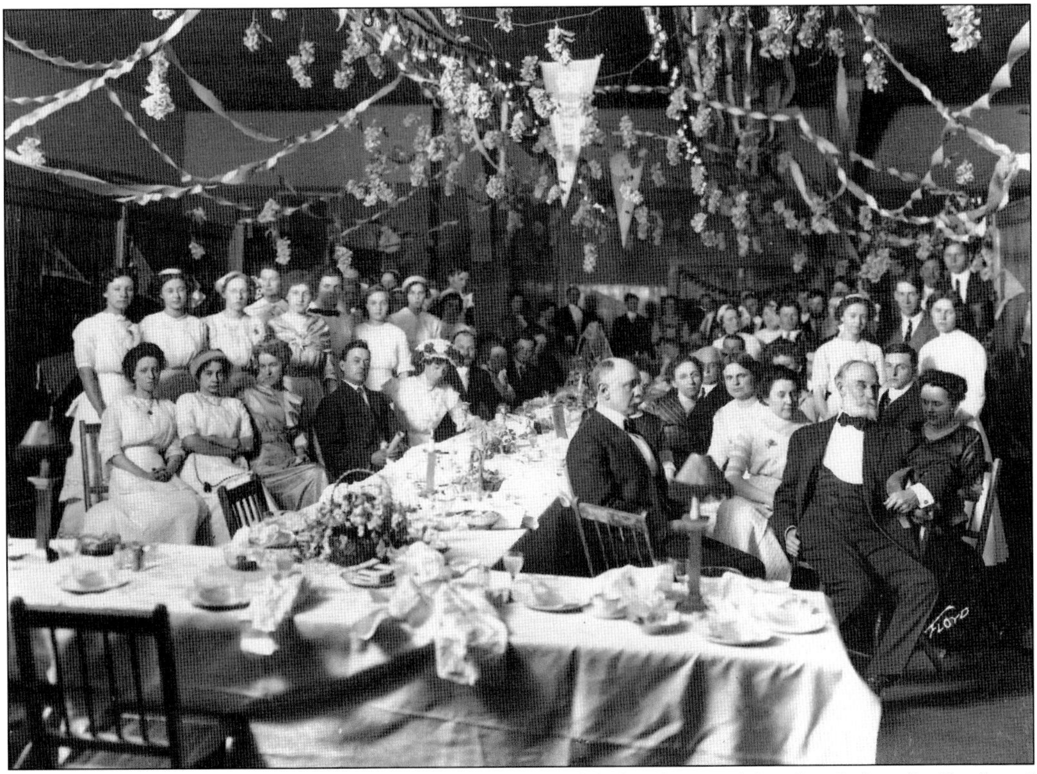

General Palmer hired Dr. Richard W. Corwin to establish a hospital for the Colorado Coal and Iron Company employees in 1881. Dr. Corwin was a pioneer in sociological medicine and is credited with several breakthroughs in the medical field. He served Pueblo for 48 years. Dr. Corwin sits at far right (leaning back in his chair). (PH-B-108-02.)

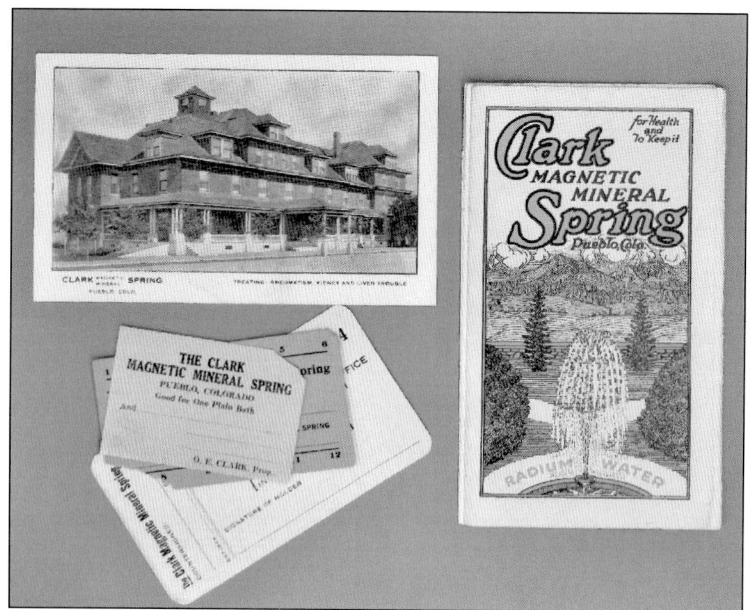

Silas Clark was drilling for oil in South Pueblo in 1879 when the oil rig struck a strong flow of artesian water. This was a valuable find for the treatment of ailments such as rheumatism and tuberculosis. About 1900, the Clark family opened a 90-room brick sanatorium and bathhouse about seven blocks from the Union Depot. Dr. Louisa R. Black managed the complex. (D0-80-001.)

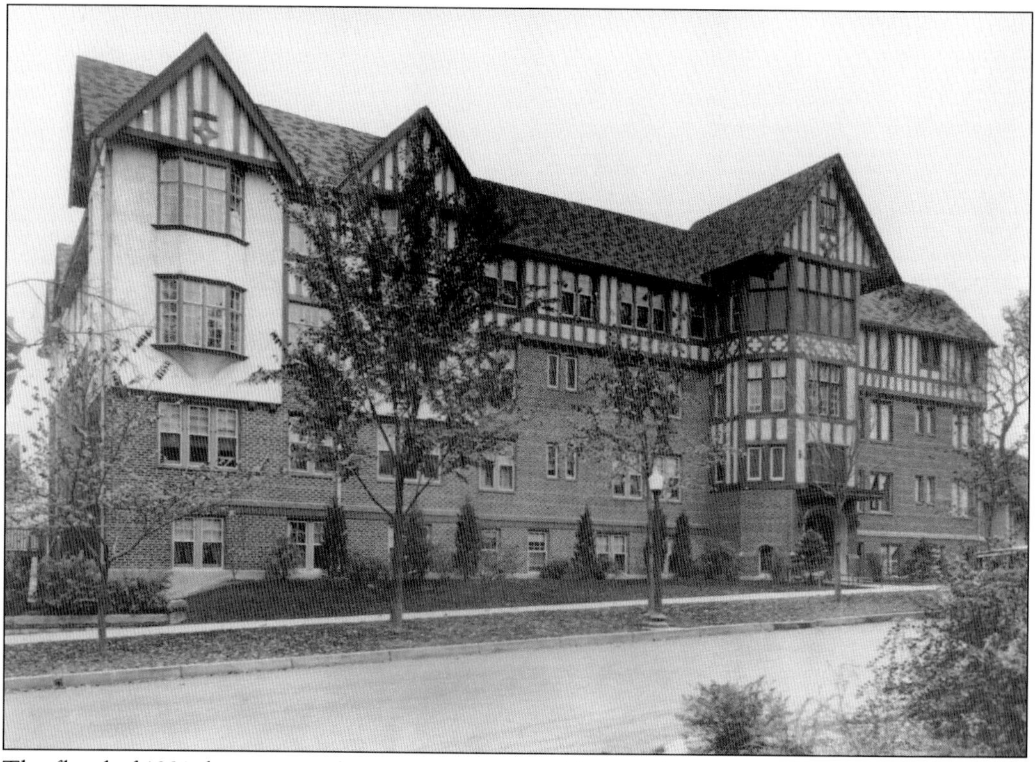

The flood of 1921 demonstrated an exceptional need for another hospital in Pueblo. A group of doctors used the Clark Sanatorium in the Grove neighborhood for a time until a new hospital building could be constructed at Seventeenth Street and Grand Avenue. It was eventually given to the Episcopal Diocese of Colorado and became Parkview Episcopal Hospital, which has expanded many times. It is no longer associated with the Episcopal Church and is now Parkview Medical Center. (PH-P-348-04.)

Three

Pueblo's Great Diversity

Pueblo developed its unique character from the people who came from all over the world to establish new lives. The 1870 United States Census occurred only months before Pueblo became a full-fledged city, and the census counted 666 residents. The population nearly quintupled to 3,217 in 1880, and exploded to 24,558 in 1890. Employment at the CF&I steel mill and smelter at the turn of the 20th century in Pueblo attracted a large number of immigrant laborers.

At one point, 40 languages were spoken in the steel mill, and more than two dozen foreign-language newspapers were published in the city. Pueblo became known as the "Melting Pot of the West." Ethnic groups included Irish, Italian, German, Slovenian, Serbian, Croatian, Greek, Jewish, Polish, Hungarian, Filipino, Japanese, African American, Chinese, and Mexican among others. The people from present-day New Mexico were considered migrants because they came from Spanish territory, Mexico, and the United States as the international border shifted. These people brought a unique culture distinct from that of present-day Mexico. Pueblo welcomed a cornucopia of ethnicities that brought different languages, religions, customs, and traditions, which were celebrated throughout the city. Many unique neighborhoods sprang up, such as the Grove, Pepper Sauce Bottoms, Goat Hill, Salt Creek, Bessemer, and Bojon Town.

Along with diversity came racial and ethnic strife, and many of the new arrivals in Pueblo experienced discrimination. The Ku Klux Klan was very active starting in the 1920s, but by the 1940s had lost its appeal. By 1960, many ethnicities had overcome the adversity, but some populations remained marginalized. The civil rights movement of the 1960s affected Pueblo greatly and was the inspiration for citizens of Spanish and Mexican descent to also work toward equal rights in the Southwest. Those who fought for change and civil rights adopted the term "Chicano." This chapter honors the diversity of the people who chose to call Pueblo home.

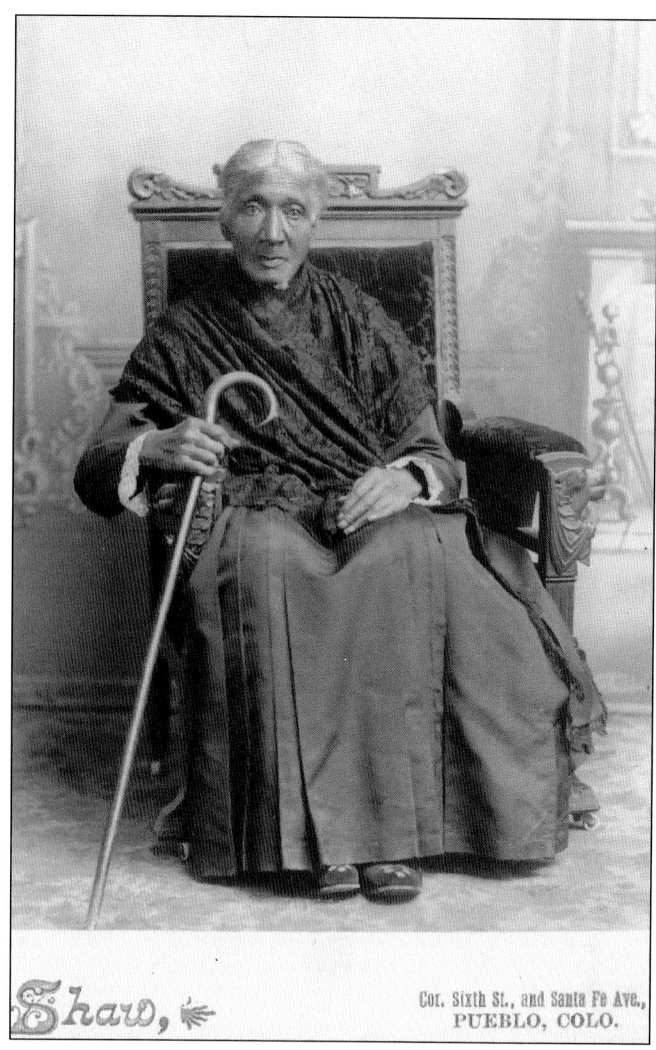

According to the 1860 census, "Aunt" Liza Boone (pictured) came to Pueblo as a slave of Albert Boone, who founded Boone, Colorado, east of Pueblo. After emancipation, she earned a living as a laundress and nursed the sick. She died in 1893 at age 86. (Denver Public Library, Western History Collection X21537; photograph by J.W. Shaw.)

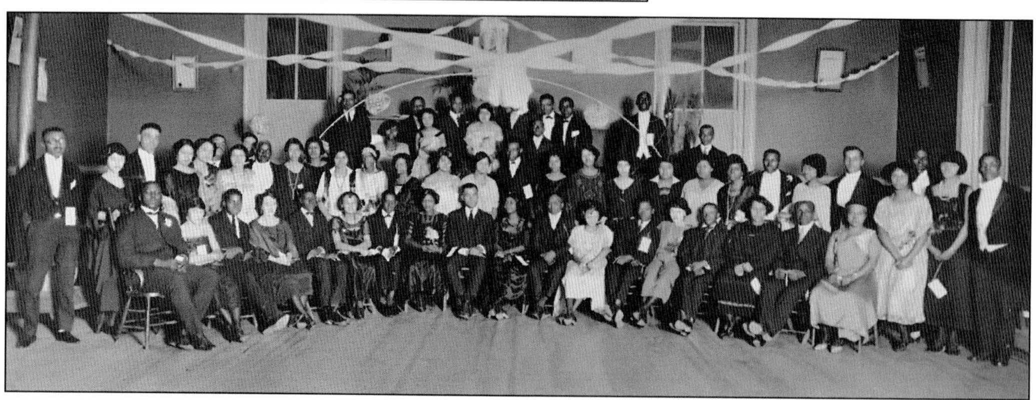

Initially, Pueblo's African American population was centered downtown, but many eventually moved to the Bessemer neighborhood. The African American population grew from 27 (1.8 percent) in 1870 to a peak of 1,689 (3.2 percent) in 1910. Shown here is an African American social club at a function in 1923. (PH-P-34-01-006.)

In 1907, the Pueblo Colorado Orphanage and Old Folks Home was incorporated. The operation grew quickly, leading the organization to purchase two homes at 2713 and 2715 North Grand Avenue and connect them via a hallway. The renamed Lincoln Home Association closed in 1963, and the home opened as a museum in the mid-1990s. The home was the only orphanage that served African American orphans in Colorado. This photograph shows an outdoor event at the orphanage. (PH-P-418-03-004.)

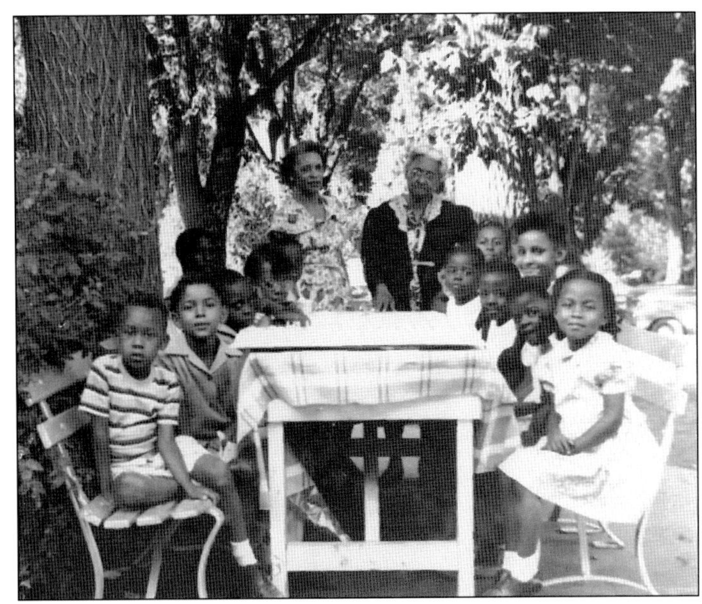

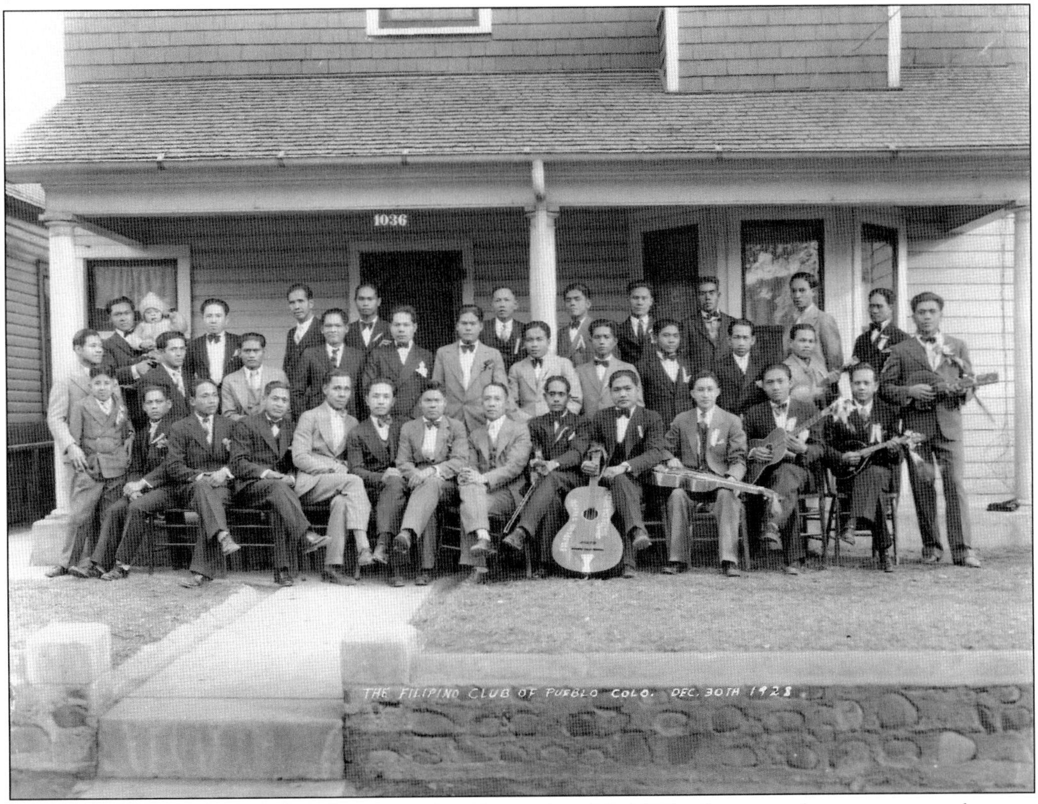

The Filipino Club of Pueblo, shown in this December 30, 1928, photograph, prepares to play at a local music festival. People of Filipino descent arrived in Pueblo following World War I, as they were considered United States' nationals and were not subject to the immigration restrictions of Asians. In Pueblo, many Filipinos lived in the Bessemer neighborhood and worked at the steel mill or smelters. (PH-P-200-01.)

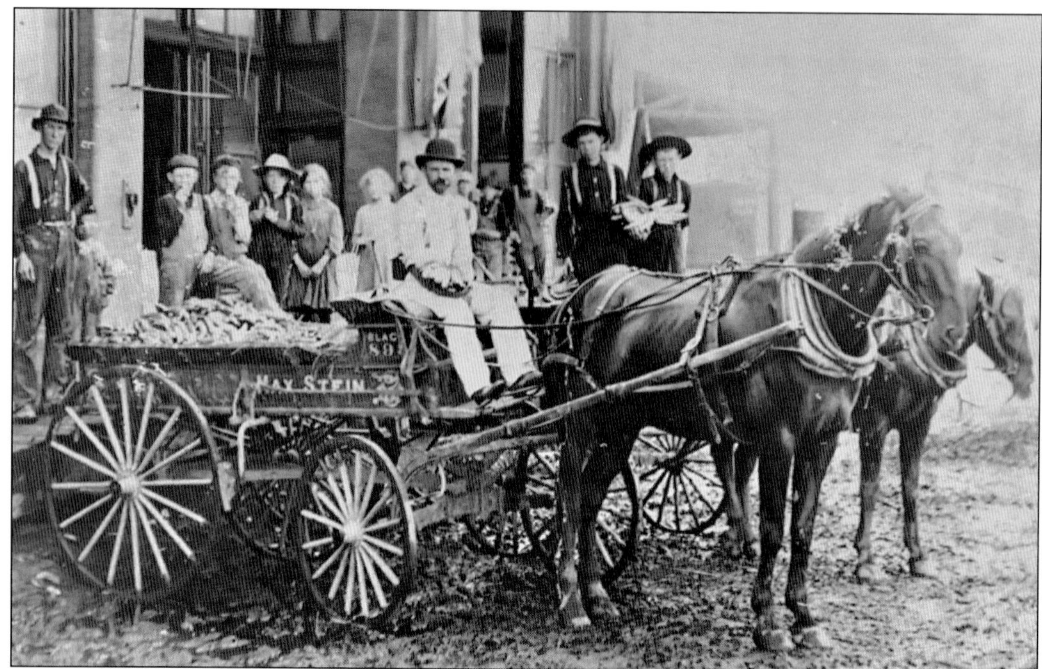

Originally, there were two synagogues in early Pueblo. Temple Emanuel, was a Reform house of worship, built in 1900 at Twelfth Street and Grand Avenue, and B'nai Jacob, the Orthodox synagogue located at 111 East Second Street (the present location of the Sangre de Cristo Arts Center). (PH-P-366-02.)

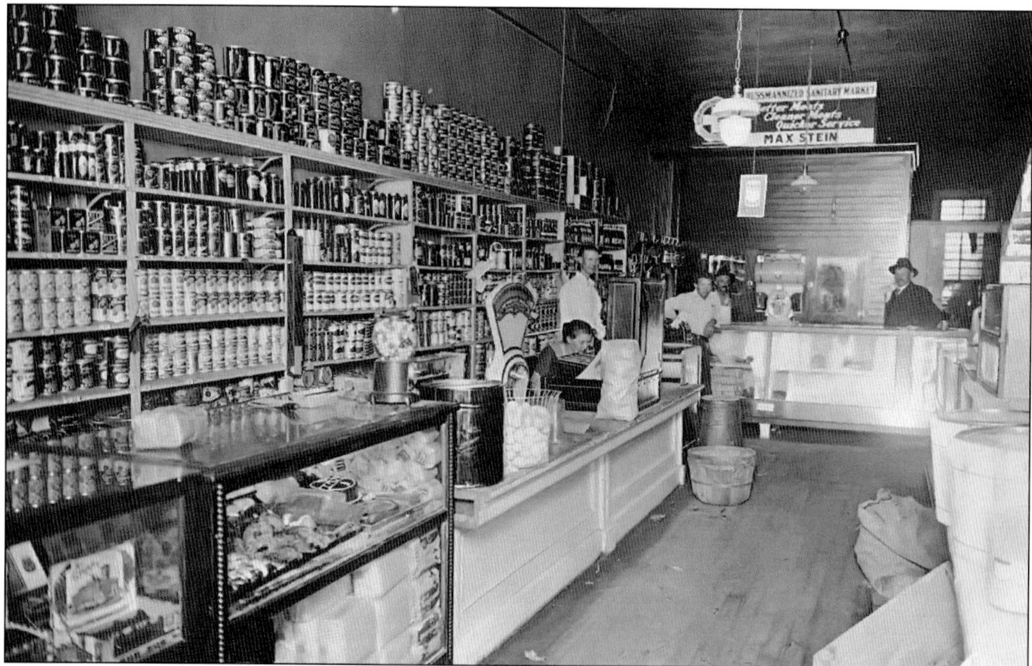

This c. 1918 image shows Stein's Market, one of the earliest grocery stores in Pueblo, located at 115 East Fourth Street. The market was a short distance over the Fountain Creek, in the Eastside Neighborhood where Pueblo's early Jewish population resided. (PH-P-366-02-001.)

The 1880 census was the first Census to count Chinese immigrants in Pueblo County. Many males were employed as laundrymen and lived in boarding houses. The 1890 City Directory lists eleven laundries owned by Chinese men throughout Pueblo. The 1897 City Directory lists Hop Lee, shown here, owning a laundry at 116 West First Street. (PH-P-160-01-001.)

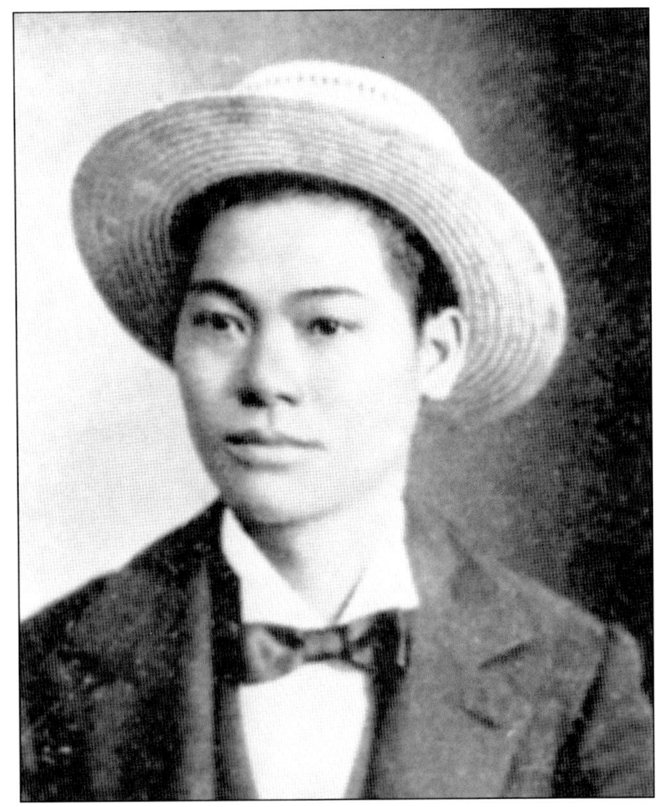

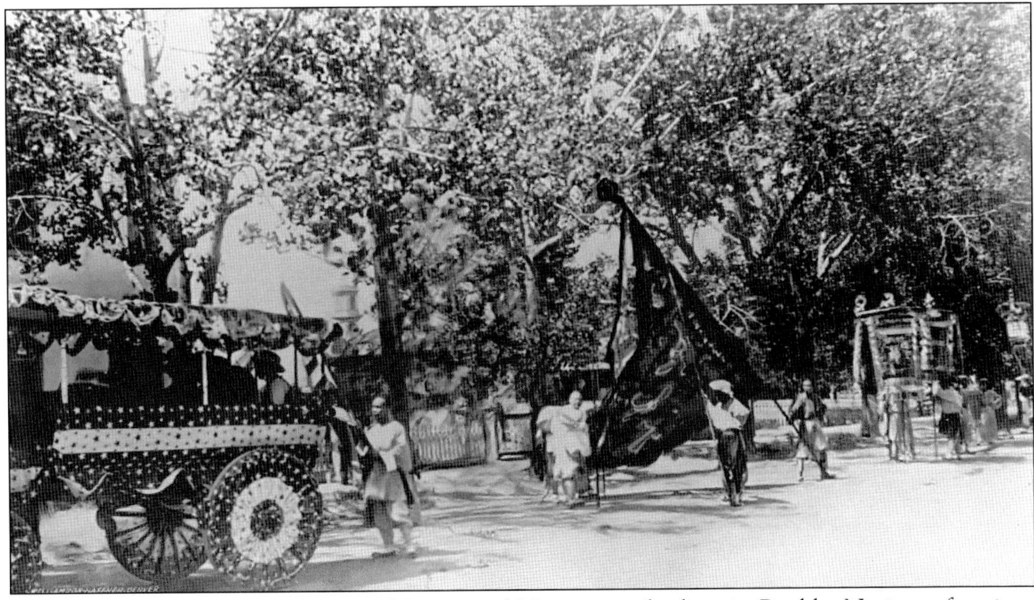

On July 5, 1897, the first Pageant of States and Nations took place in Pueblo. Natives of various states and foreign countries who took up residence in Pueblo designed floats celebrating their heritage and the birth of American independence. This photograph shows a float from the pageant representing Chinese heritage with a "celestial band" and banners, which won second place (PH-P-160-01-001.)

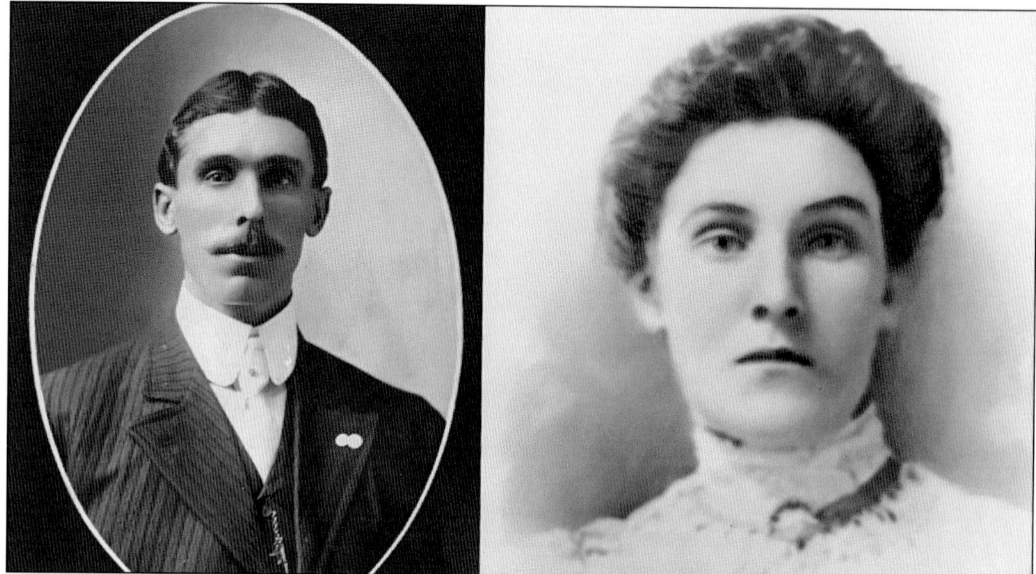

Most Irish who arrived in Pueblo were first-generation Americans. The census records show that their jobs had improved compared to their parents who fled Ireland because of the potato famine. John Joseph and his wife, Catherine Mary Sheehan, are pictured around 1906. (PH-P-364-02.)

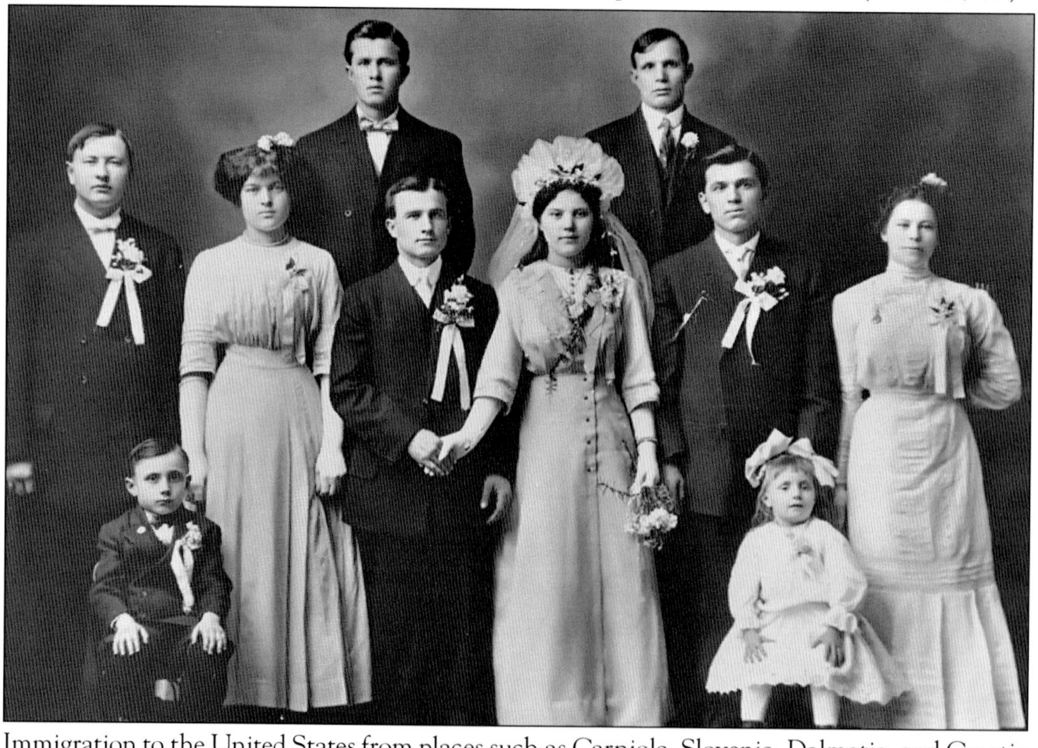

Immigration to the United States from places such as Carniola, Slovenia, Dalmatia, and Croatia began in the 1880s. Thousands of Eastern European immigrants came to Pueblo to work in the smelting and steel industry. The neighborhood near Eiler's smelter has a rich history and is an area of Pueblo where many people of Slovenian descent settled, thrived, built businesses, and raised families. Shown here is a photograph of the Sajbel and Rajz families. (PH-P-576-02.)

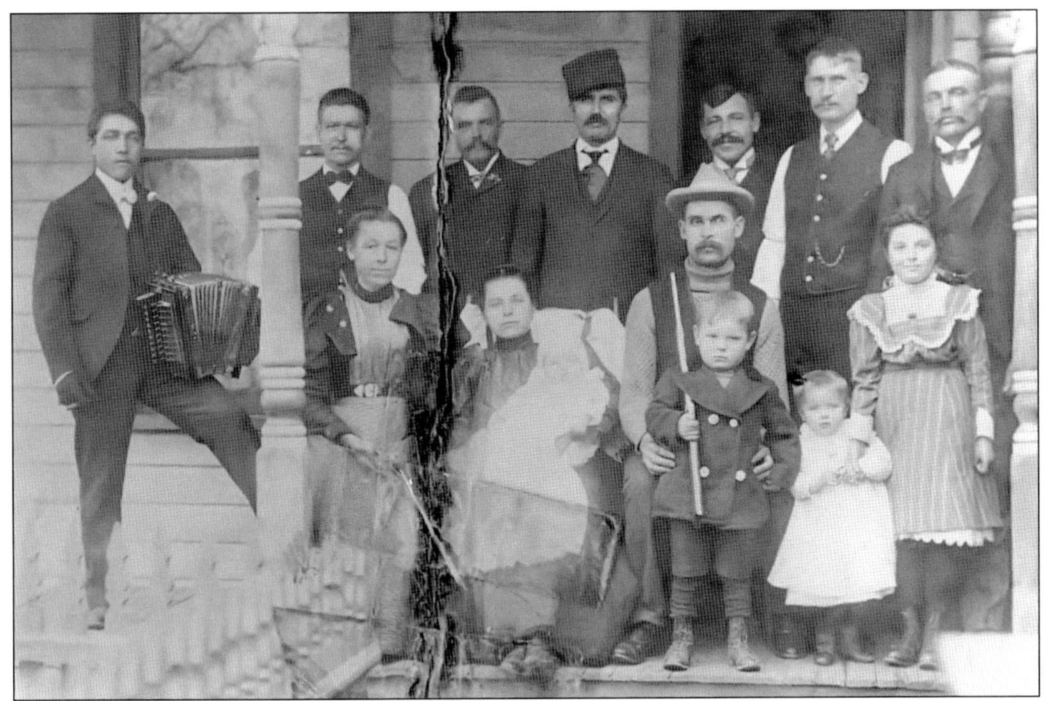

The Eiler's neighborhood became known as "Bojon Town." "Bojon" is a slang term referring to those of Slovenian descent. One explanation for the term is that when traveling to Paris, the Parisians described Slovenians as "Quels beaux gens!" ("What handsome people!"). When declaring themselves at immigration points, they chose to call themselves "beaux gens," which immigration officials understood as "Bojons," a term now embraced by Slovenian Americans from Pueblo. Shown here in 1902 are some members of the Miketa family of Slovenian descent. (PH-P-576-02.)

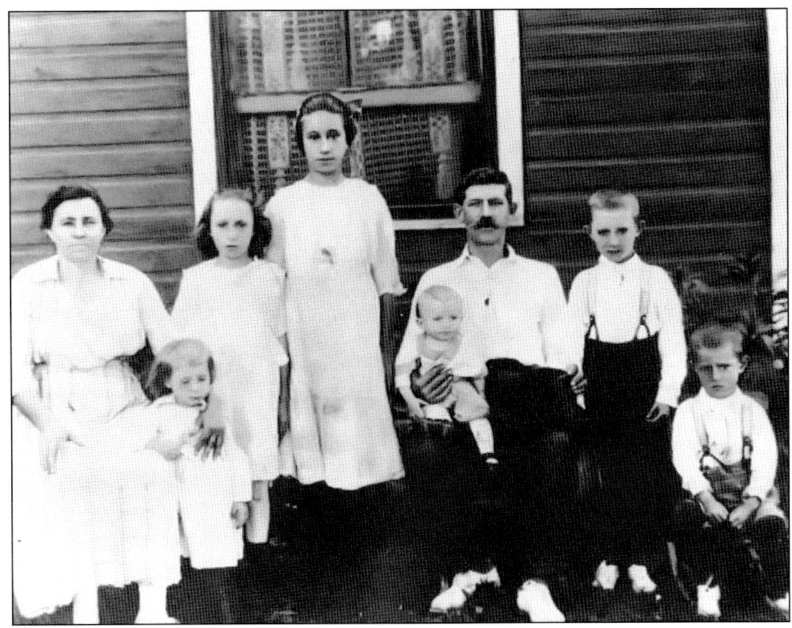

The Yengich family hailed from Croatia. This photograph was taken in 1920 at the family home at 1901 East Abriendo Avenue. Shown are Mary (maiden name Stelinovich); Anne (age 3); Marge (age 9); Mildred (age 12); Duja (Dewey); Sam on lap; Joe (age 8); Jack (age 5). (PH-P-805-01.)

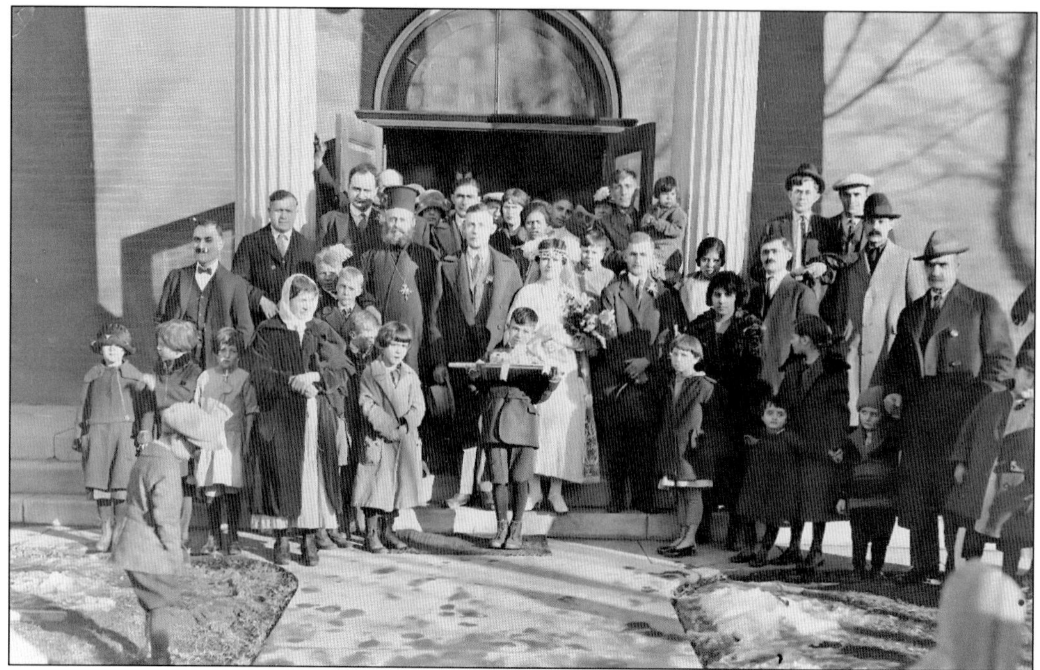

Shown here is the wedding of Simos Lymberopulos (Sam Leber) to Angelina Margarite in January 1925 in front of St. John's Greek Orthodox Church. In 1903, the Greek Orthodox Community Association of Pueblo was formed, and in 1905 it was registered with the state. The three goals of this new corporation were to build a church, provide cemetery facilities, and to help Greeks establish themselves in the city. (Maria Sanchez Tucker.)

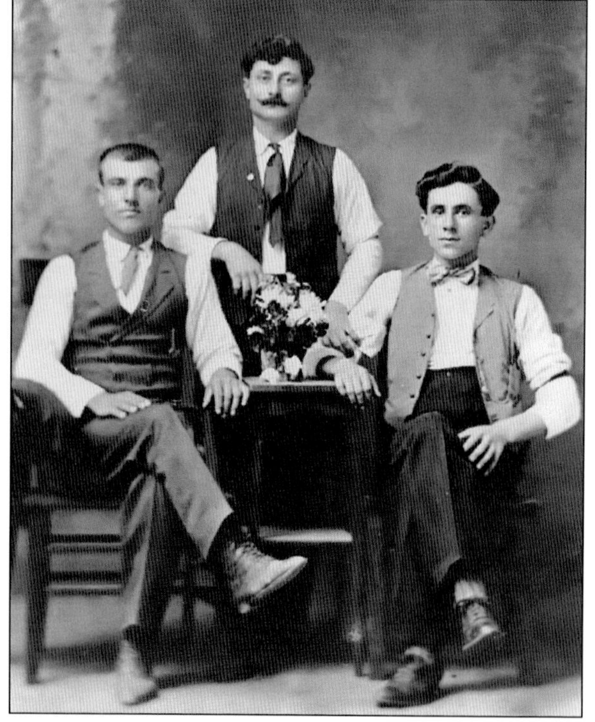

The Greek gentlemen in this c. 1907 image are identified as, from left to right, Eddie Kouris, John Rougas, and Gus Poulos. In an interview, Rougas stated that when he and his cousins arrived in Pueblo they rented a house at 1127 Abriendo Avenue. His first job in Pueblo was in the wire mill department at CF&I. (PH-P-308-01.)

Johanna Chujeba, from Teschen, Austria (now Poland), immigrated to the United States in 1909. She is shown here wearing a traditional Polish dress. People of Polish descent appear to be one of the later groups to migrate to Pueblo. While many other ethnic groups migrated in the last few decades of the 1800s, many Polish people waited until the first or second decade of the 1900s. (PH-P-447-01-003.)

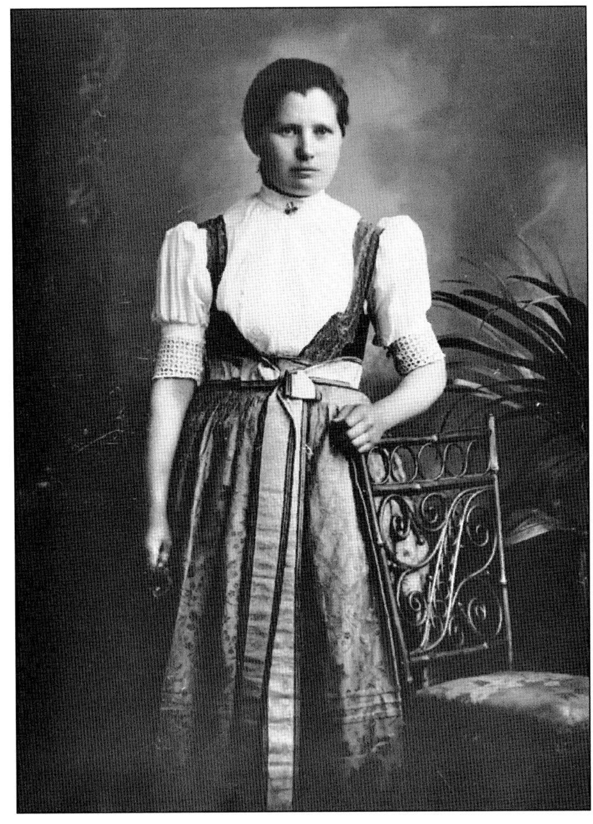

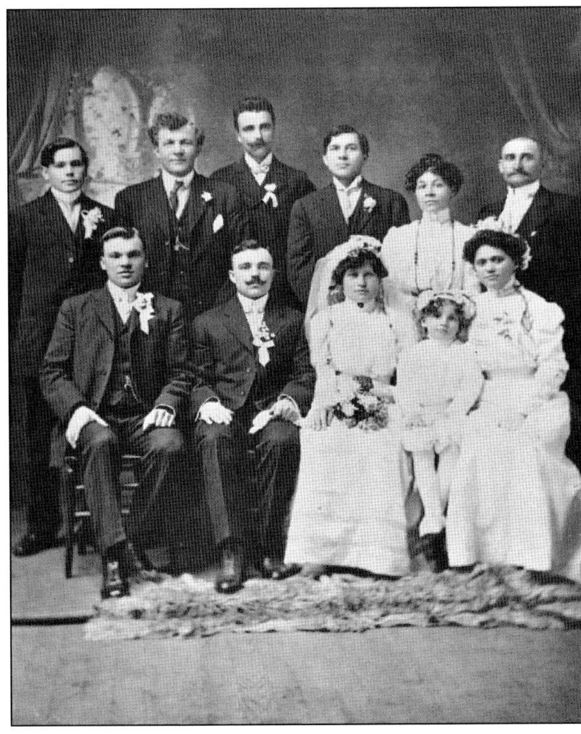

This photograph shows the Mendrick and Chujeba wedding. The bride and groom are John Mendrick and Johanna Chujeba. A naturalization certificate shows that John became a citizen on October 11, 1921. (PH-P-447-01-001.)

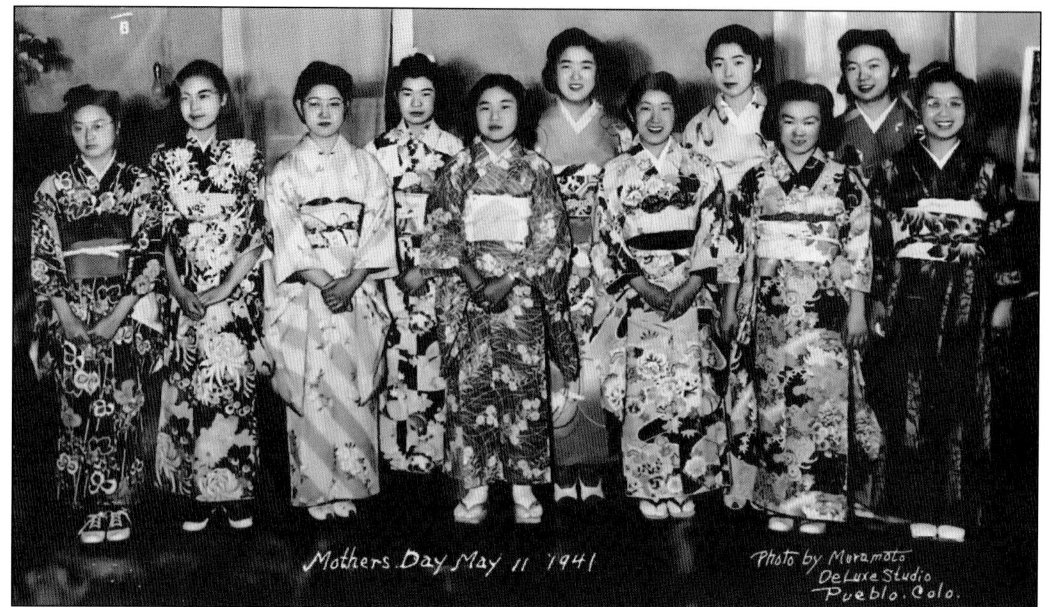

Japanese women are pictured on Mother's Day, May 11, 1941. This photograph was taken by Frank D. Muramoto, who owned a photography studio in Pueblo from 1912 until 1958. Born in Japan in 1905, Muramoto came to the United States at age 18. Before coming to Pueblo, he lived in Illinois, where he worked as a houseboy for Frank Lloyd Wright. (PH-P-177-02.)

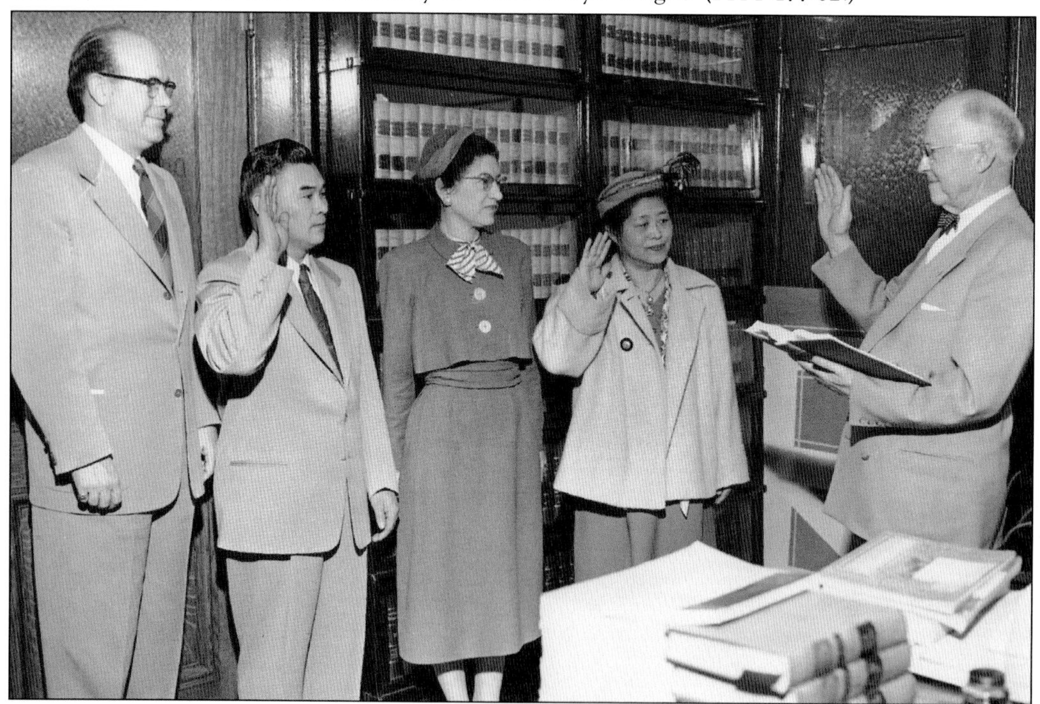

Shown here is a naturalization ceremony in Pueblo about 1960 in which Sam Futamata (second from left) and a woman identified as Mrs. Muramoto (second from right) are being sworn in as United States citizens. Also pictured are their teacher, Victoria Christiano Marion; their sponsor Frank Hoag Jr. (left) publisher of the *Pueblo Chieftain*; and Judge J.A. Phelps. (PH-P-177-02.)

Charles Nelson, a Swedish soldier and later a Pueblo immigrant, is pictured here during World War I. Around 1900, the Swedish community was centered in the 800 block of East Abriendo Avenue. The community included a grocery store, Tabor Lutheran Church, and a Swedish Free Mission. (PH-P-749-02.)

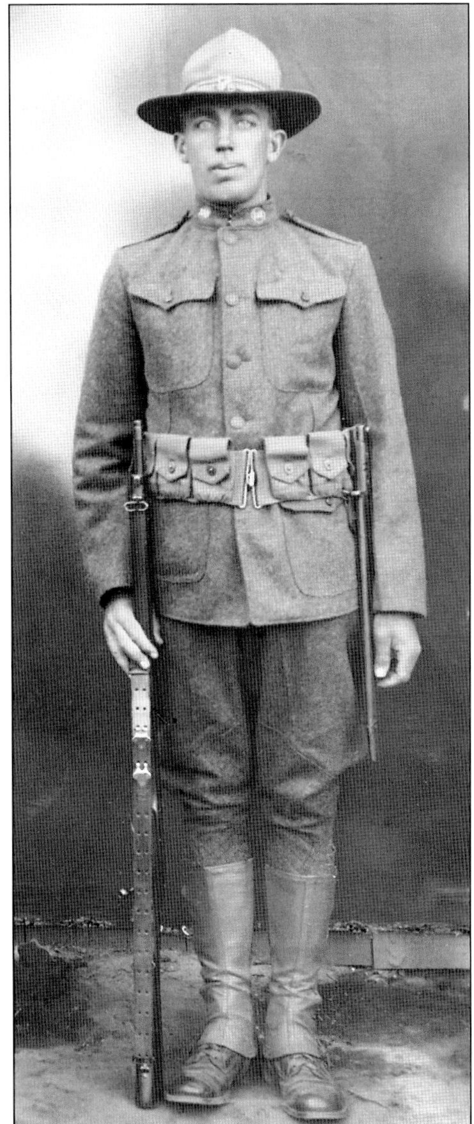

First- and second-generation German families were distinguished in Pueblo by their music, art, and customs. For several years, Puebloans sponsored a Grand Reunion of States and Nations on Independence Day. Many nationalities and former residents of other states joined in a parade of floats, bands, and marching units. This 1898 photograph shows a horse-drawn float prepared by Pueblo Germans to welcome newer arrivals from Germany. (PH-P-304-02-001.)

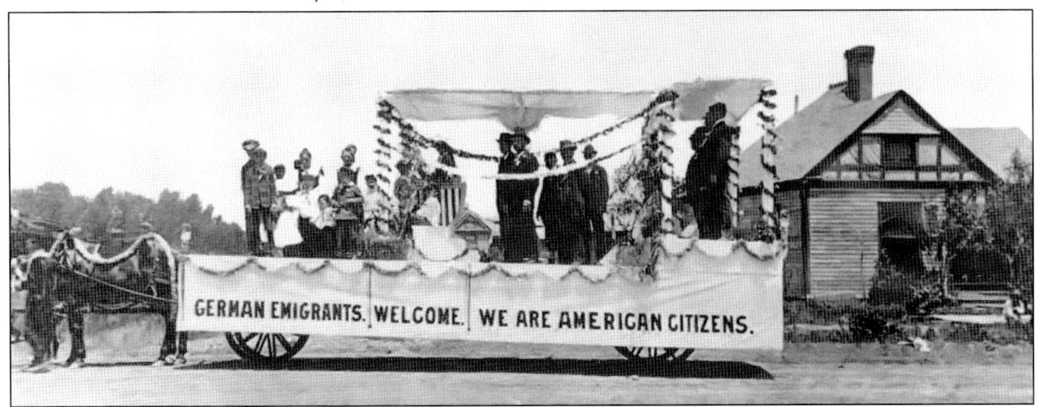

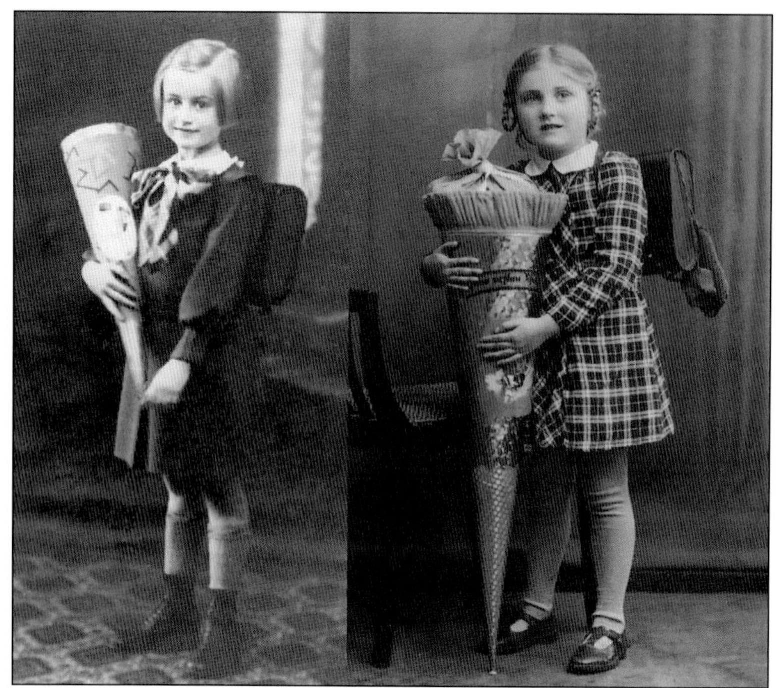

Like all ethnic groups, Germans brought several traditions with them. Two children, Erika Leist (left) and Lolita Kessler, are shown holding a tubular cone filled with candy. There was a tradition of giving children this cone on the first day of kindergarten. Some Germans still continue this tradition in Pueblo. (Left, Charlene Garcia Simms for Leist; right, German American Club of Pueblo for Kessler.)

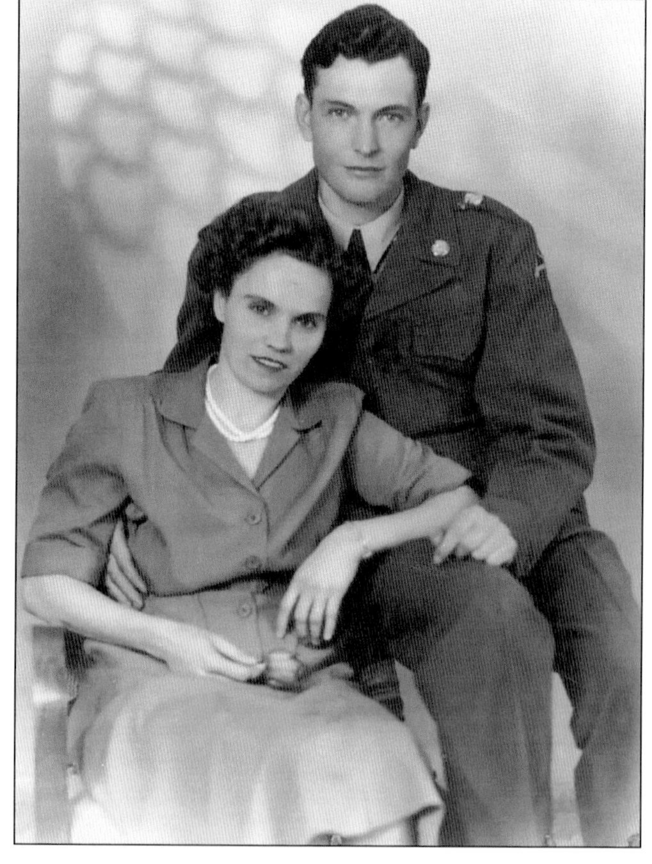

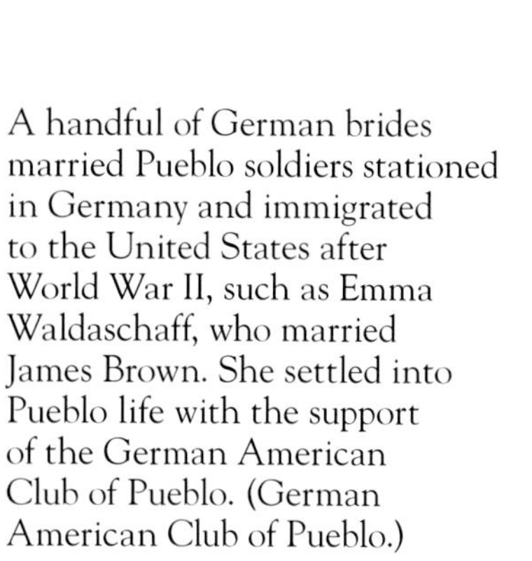

A handful of German brides married Pueblo soldiers stationed in Germany and immigrated to the United States after World War II, such as Emma Waldaschaff, who married James Brown. She settled into Pueblo life with the support of the German American Club of Pueblo. (German American Club of Pueblo.)

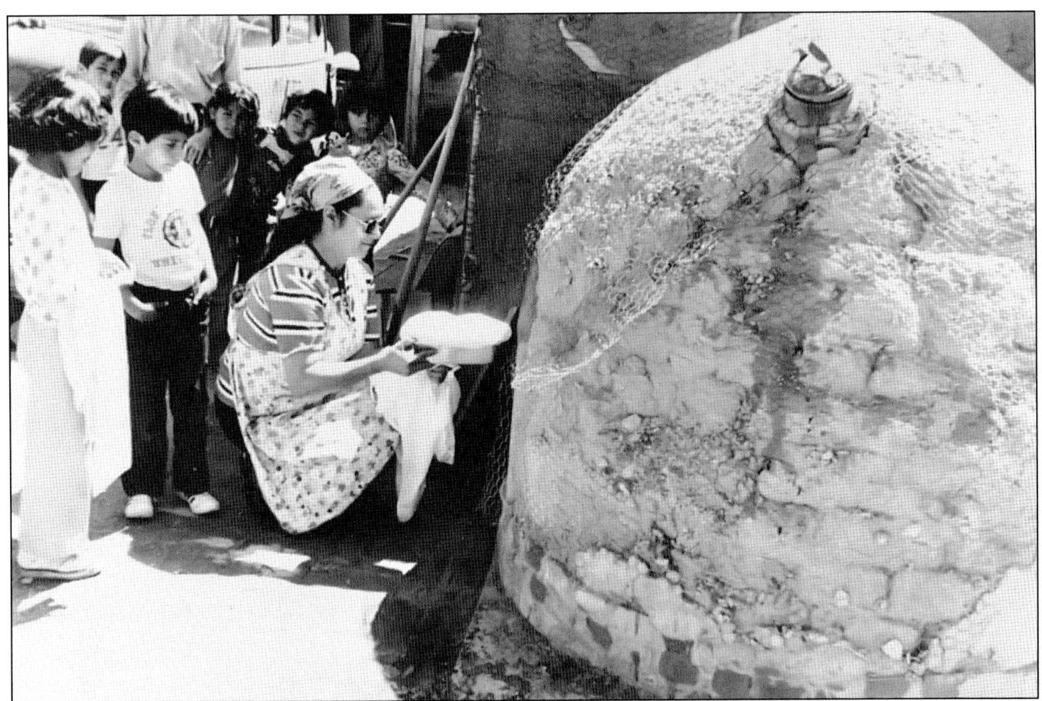

A woman in the Salt Creek neighborhood teaches children how to bake in an outside oven (*horno*) made of adobe bricks. Before baking, the oven was heated for a few hours. Bread and pastries were placed in the ovens, and the opening was then covered. The hot walls radiated enough heat for baking. (PH-P-370-04-005.)

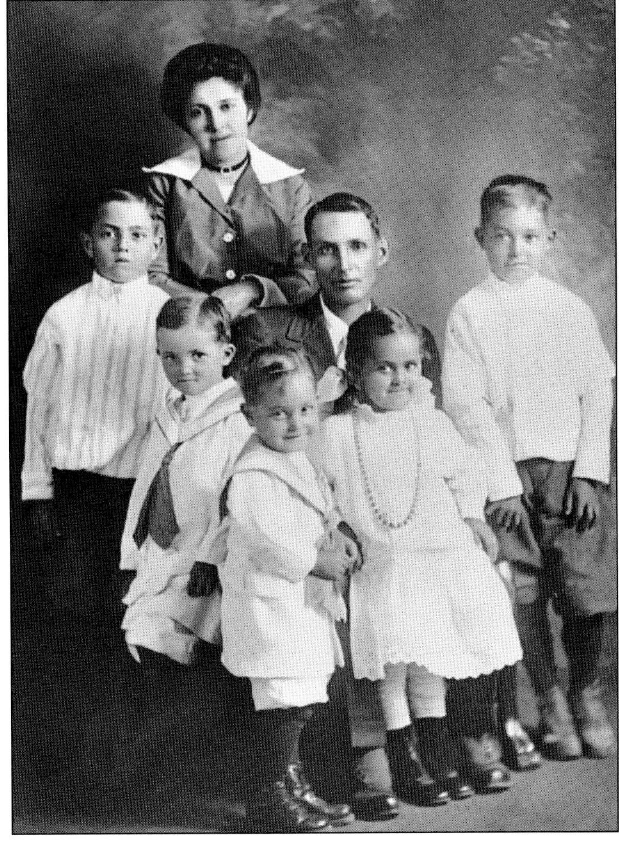

The Martinez family lived in the Salt Creek neighborhood. They were descendants of the first people who settled in the neighborhood, located immediately east of the CF&I steelworks. Most of the people worked in the smelters or on the farms of the St. Charles Mesa. An influx of Mexican immigrants and New Mexico residents arrived in Pueblo in the 1940s to work at the steel mill and the Pueblo Army Depot. (PH-P-370-08-001.)

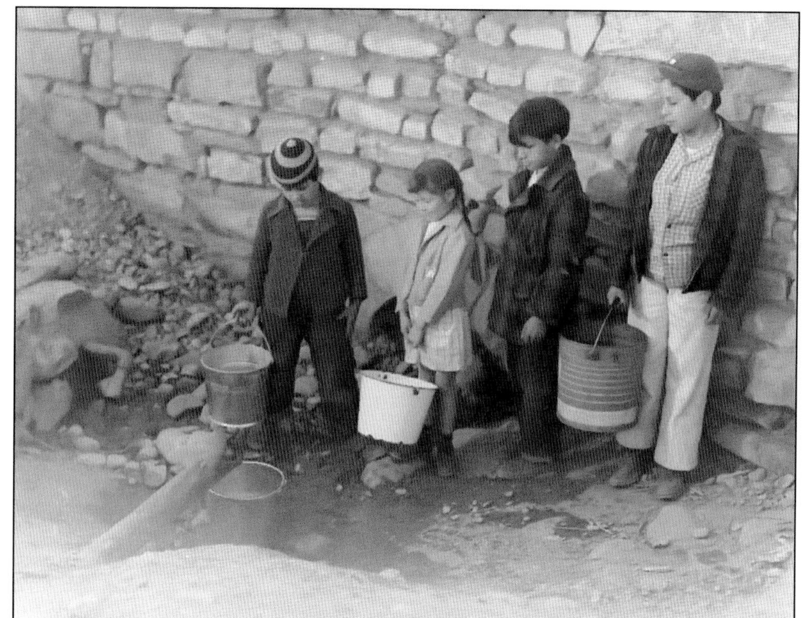

These children are waiting to get water from el Ojito (the Eye), a natural spring from which Salt Creek residents obtained water for cooking and drinking. Most immigrants from Mexico and migrants from New Mexico settled in Salt Creek. Several descendants of the first settlers still live there. (Jovita Chavez.)

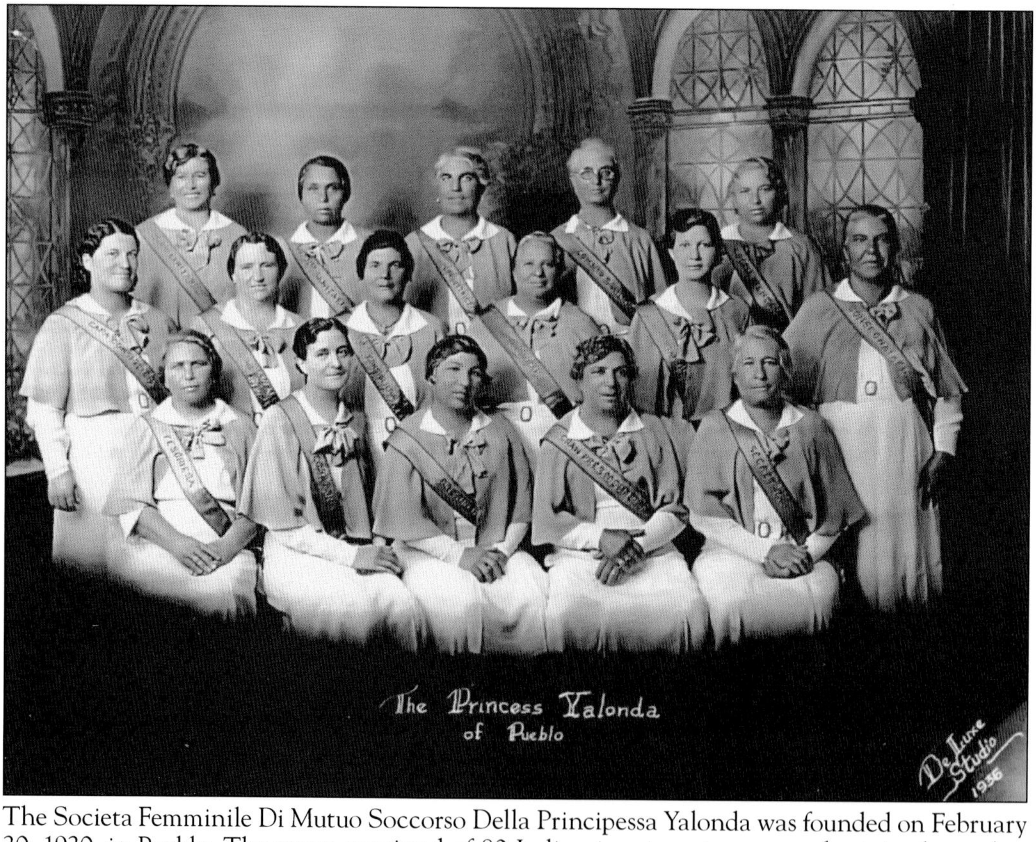

The Societa Femminile Di Mutuo Soccorso Della Principessa Yalonda was founded on February 20, 1920, in Pueblo. The group consisted of 80 Italian immigrant women who joined together for mutual benefit. The club was named after Princess Yalonda of Savoy, daughter of King Victor Emmanuel III of Italy. The group disbanded on March 22, 1986. (A-008 Box 87 3.00.)

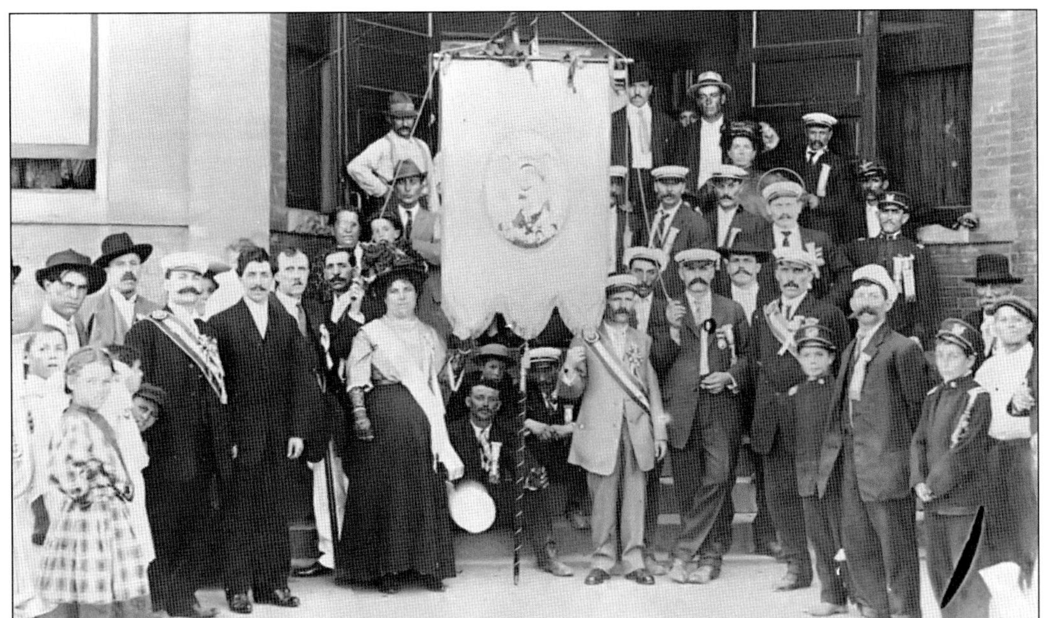

With the railroad and steel mill came a new wave of immigrants. A large number were Italians. Only five Italians were recorded in the census of 1880. The 1885 Colorado census counted 140 Italians, and by 1900, the number rose to 761 Italians. The Independent Sicilian Society shown here was formed in 1899 for the advancement of everyone's good and cooperation for the common welfare. (PH-P-365-01.)

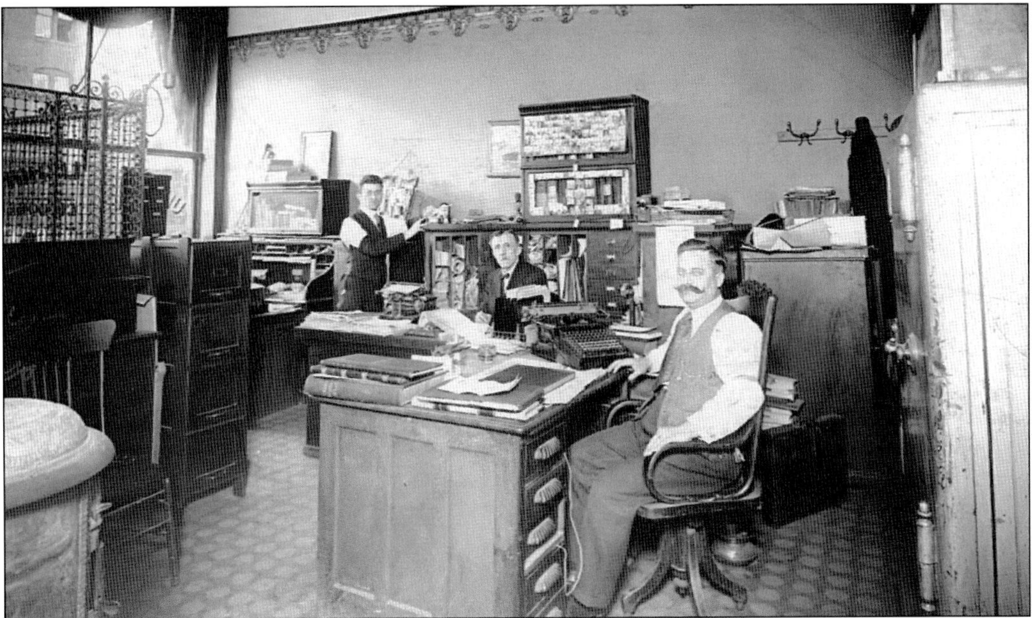

Vincent Massari (left), Hector Chiariglione (center), and Joseph Battaglia are pictured at the offices of *L'Unione*, one of the foreign-language newspapers published at the turn of the 20th century. Chiariglione founded *L'Unione* in 1897, when he published 400 copies. The 1921 flood nearly destroyed the newspaper, placing the building under 11 feet of water. Chiariglione sold the newspaper to Massari, who later became a state senator. (PH-P-94-13-09.)

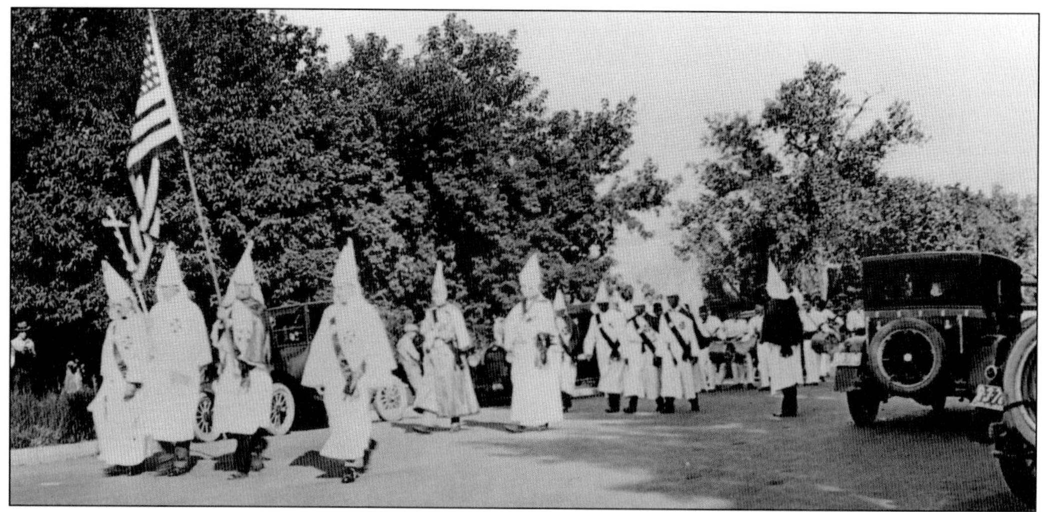

While most Pueblo residents celebrated the ethnic diversity of the city, others refused. The Ku Klux Klan (shown here in a funeral procession) infiltrated the community in the 1920s. Most of the group's efforts toward economic, political, and social control in Pueblo centered on Catholics, though Jewish, African American, and other minority populations were also targeted. At the height of the Klan's popularity in Pueblo, immigrants accounted for 17 percent of the city and another 17 percent were second-generation Americans. (PH-P-368-02_001.)

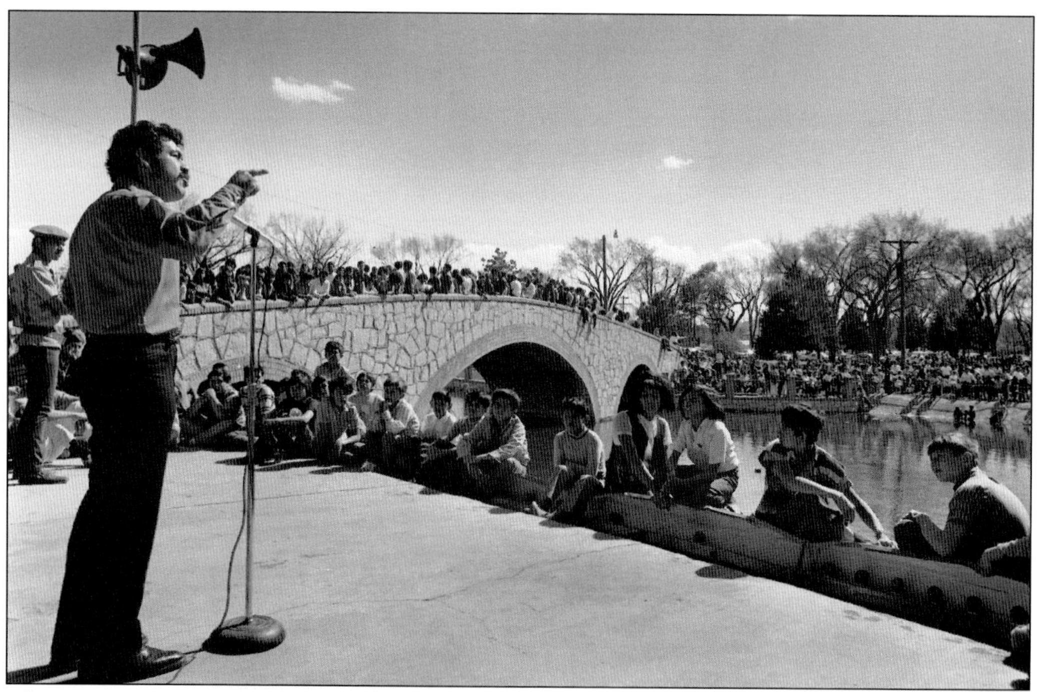

Chicano activist Rodolfo "Corky" Gonzales is shown during a speech calling for equality for Chicanos at a Cinco de Mayo event at Mineral Palace Park in the late 1960s. Pueblo attracted national speakers in the Chicano Movement such as Gonzales from Denver's Crusade for Justice and Cesar Chavez and Dolores Huerta of the United Farm Workers. Many people from Pueblo participated in the Chicano movement, fighting to end discrimination and inequality. (PH-B-168-02_001.)

Four

Growth and Stability

The first established residents of Pueblo valued religion and education as means of stability and permanence. Before constructing churches and schools, residents met informally in homes or halls and even in the old courthouse. The Episcopalians constructed the first formal church in Pueblo in 1868 and dedicated it as St. Peter's Church. Other denominations soon followed.

The first public school in Pueblo measured only 16 feet by 20 feet and was constructed in 1862 at 421 North Santa Fe Avenue. This building was doomed to inadequacy by the burgeoning town. By 1869, the "Adobe School" opened at the intersection of West Eleventh and Court Streets and accommodated 80 students. Centennial School replaced the smaller "Adobe School" in 1876, and various authorities constructed a plethora of both secular and religious educational facilities in the following decades.

In 1868, Dr. Michael Beshoar began Pueblo's first newspaper, named the *Colorado Chieftain*. Local magnates and entrepreneurs formed the equivalent of a chamber of commerce on January 20, 1869, and named it the Board of Trade of Southern Colorado. Growth and stability were dependent on capital investment from the eastern board and beyond. According to the *Historical Descriptive Review of Colorado's Enterprising Cities*, "the eleventh census accredits Pueblo with the most rapid increase in population since 1880 of any city in the union."

A growing and lively town, in addition to industry, required a bustling commercial sector. John and Mahlon Thatcher established the first bank in Pueblo in 1871, setting the stage for future economic and commercial growth. The city established a police department in 1880, though a sheriff served the needs of law enforcement beginning in 1862. The first fire department organized in 1873 and was composed of volunteers; the city would not establish a paid fire department until 1889. Numerous fraternal organizations emerged within the city, and several entrepreneurs supplied Pueblo residents with most everything imaginable at the time.

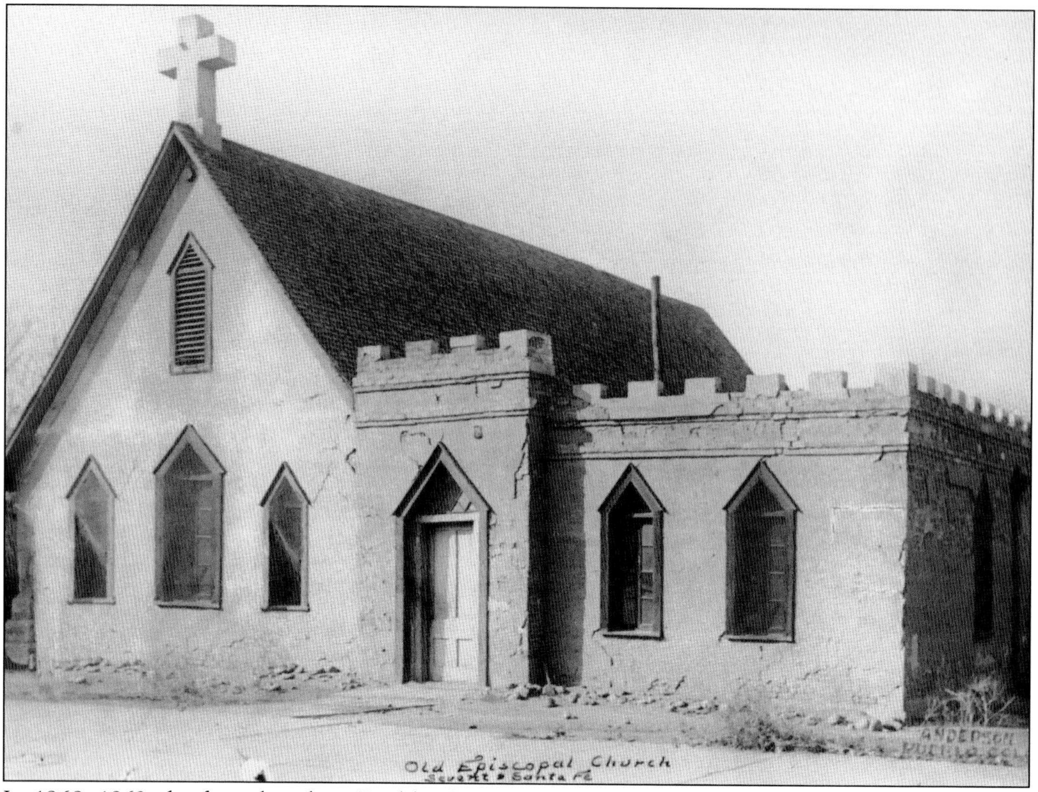

In 1868–1869, the first church in Pueblo, St. Peter's Episcopal Church, was built at Seventh and Santa Fe Avenues. The building included a bell that rang for church services, to announce the arrival of the mail stage, and for official town meetings. Other early churches were established by Methodists, Presbyterians, and Catholics. By 1900, there were 45 churches listed in the city directory. (PH-P-166-01-002.)

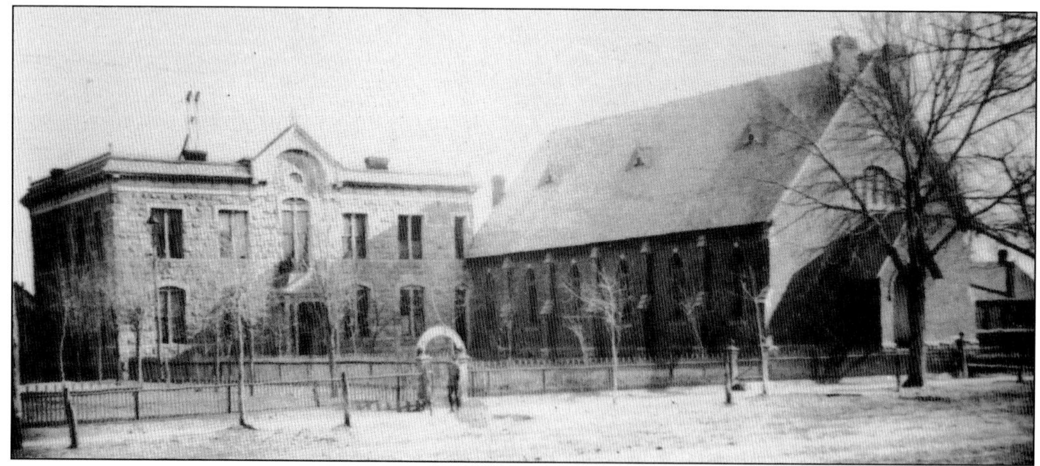

Pictured here is St. Patrick's Catholic Church, which served a predominantly Irish population. It was established in 1882 when the church was constructed. The combination rectory and school building, seen here at the left, dates to 1884. Both buildings are extant yet vacant as of this writing. Pueblo churches provided immigrants with a place where a common language was spoken and similar traditions were shared. (PH-P-166-01-002.)

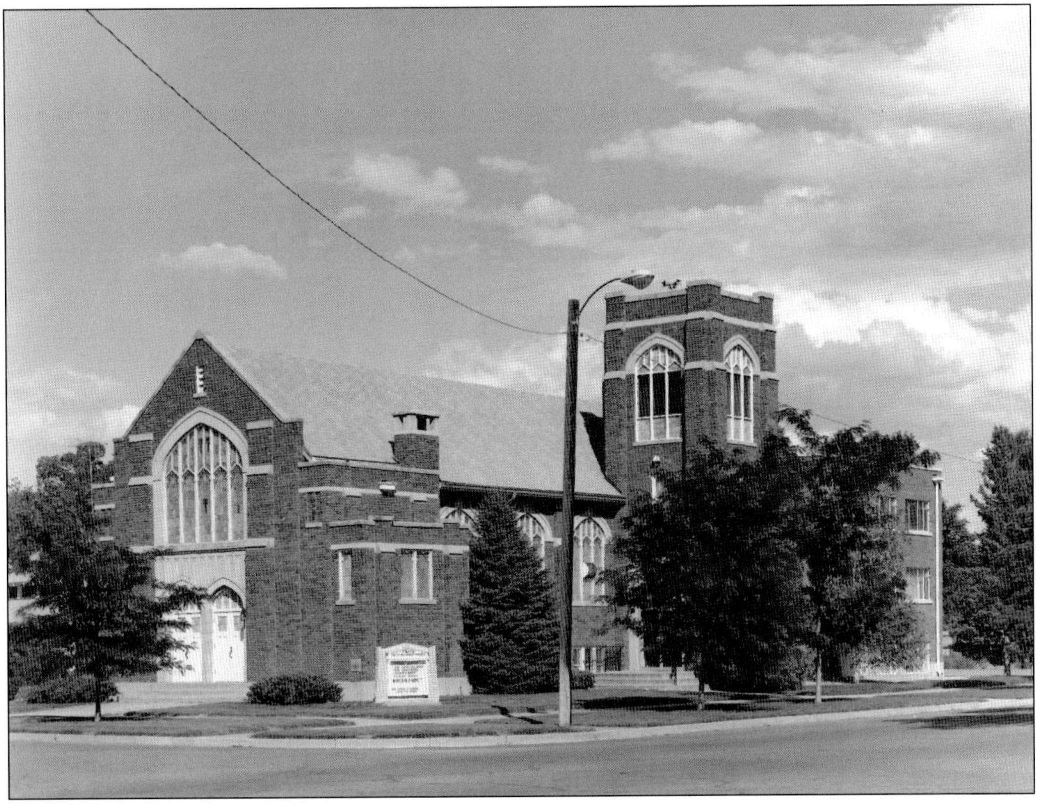

Dating to 1861, the First Methodist Episcopal Church is the oldest Protestant congregation denomination in the city of Pueblo. The congregation lacked a formal home until 1868, at which time it constructed an adobe building, the second church building in Pueblo. The church's second building was dedicated in 1888, and the steeple was constructed the following year. This building was replaced with the current building in 1923 (pictured). The congregation would later evolve into the First United Methodist Church. (PH-P-178-04_001.)

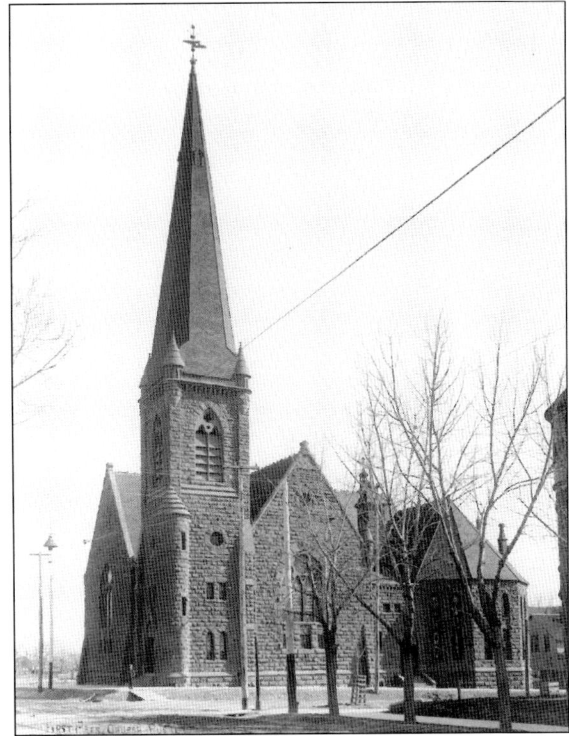

Pastor Sheldon Jackson founded the First Presbyterian Church of Pueblo in 1870. Jackson delivered the congregation's first sermon in the quaint courthouse on February 27 of that year. It took merely a year for the congregation to grow large enough to add a Sunday school. The monumental building pictured here was constructed in 1890. (PH-P-171-05_001.)

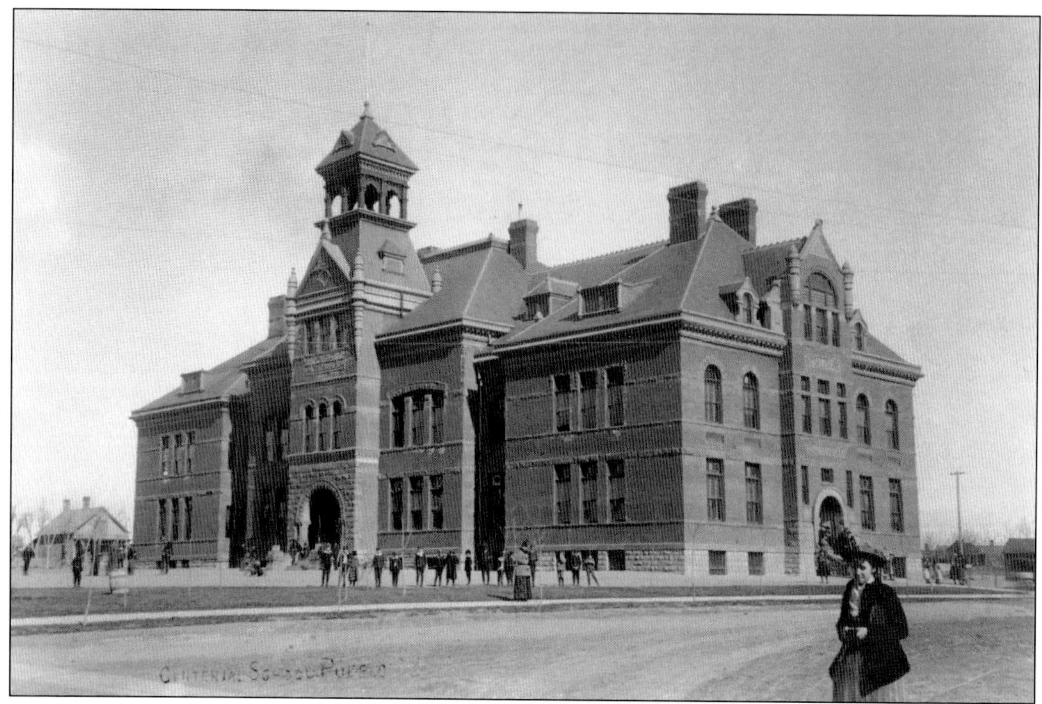

Centennial High School opened in 1876 and was named as such because Colorado gained statehood the year the school opened, 100 years after the founding of the United States. Pictured here is the original school building located at 315 West Eleventh Street, later replaced by a school district office building. (PH-P-509-02-002.)

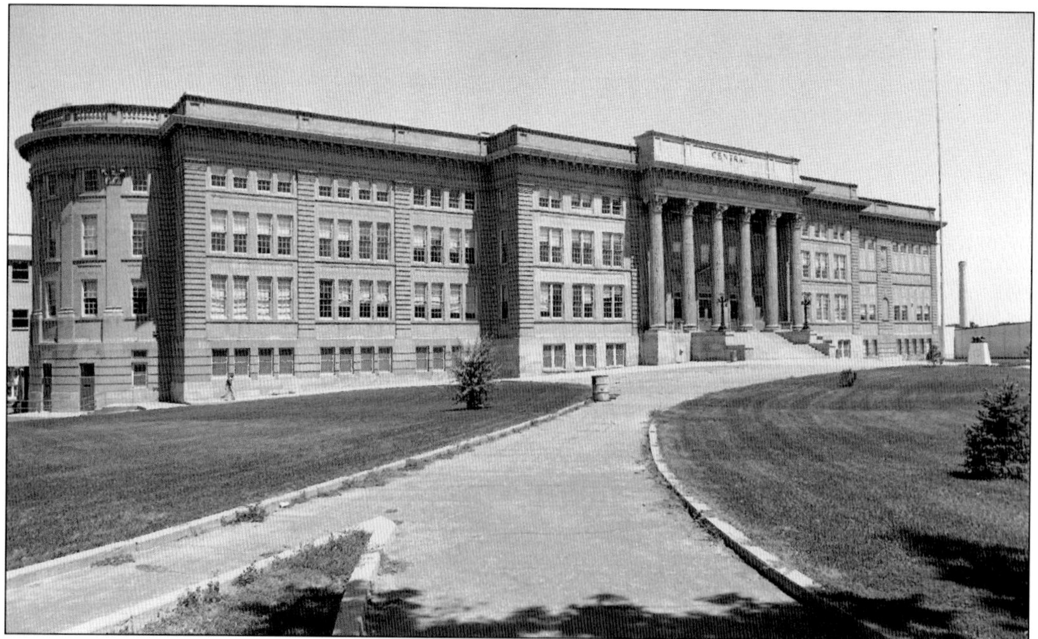

Central High School at 216 East Orman Avenue was built in stages. The first stage opened in 1906, and subsequent stages opened by 1912. This building replaced a smaller, inadequate one located at 431 East Pitkin Avenue. (PH-P-512-04.)

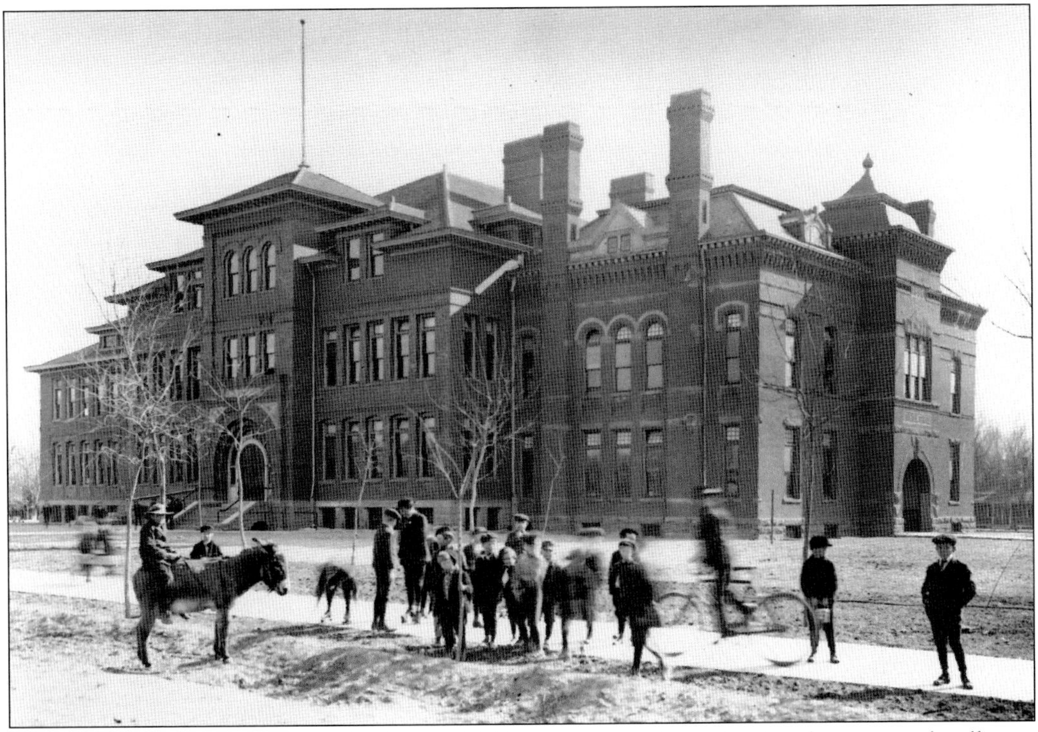

Fountain Elementary School has had several different incarnations. The first four-room schoolhouse opened in 1882, and the local district doubled the size of the school with an addition to the front facade by 1890. Additions to the building occurred from the early 1900s through the baby boom period. The structure was eventually replaced in the early 1970s by a building three blocks away. (PH-P-530-03-003.)

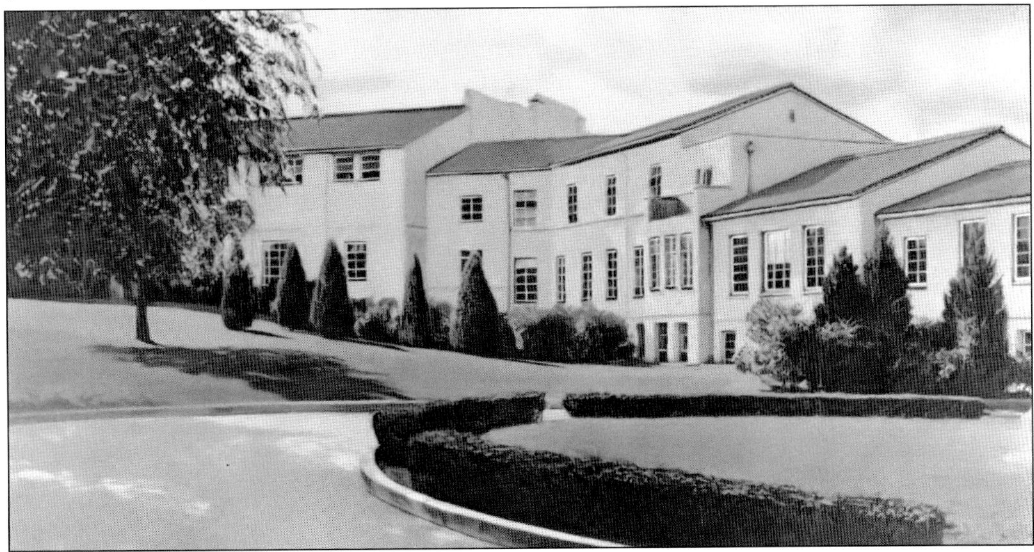

Pueblo Junior College opened in 1933 and eventually evolved into Colorado State University-Pueblo. The first students met on the third floor of the courthouse until 1935, when a new site was found on West Orman Avenue, the current location of Pueblo Community College. (PH-P-557-05-004.)

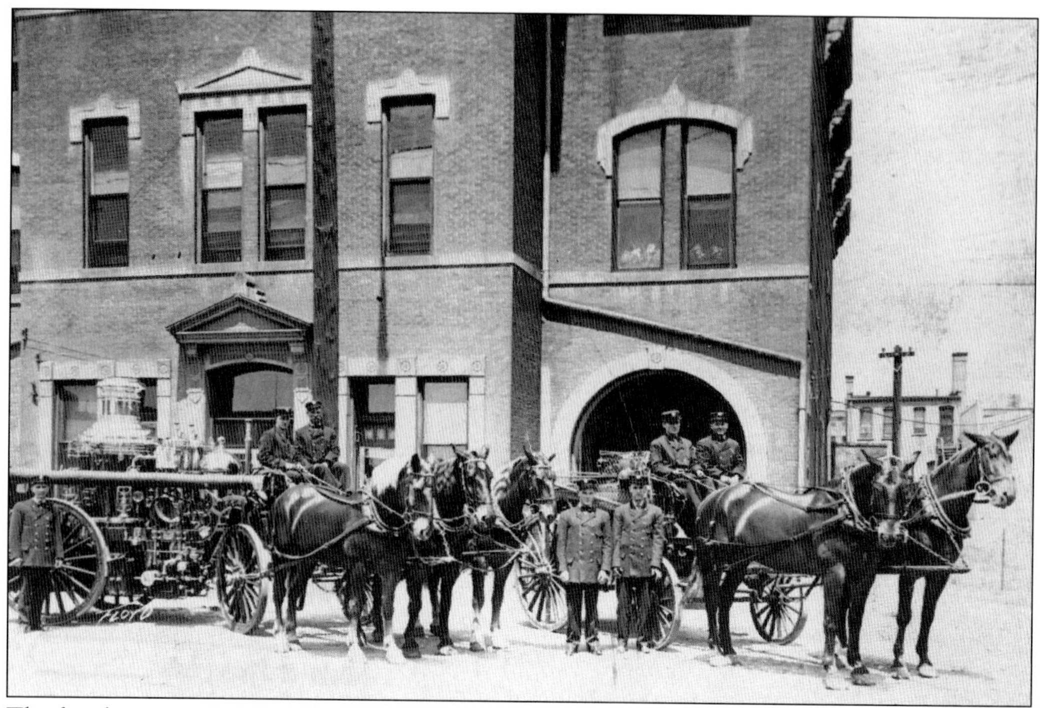

The fire department was a welcome addition to Pueblo. Powerful horses, sturdy wagons, and brave men answered fire alarms in Pueblo's earlier years. Three horses at left are hitched to a steam pumper. On the way to a fire, a blaze under the upright boiler created steam that operated a pump to increase water pressure. The wagon on the right carried hoses and ladders. This photograph was taken in front of the consolidated city hall at Central Main Street and City Hall Place. (PH-P-270-020.)

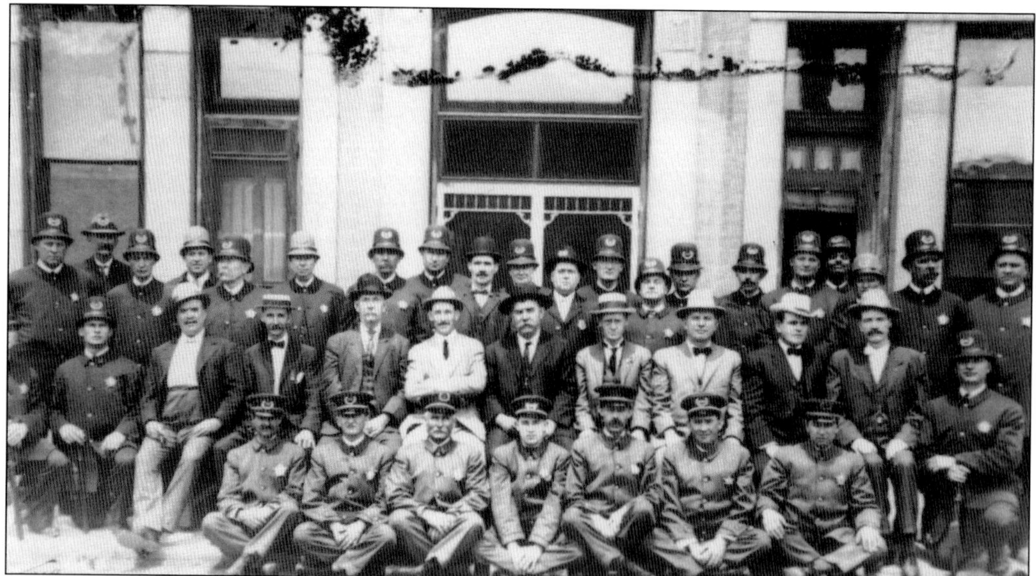

Law enforcement started once Pueblo was established as a town. The first appointed sheriff was John B. Rice in 1862. Pueblo's police department was created in 1880, but the first town marshal, Daniel P. Wooton, was not appointed until 1886. (PH-P-472-10-001.)

The first edition of the *Colorado Chieftain* was printed June 1, 1868, and was the first newspaper published in southern Colorado. This weekly publication was founded by Dr. Michael Beshoar and enlisted the assistance of Sam McBride as printer. The edition provides an account of the geography and history of southern Colorado and reported on the death of Kit Carson. (SC0999.)

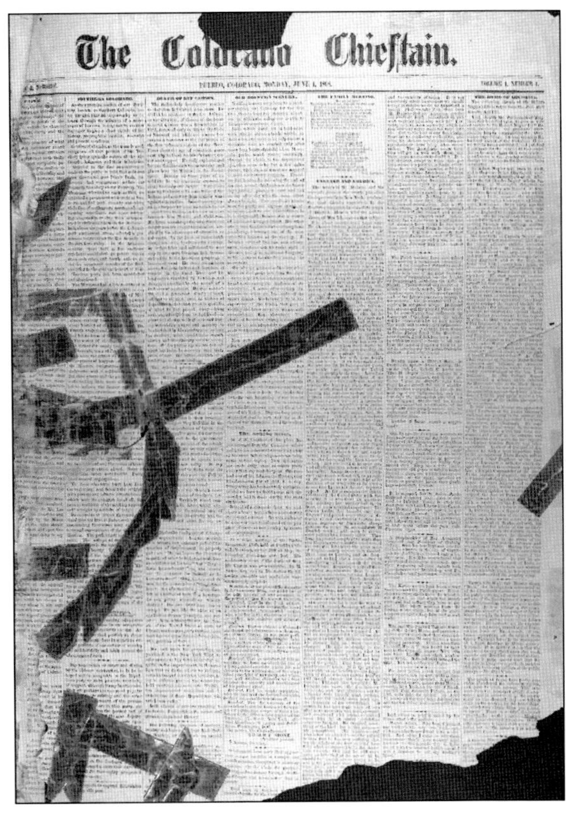

The Colorado Chieftain.

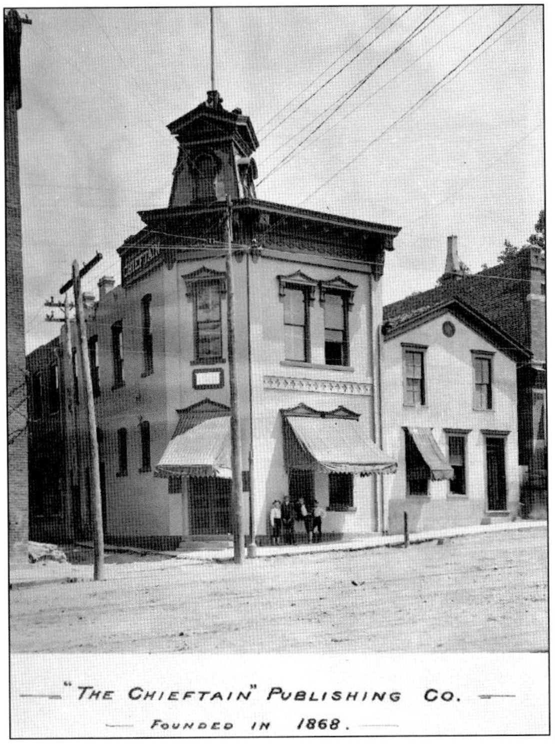

The *Colorado Chieftain* became the *Pueblo Chieftain*, a daily newspaper, in 1872. As Pueblo grew, it had a variety of locally published newspapers, including those printed in other languages. The *Chieftain*'s competitor, the *Star-Journal*, consolidated with the *Pueblo Chieftain* under the direction of Frank Hoag Sr. in 1933. The newspaper remained a family endeavor with Frank S. Hoag Jr. and, later, Robert Hoag Rawlings eventually becoming publishers of the now oldest daily newspaper in Colorado. (PH-P-415-03_001.)

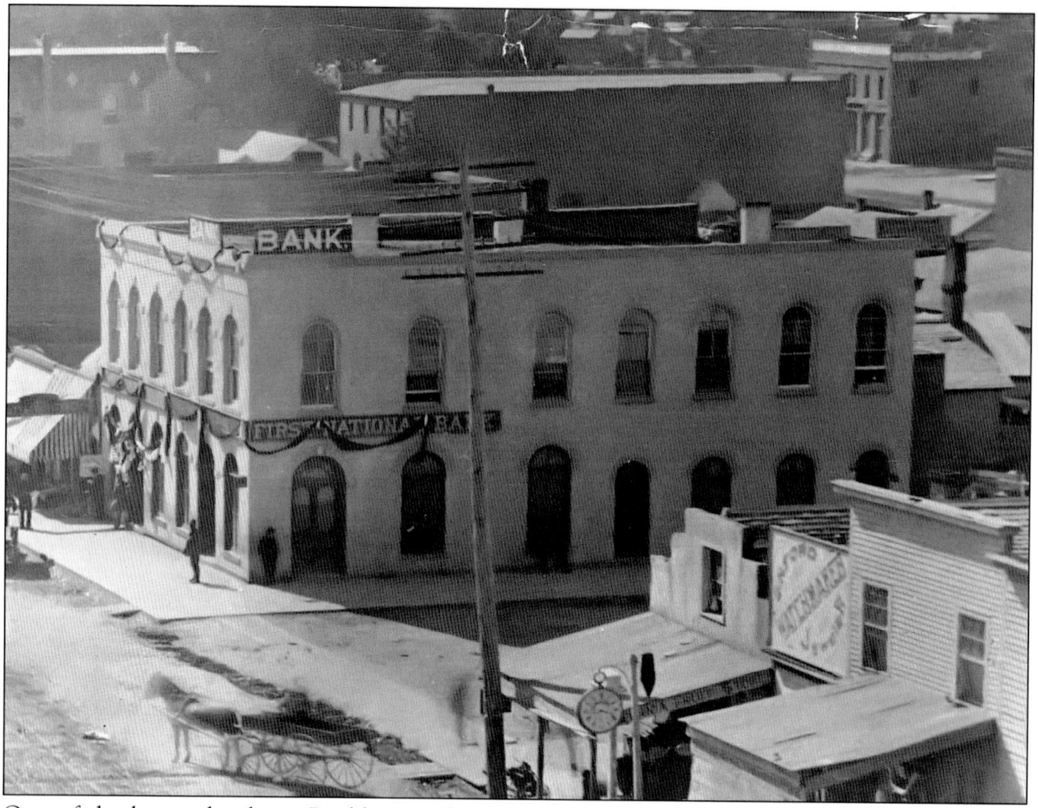

One of the largest banks in Pueblo was the First National Bank, founded by brothers Mahlon and John Thatcher. The second floor of the building, which was located at the southwest corner of West Fourth Street and Santa Fe Avenue, served as the Lodge Hall of Pueblo Masonic Lodge No. 17 for many years. By 1886, Pueblo boasted six banks. (PH-P-603-04-004.)

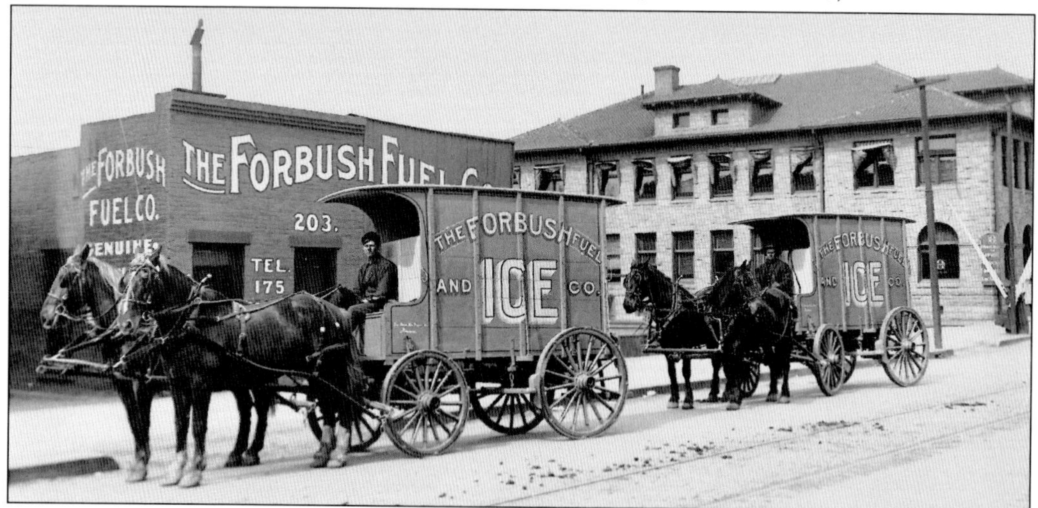

Pueblo featured several different icehouses, which collected ice in the winter months and delivered the product to homes in the warmer months. Horse-drawn wagons such as those of the Forbush Fuel and Ice Company provided delivery in the years before refrigerators and freezers were commonplace in Pueblo kitchens and eventually rendered icehouses obsolete. (PH-P-65-02-006.)

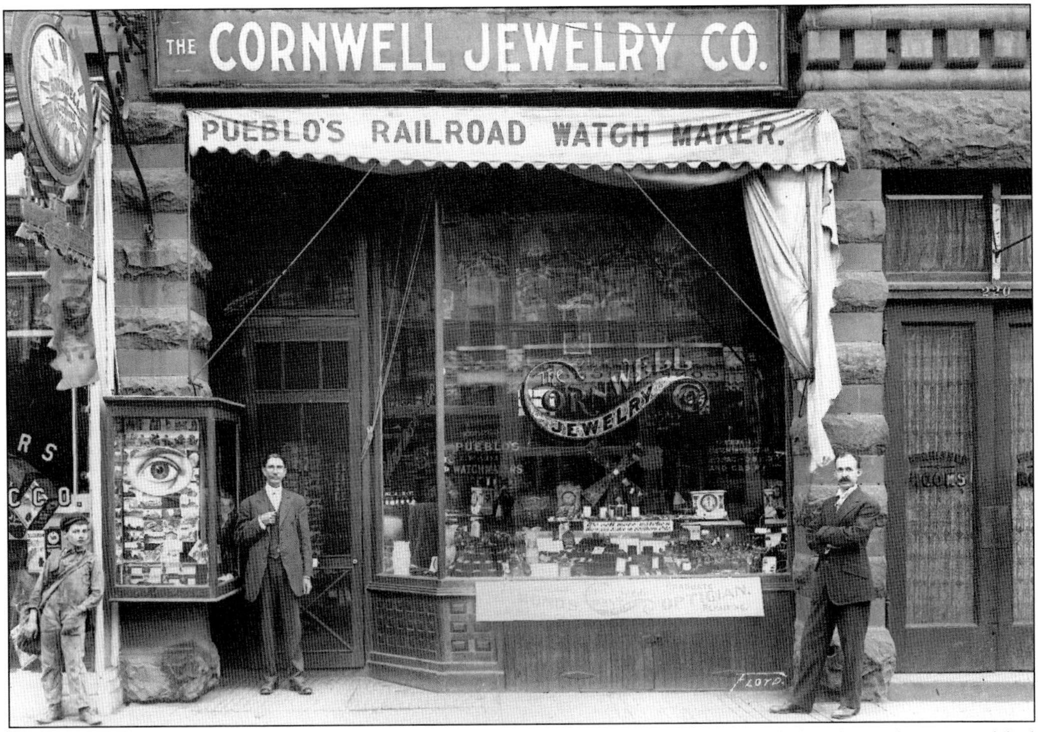

The Cornwell Jewelry Company was one of several jewelers in Pueblo, and the shop also assembled railroad watches. A very interesting hidden gem in this photograph is the newsie to the left of the picture. Newsies were young boys who sold the newspaper and for special editions shouted, "Extra! Extra! Read all about it." (PH-P-662-20-003.)

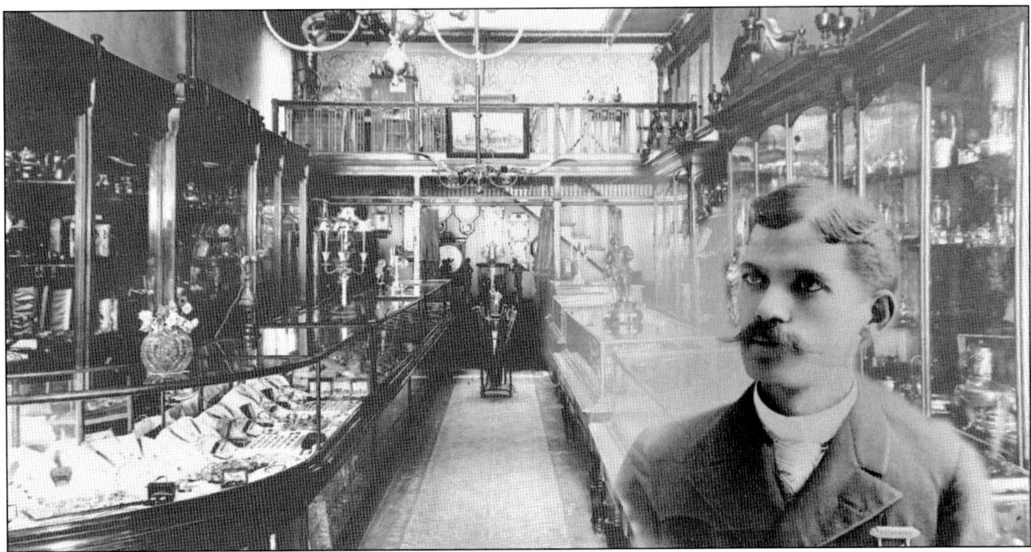

Charles Otero operated a jewelry store at 303 Santa Fe Avenue but later moved to the Opera House Block at Fourth and Main Streets. Otero crafted fine jewelry, served as Pueblo's fire chief in 1880, and played the tuba in the nationally known Cowboy Band. Otero crafted a $5,000 miniature of the Mineral Palace for display at the Chicago World's Fair in 1893. (PH-P-265-06-00 and PH-B-322-01.)

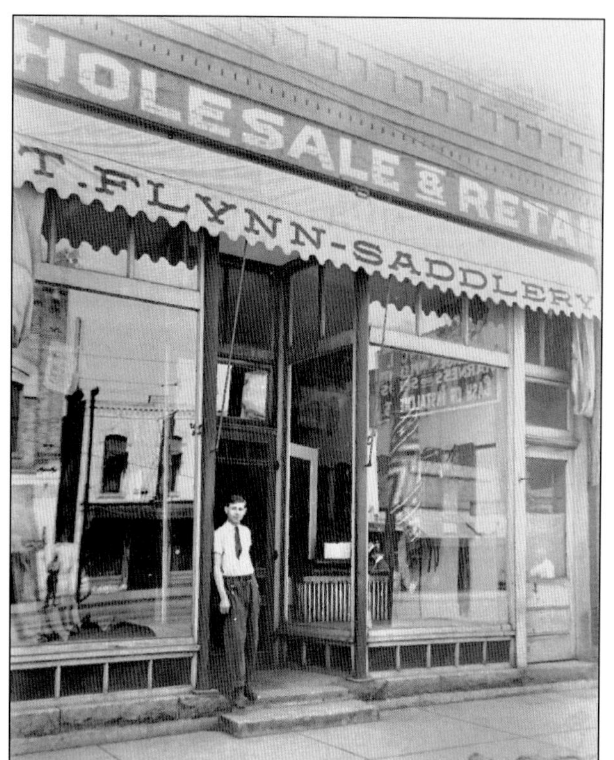

At one time, Pueblo was known as the saddle-making capital of the world. Some of the best-known saddlemakers were Samuel C. Gallup, Robert Frazier, and Thomas Flynn. In 1880, Frazier and Gallup merged and kept the partnership for 10 years. All three made the Pueblo-style saddle developed by Samuel C. Gallup. T. Flynn-Saddlery, pictured here, lasted into the 1930s. (PH-P-132-08-006.)

The Paris Café replaced a Chinese restaurant located at 312 North Union Avenue when the Todero family took ownership about 1914. "Tables for ladies" is advertised on the window since it was not considered dignified for ladies to sit at stools. The restaurant's menu included steak for less than $2 and pancakes and coffee for 10¢. (PH-P-760-3-001.)

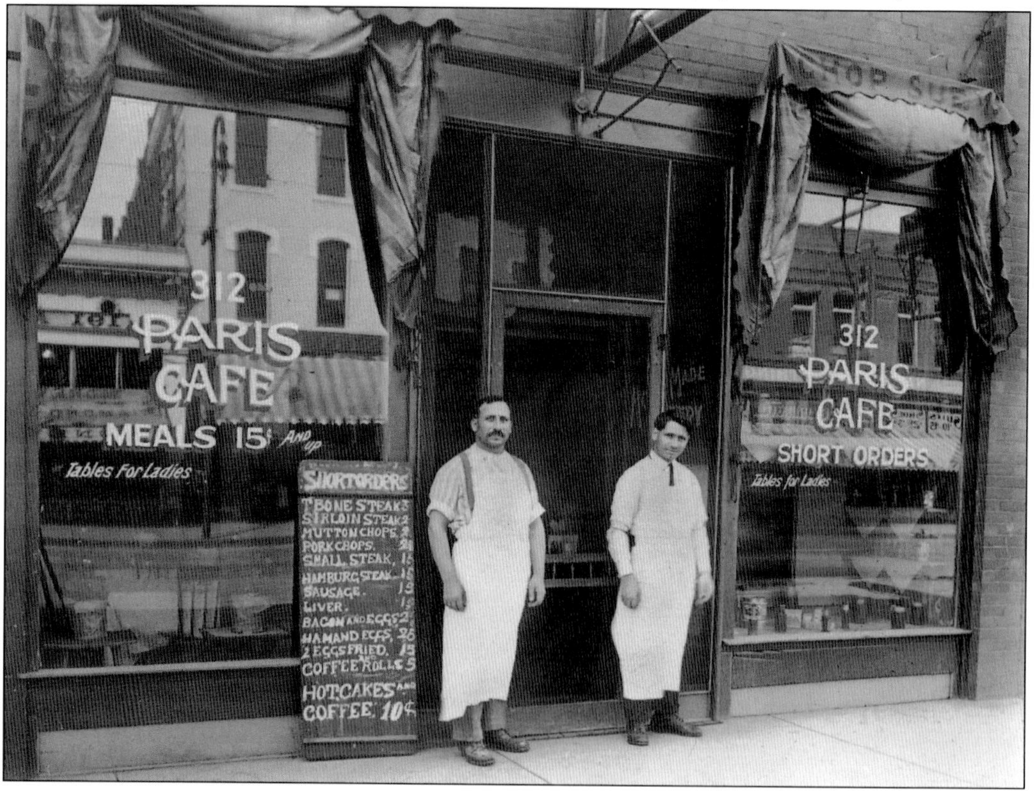

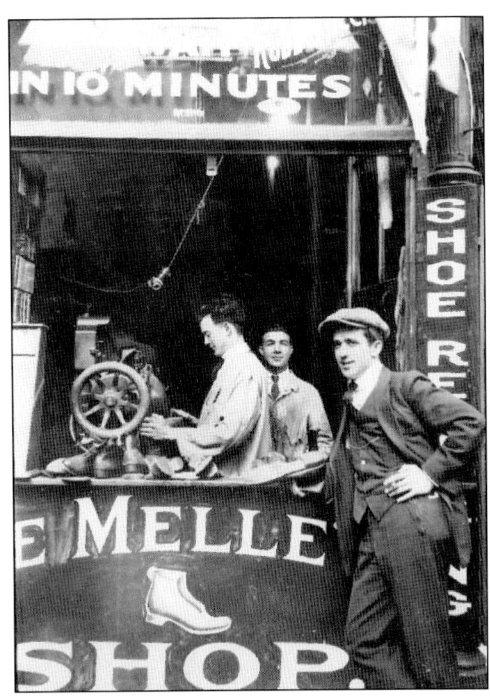

Shoes were essential attire for any working man. Several proprietors capitalized on the influx of workers just prior to the turn of the 20th century by catering to this burgeoning market. Cobblers practiced their craft along Union Avenue, and downtown Pueblo, and in neighborhoods like Bessemer. The Melley Shoe Shop, pictured here at 313 West Northern Avenue, advertised shoe repair in 10 minutes "while you wait." (PH-P-133-01-001.)

No maturing city would be complete without secret and benevolent societies. There were nine such organizations and 21 chapters in Pueblo in 1890, and those numbers grew to 19 different organizations and over 50 chapters by 1900. The number of organizations exploded to 33 by 1910 with approximately 85 different chapters. This photograph was taken on the lawn of the McClelland Library on October 2, 1909, during an Elks reunion. (PH-P-199-05_001.)

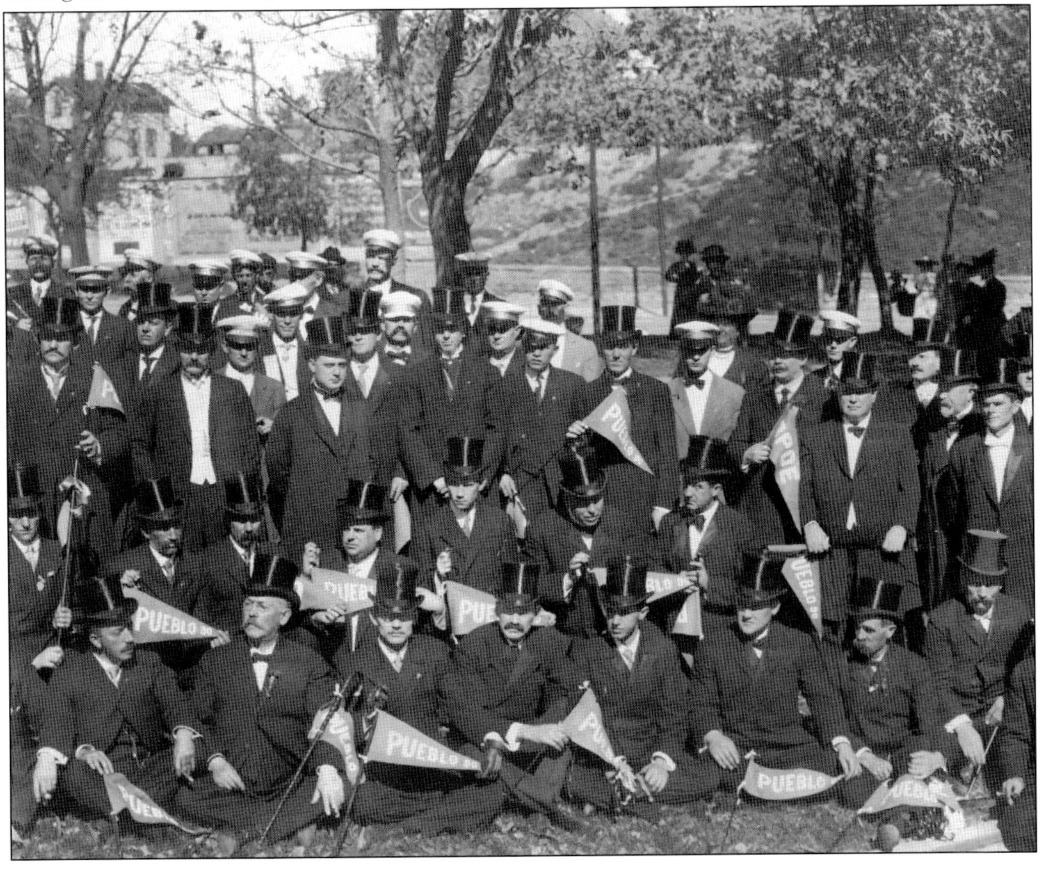

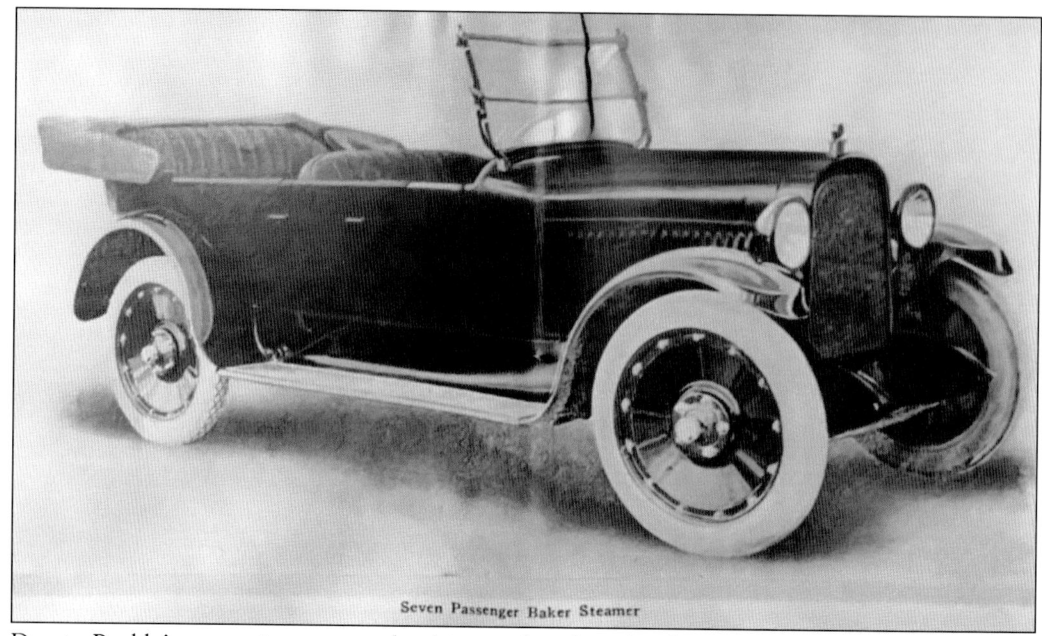
Seven Passenger Baker Steamer

Due to Pueblo's reputation as a steelmaking, railroad, and industrial hub, Dr. Hartley O. Baker decided to construct an automobile plant here. The Baker Steam Motor Car Company produced steam-powered automobiles at a plant near the western end of Twenty-Ninth Street from 1918 until 1926. The company initially produced a seven-passenger touring car as well as prototypes of delivery vehicles and multi-passenger buses. (PH-P-71-01-001.)

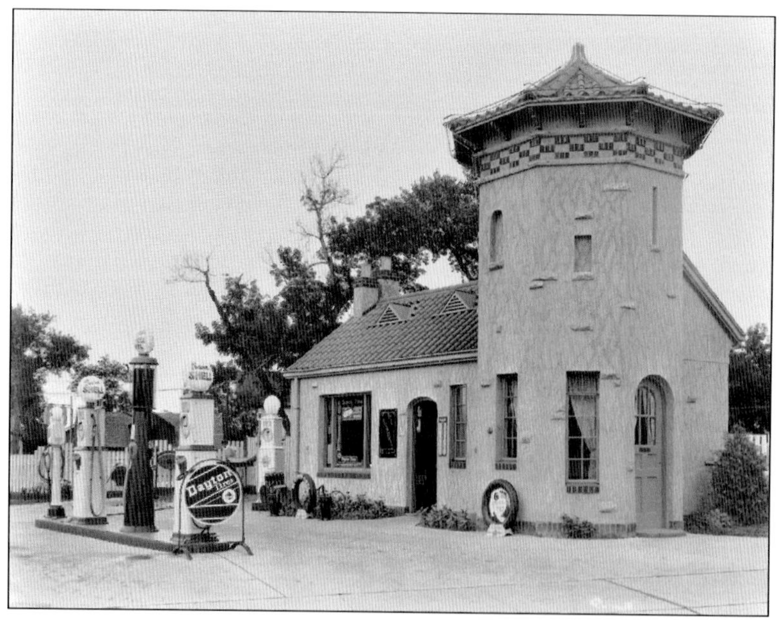

The influx of automobiles on Pueblo's streets meant an increase in the number of refueling and service stations across the city. This station was located at 200 East Abriendo, just a short walk from where the Rawlings Library now stands. In the 1920s, it was a Shell station advertising Dayton Tires. (PH-P-93-02-002.)

Five

The Progressive Era and the City Beautiful Movement

Many of the people responsible for Pueblo's commercial growth also funded and secured civic improvements, improving the quality of life and leaving a lasting legacy. Andrew McClelland was one of those benefactors who helped contribute to many endeavors. On April 10, 1891, a library named after McClelland opened on the fourth floor of the Board of Trade Building.

The Victorian-era building boom of the 1880s and 1890s created neighborhoods of small cottages and stately mansions across Pueblo. On September 28, 1896, with the City Beautiful Movement firmly underway, the city adopted an ordinance creating City Park. The movement led to the establishment of parks throughout the city, with one in nearly every neighborhood. While some parks were small, others were elaborate, like Minnequa Park, which boasted a lake and an amusement park on the north shore.

In addition to the numerous opera houses that kept with the opulent trends of the period, there were also small hotels, boardinghouses, and brothels. A planned resort called the Fountain Lake Hotel was constructed but never operated as a hotel. The successful Grand Hotel changed its name to the Congress Hotel, where attendees of the 1910 National Irrigation Congress stayed. The extant Vail Hotel is a testament to Pueblo's former grandeur and is shown on the cover of this book. Two other monumental buildings are the Pueblo County Courthouse built in 1912, and the combination City and Memorial Hall built in 1917. Memorial Hall was named to commemorate the effort of all the heroes, domestic and abroad, of World War I.

The Colorado Mineral Palace opened in 1891 to display minerals found in the state and to show the importance of mining and minerals in Colorado's economy. The structure occupied one city block, and though it opened to much fanfare, the building was underfunded and improperly maintained through the economic hardships of the Great Depression and fell into disrepair. Crews razed the dilapidated building in 1942, with much of the scrap iron going to the World War II effort.

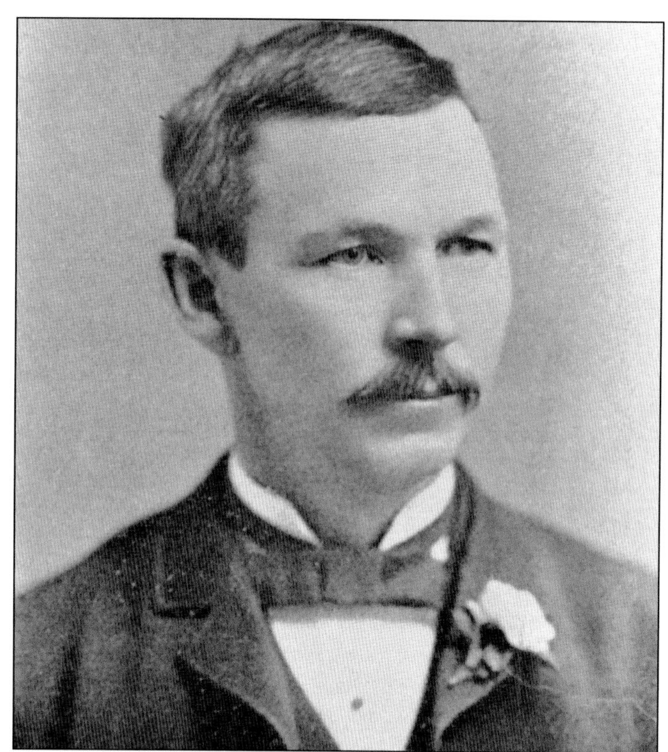

Andrew McClelland invested heavily in Pueblo, both in business and philanthropic matters. He secured the right-of-way for the Missouri Pacific Railroad to come to the city and funded construction of the Board of Trade Building in 1891. This was an organization in which he served as president. (PH-B-282-02_001.)

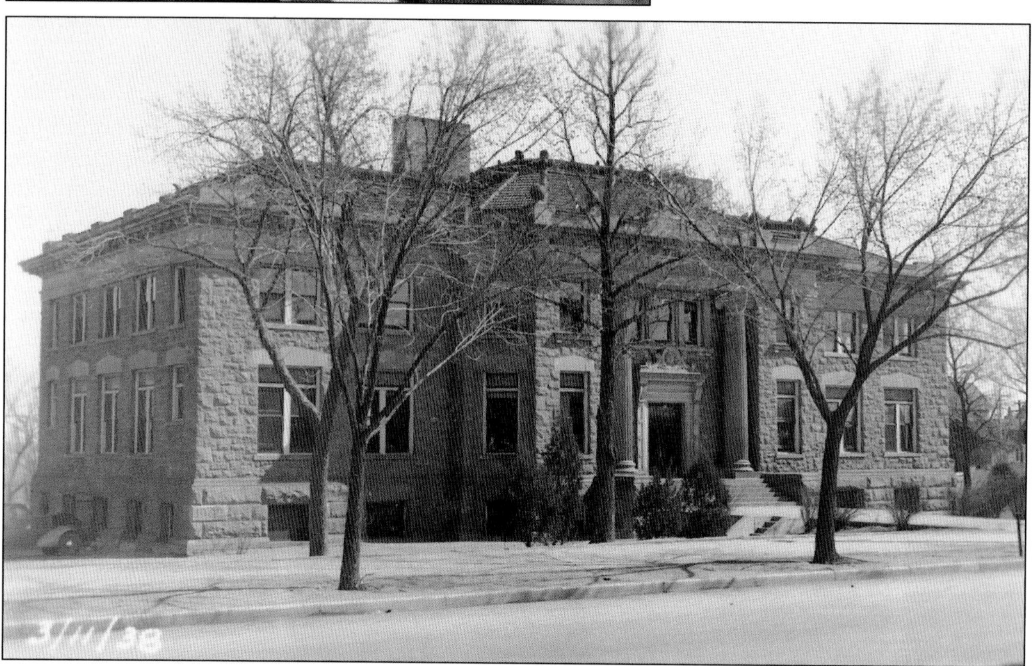

On June 26, 1893, Pueblo City Council passed the McClelland Public Library Ordinance. Books now circulated for free: previously, only reading at the library was free, with a $5 annual fee to check out books. In 1902, Andrew Carnegie gave $60,000, with some funding from McClelland, for a new building to house the McClelland Public Library. The library at the new location was dedicated on January 20, 1904. (A-001 4.3.00001.)

A group of concerned citizens met to address the problem of a sizeable population of parentless children and established an orphanage in 1905. Andrew McClelland offered the group a building valued at $20,000 for $5,000, if the orphanage made $2,500 in repairs. The group had raised nearly the entire amount when Columbia Jane, McClelland's wife, donated $5,000. The orphanage eventually evolved into the McClelland School. (PH-P-419-02-001.)

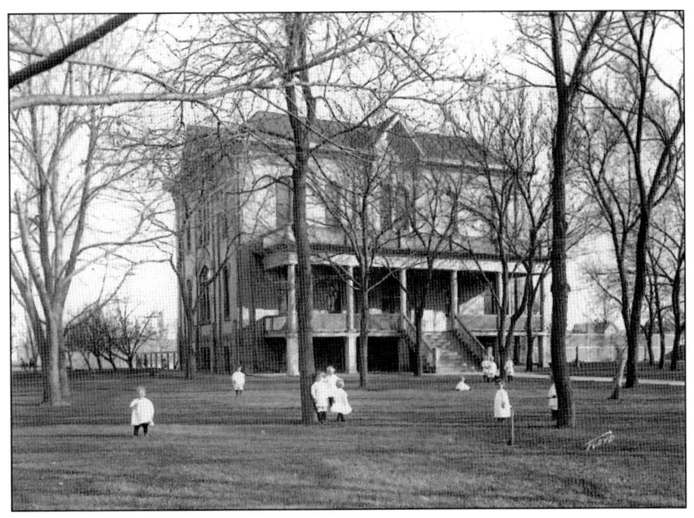

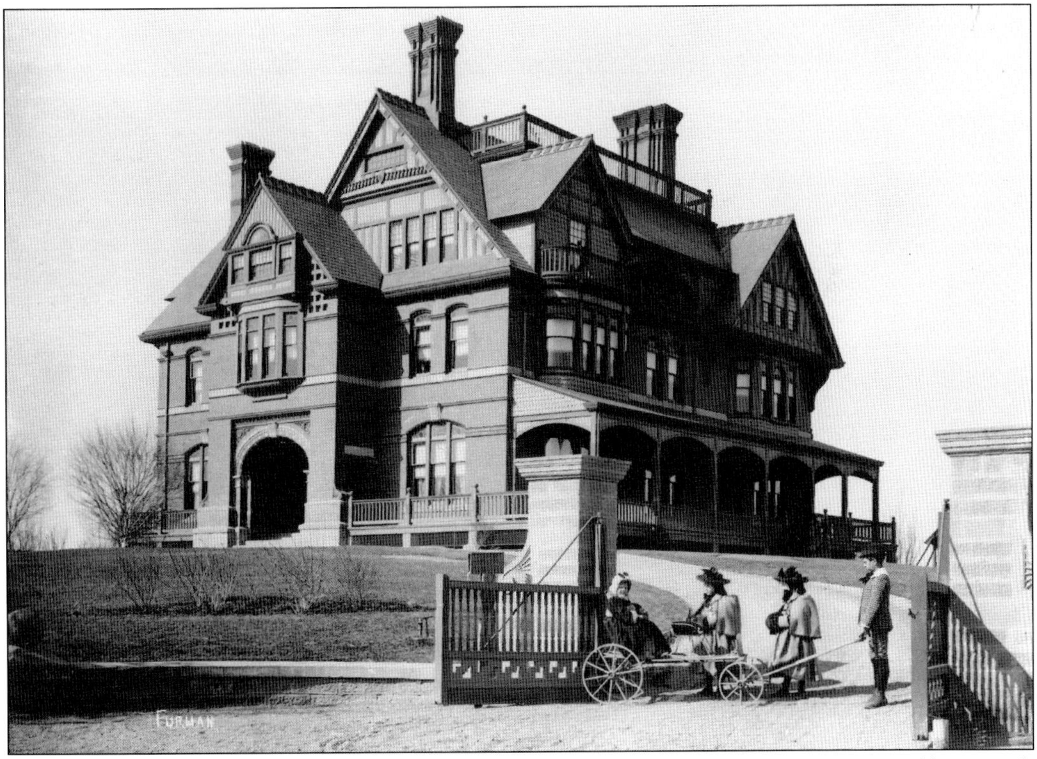

Business magnate Mahlon D. Thatcher erected his home near the highest point in Pueblo's North Side neighborhood and aptly named the residence Hillcrest. It was situated on Greenwood Street between Fifteenth and Sixteenth Streets. Henry Hudson Holly designed the 41-room Queen Anne house built in 1881. The house changed hands several times and was used for commercial purposes before being demolished in 1976. (PH-P-772-02-001.)

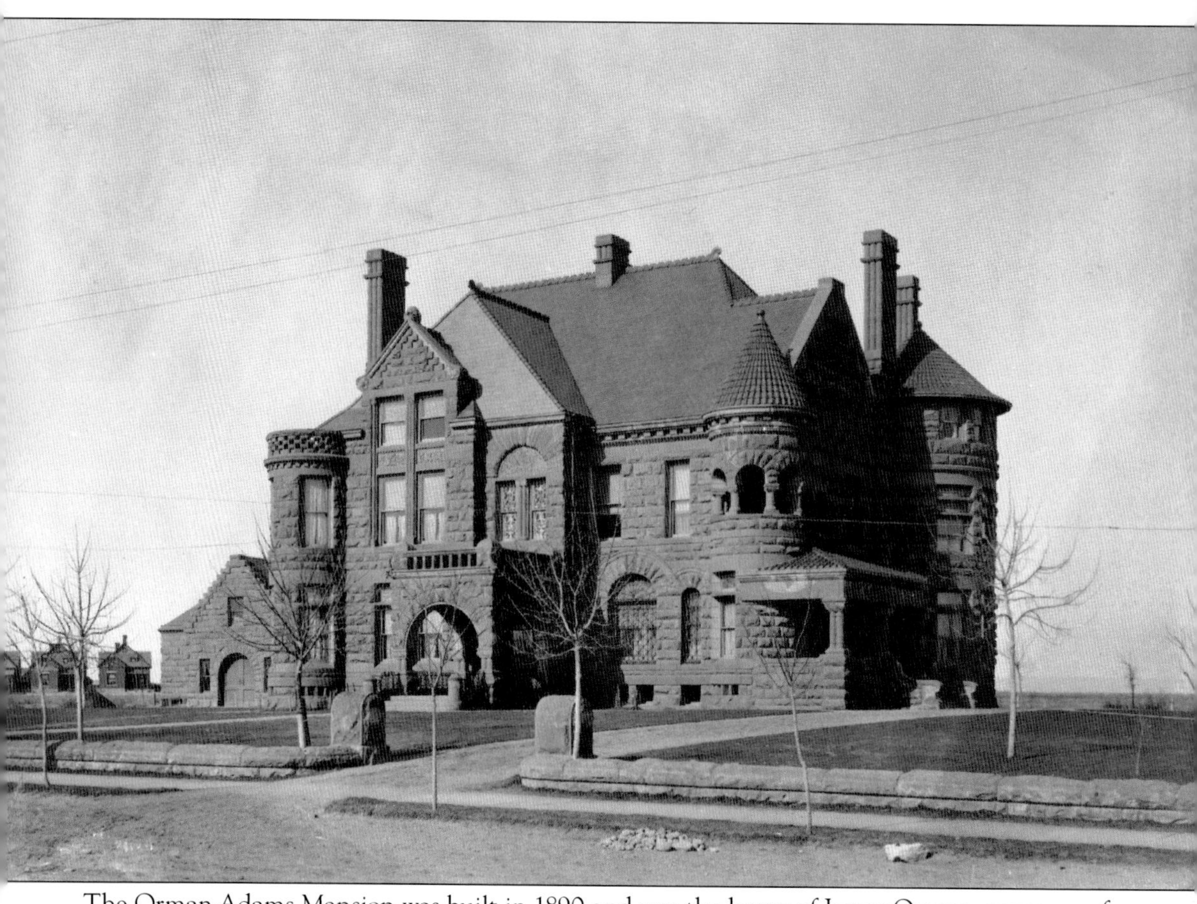

The Orman-Adams Mansion was built in 1890 and was the home of James Orman, governor of Colorado from 1901 until 1903. Orman lived there until 1918, when he sold the mansion to Alva Adams, also a governor of Colorado—at three different times. Alva B. Adams, the son of Alva Adams, also lived here. The younger Adams served as United States senator by appointment from 1922 to 1924 and by election from 1932 until 1941. From 1952 until 1979, the building was used by Pueblo School District 60 as an administration facility. It is now a private residence. The Orman-Adams Mansion was listed in the National Register of Historic Places in 1976. (PH-P-776-02-002.)

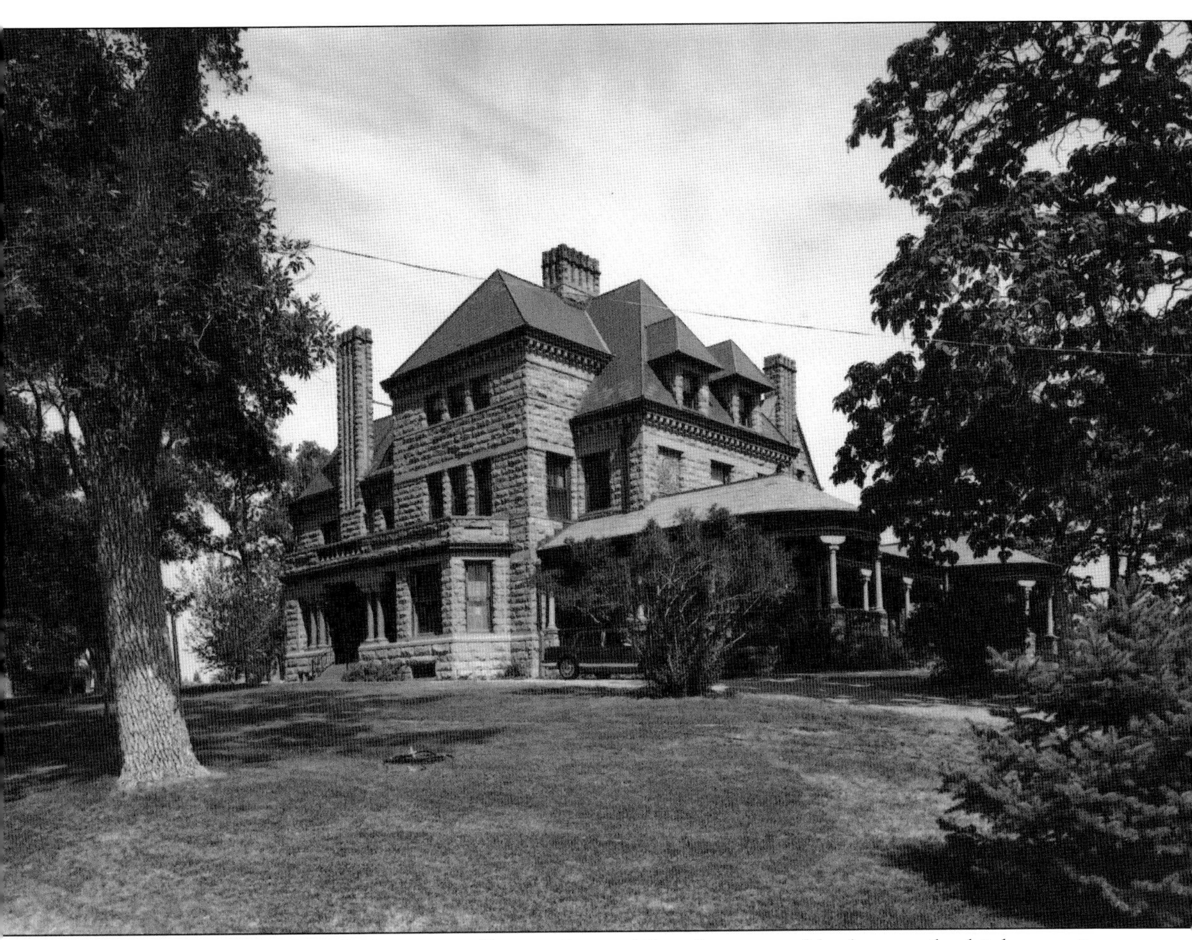

Rosemount, pronounced "Rosemont," is in the middle of a square block near the highest point in Pueblo's North Side neighborhood. It was built between 1891 and 1893 by John A. Thatcher for his family. Thatcher was a merchant, banker, cattleman, railroader, and community leader in Pueblo who was involved in starting many enterprises. The mansion and its accompanying carriage house are now a Victorian-era museum called Rosemount, with a plethora of the original furnishings on display. Rosemount was listed in the National Register of Historic Places in 1974. (PH-P-392-03.)

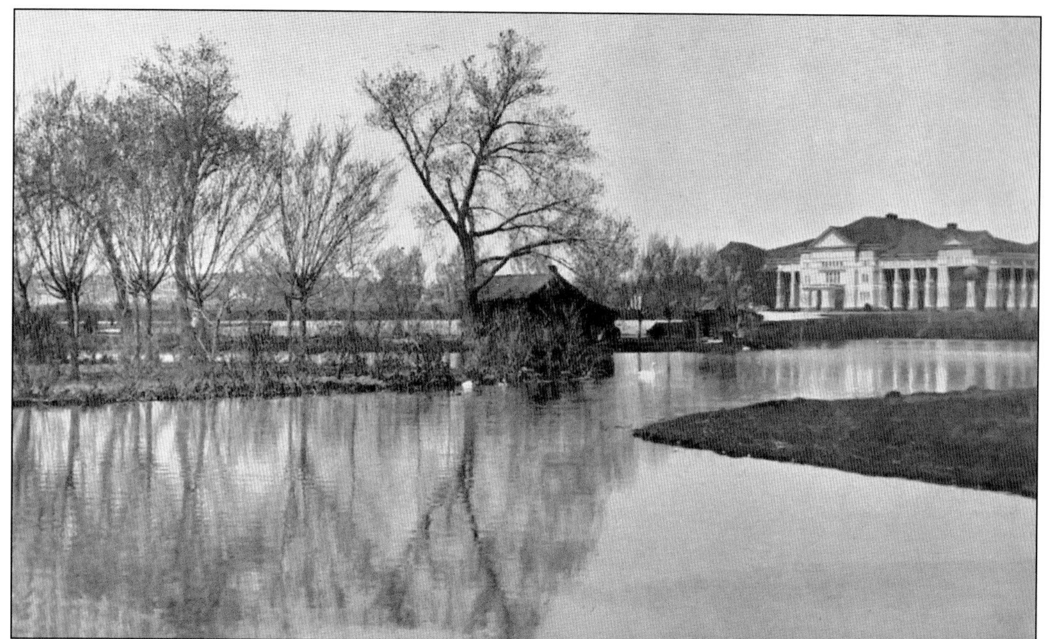

When the Colorado Mineral Palace was first built in 1890, Lake Clara was southeast of Mineral Palace. The surrounding Mineral Palace Park was established in 1896. The Pueblo Parks Commission named Lake Clara for Clara M. Latshaw, one of the founding commissioners. The construction of Interstate 25 reduced the size of Lake Clara. (PH-P-756-04_007.)

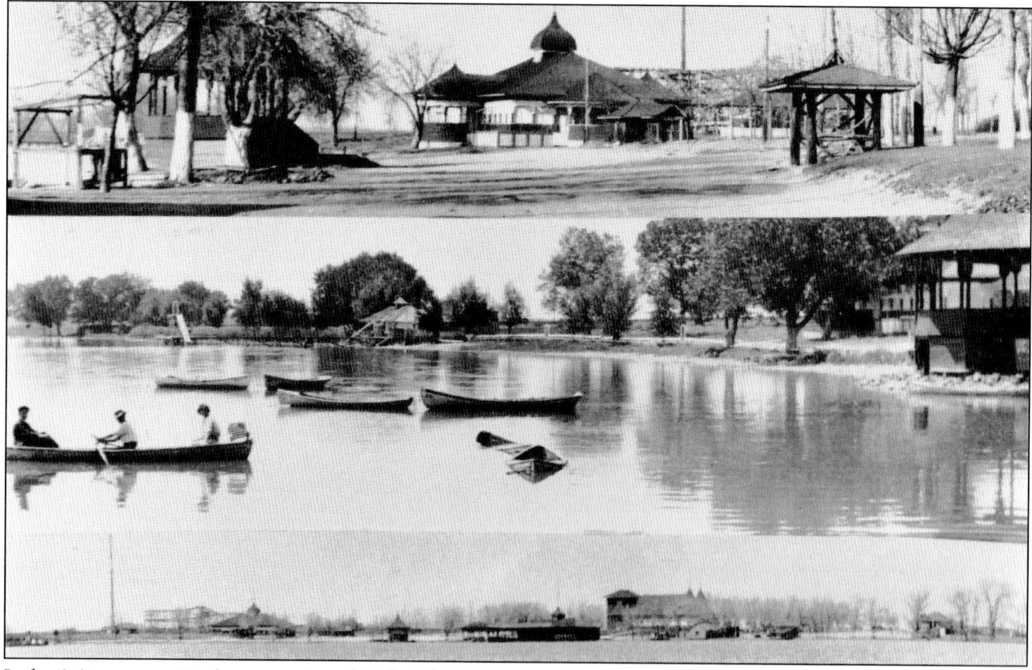

Lake Minnequa Park opened in 1902. The area featured fishing and boating, and a pavilion for dancing, parties, and stage productions. Picnic areas were available for family outings, and the park was just a five-minute trolley ride from the center of town. Attendance declined throughout the Depression, leading the city to sell off part of the property. (PH-P-726-03.)

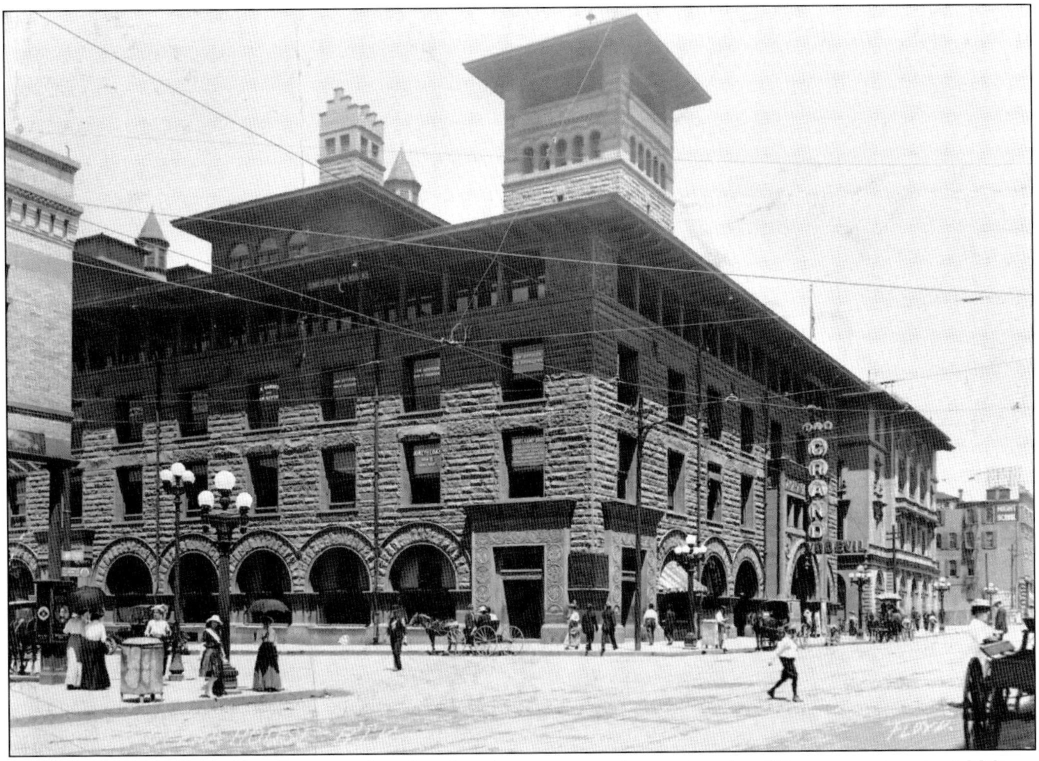

The Grand Opera House was said to be the finest opera house in the West, opening in 1890 on the corner of Fourth and Main Streets. The architectural firm Adler and Sullivan of Chicago was hired to design the building, with Louis Sullivan taking the lead. Sullivan utilized sandstone from Manitou upon a base of gray granite. Behind the tower, but not visible here, was the grand ballroom. (PH-P-09-09-009.)

A fire at the Grand Opera House erupted on March 1, 1922. With the reported temperature 29 degrees below zero, icicles formed while water dripped from the building, causing an eerie effect. The fire destroyed the building within 45 minutes of being first reported and displaced dozens of businesses. Up in smoke went the 1,100-seat auditorium that rivaled those in cities such as Denver and Chicago. (PH-P-709-08-003.)

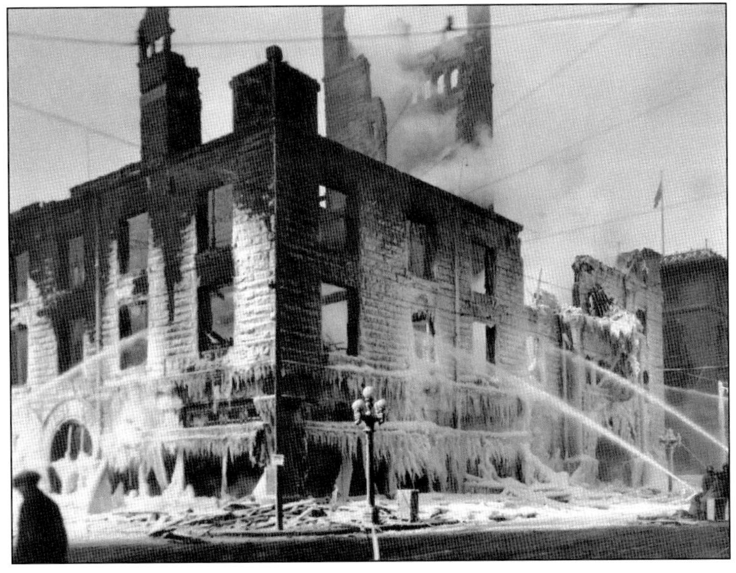

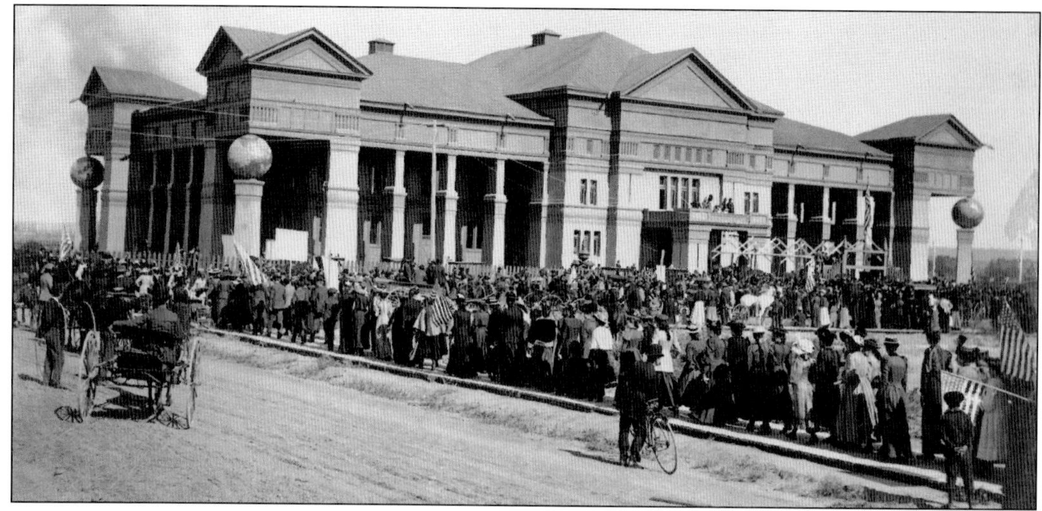

The Colorado Mineral Palace opened on July 4, 1891. It was a one-story frame building that encompassed an entire city block with sheet iron facing on the north side and a dome on top. Each corner had a stone pillar topped with a globe. The building also featured electricity. There were mineral displays along the walls and a majestic fountain in front of the building. (PH-P-433-05-009.)

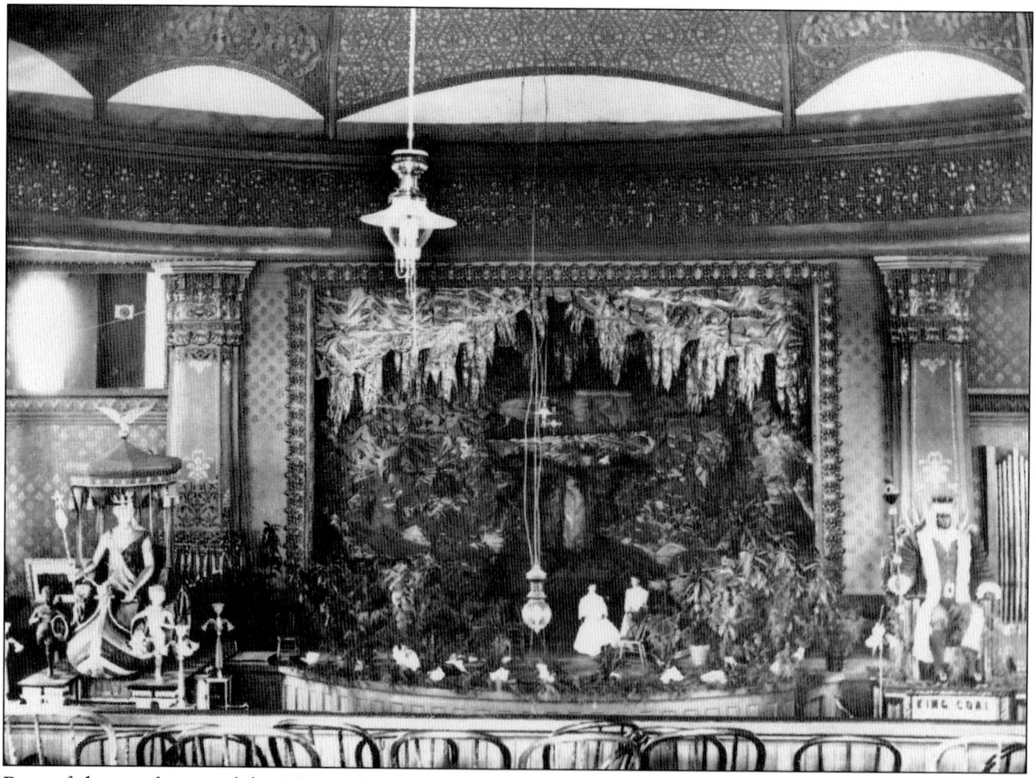

Part of the opulence of the Mineral Palace can be seen in this photograph. Larger-than-life, Queen Silver (seen on the left of this photograph) came from Aspen, and King Coal (to the Queen's left) came from Trinidad. They both reigned on thrones within the palace until demolition occurred in the early 1940s. What happened to the sculptures remains a mystery. (PH-P-434-03-005.)

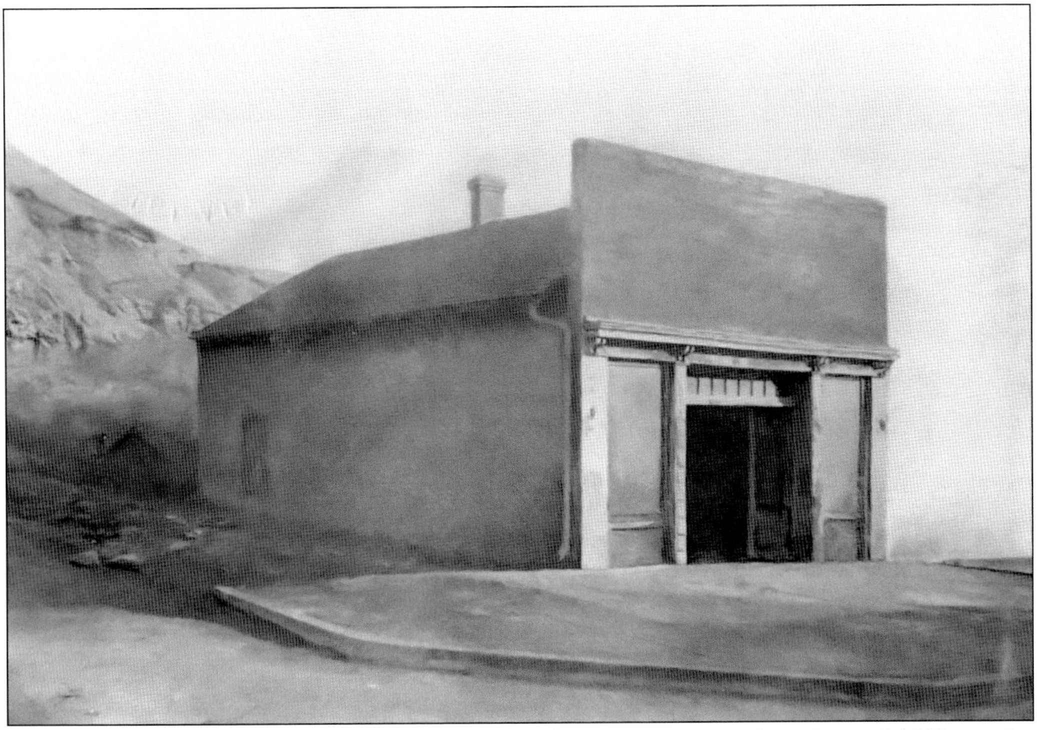

This image shows the first Pueblo County Courthouse, constructed in the mid-1860s in the middle of Santa Fe Avenue near Third Street. Pueblo County purchased the building from a local proprietor (hence the commercial appearance) for $1,100, with funds from a forfeited bail. (PH-P-458-09-002.)

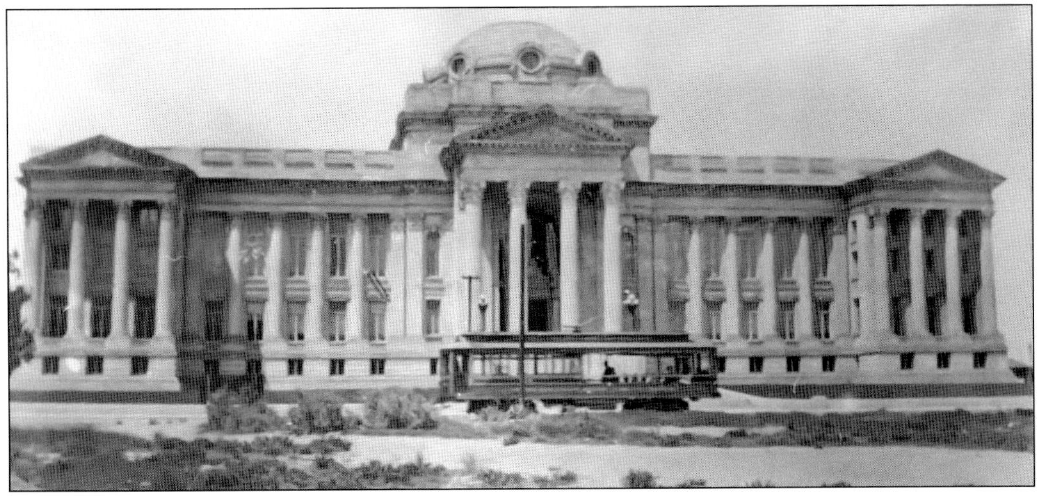

Opened in 1912, the current Pueblo County Courthouse covers an entire city block. Masons constructed the building from nearby Turkey Creek sandstone and pink marble from Beulah. The interior features several historical murals painted by Charles Schnoor that depict the cattle trade, manufacturing, and industry of Pueblo. The courthouse was listed in the National Register of Historic Places in 1975. (PH-P-458-08-002.)

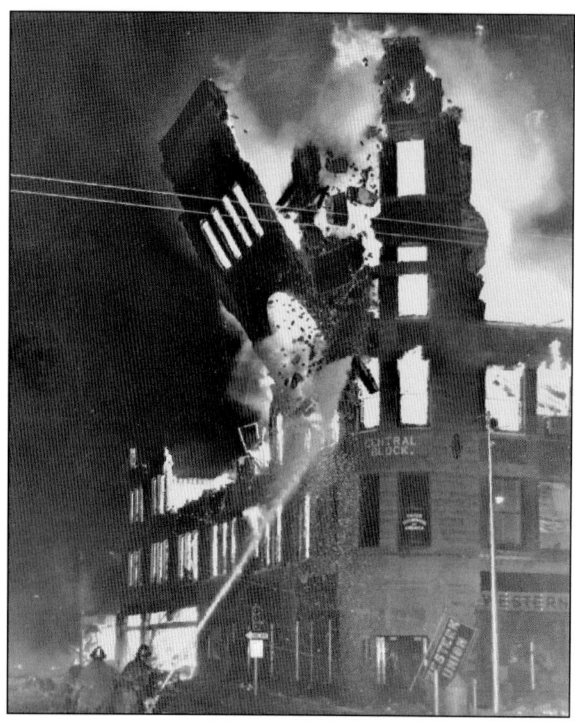

Sadly, many Pueblo buildings suffered fire damage throughout the years. This is an image of the Central Block as it burned during the night of August 29, 1953. Located at the corner of Second and Main Streets, the Central Block opened in 1889. The *Pueblo Chieftain* photographer, Bud Hawkins, earned second place in a photography contest sponsored by the National Press Photographer's Association for this image. (PH-P-3904-002.)

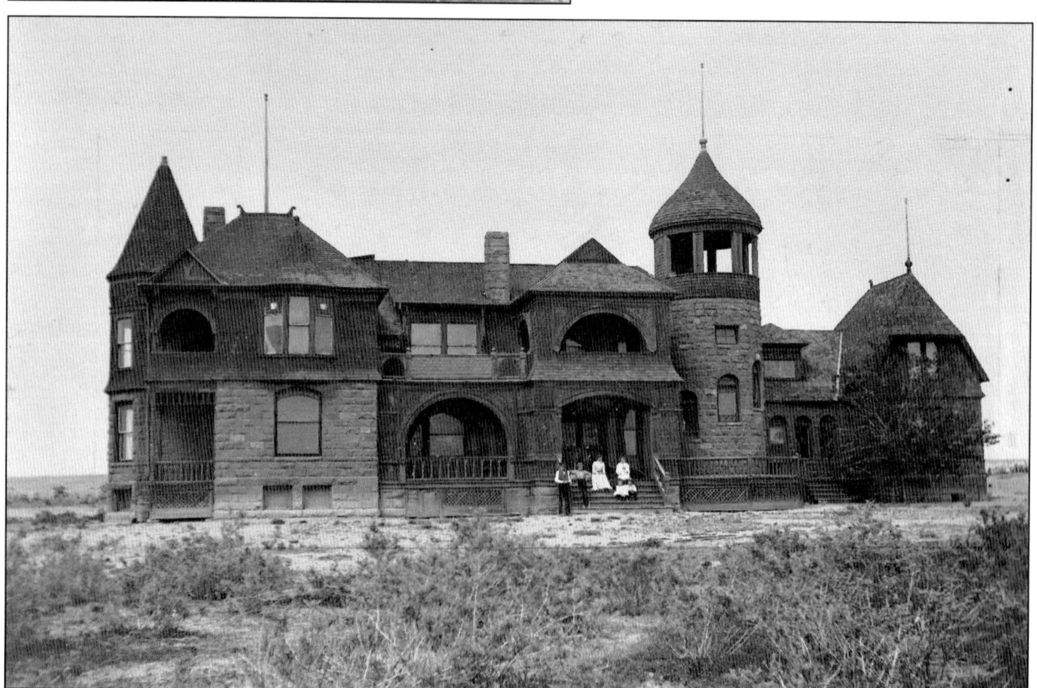

Located in the area now known as University Park, the Fountain Lake Hotel was built about 1889 adjacent to an artificial lake filled by water from Fountain Creek. The anticipated real estate boom did not occur due to its distant location, and the planned resort was an utter failure. During early Prohibition, it became a roadhouse and speakeasy. The building burned down in 1926. (PH-P-354-02.)

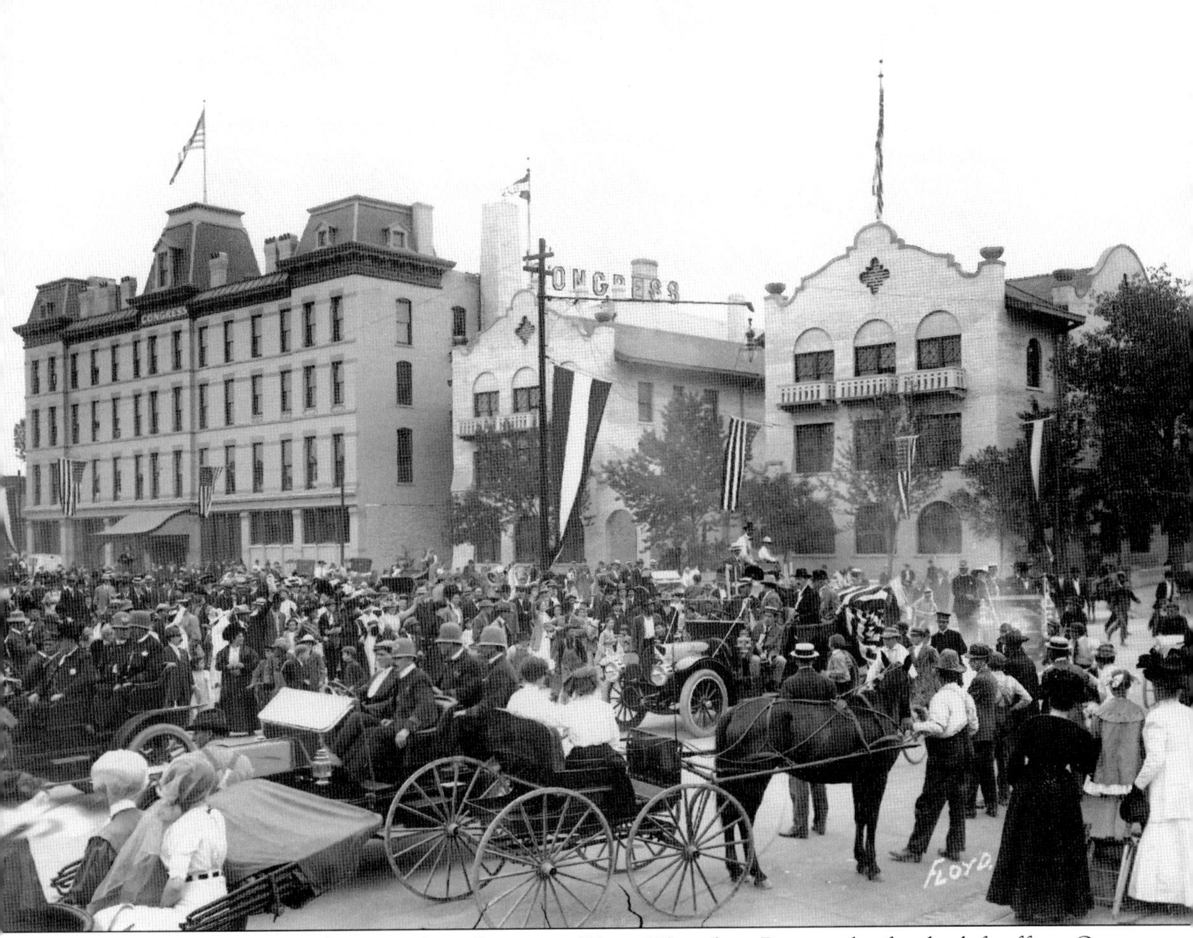

The occasion in this photograph is the visit of Pres. Theodore Roosevelt after he left office. On August 30, 1910, he was in Pueblo to dedicate the cornerstone at the newly built Young Men's Christian Association building. He can be seen through the crowd to the right in one of the latest-model touring cars. Formerly the Grand Hotel, the Congress Hotel seen in the background was named after the National Irrigation Congress that convened in Pueblo the last week of September 1910. (PH-Ph-352-03_001.)

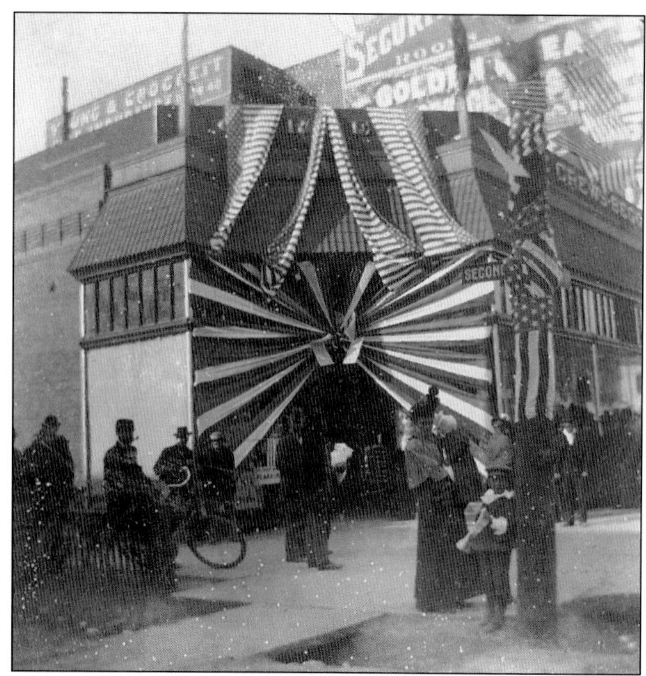

Crews-Beggs, arguably the most popular department store in Pueblo, opened on March 4, 1888, in the basement of the Fifth Avenue Hotel at Fifth Street and Santa Fe Avenue. The store moved two more times before settling into a two-story building on Main Street. In 1901, there was a fire, and the store was rebuilt and enlarged to four stories. It closed in the 1970s. (PH-P-662-19-004.)

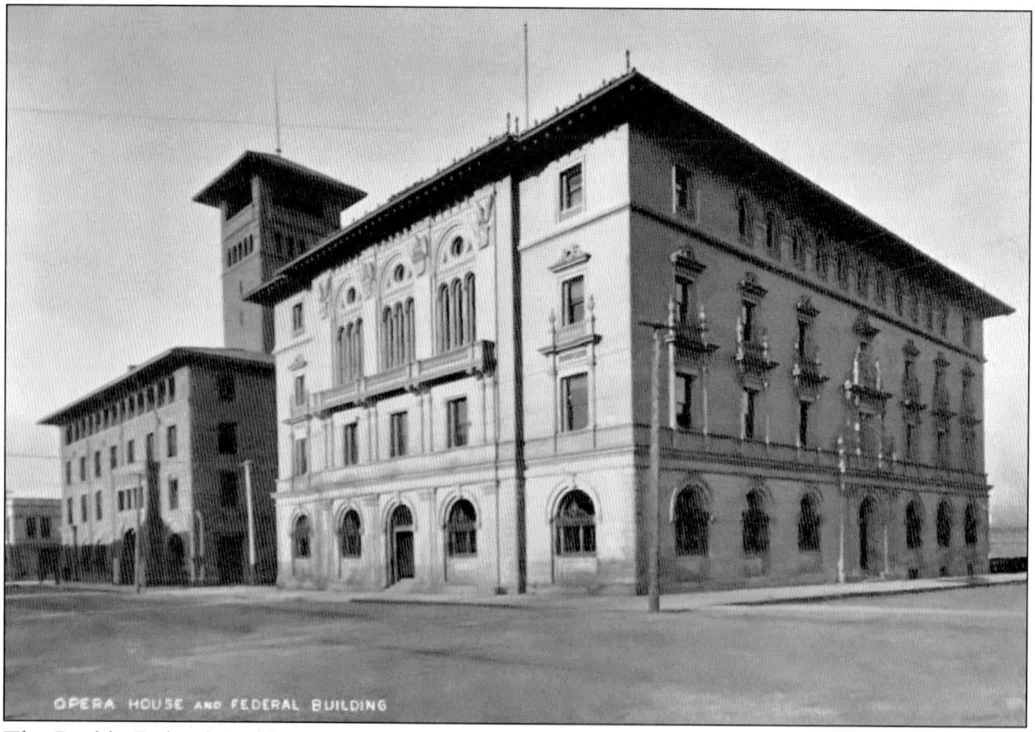

OPERA HOUSE AND FEDERAL BUILDING

The Pueblo Federal Building lies at the southwest corner of Fifth and Main Streets. Completed in 1897, the building cost $275,000. Widely known to locals as the Post Office Building, it also housed offices for the Internal Revenue Service, US Land Office, US Marshals Service, US Pension Bureau, US Weather Bureau, district court, and the Civil Service Commission. (From a 1902 booklet published by Bonney and Haines.)

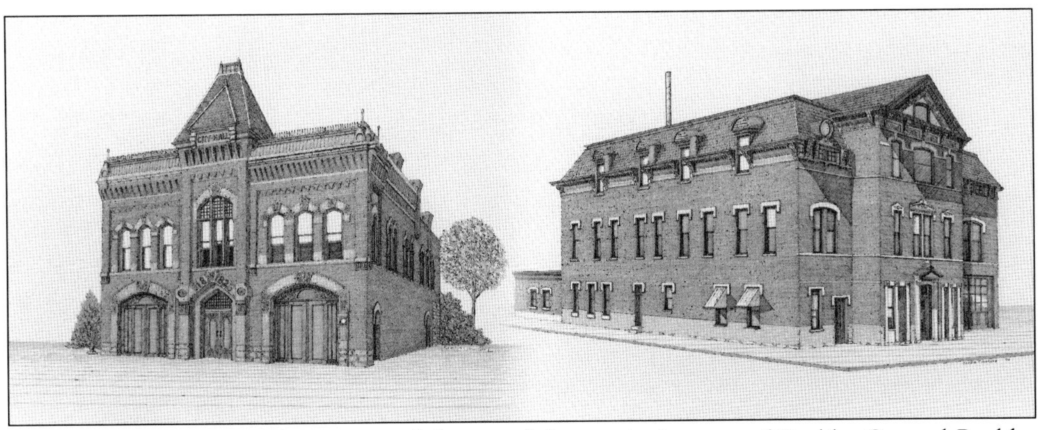

The current city of Pueblo is a consolidation of the original towns of Pueblo, Central Pueblo, South Pueblo, and Bessemer. Shown here are the two previous Pueblo City Halls. The first city hall (left) was constructed in 1882 and cost approximately $10,000. The Articles of Consolidation between Pueblo, South Pueblo, and Central Pueblo called for construction of a "consolidated" city hall (right). Construction was completed in 1889. (Pueblo County Historical Society.)

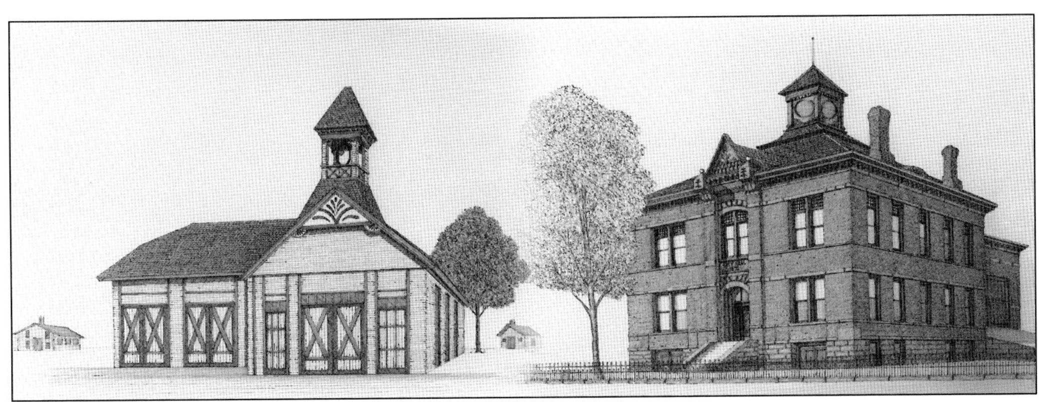

The City of Pueblo annexed the city of Bessemer in 1894, following a favorable vote by the residents of both cities. The modest structure on the left was constructed following the incorporation of Bessemer in 1886. The more stately and functional building on the right replaced the first city hall building in 1895. The Work Projects Administration demolished the second building in 1939–1940. (Pueblo County Historical Society.)

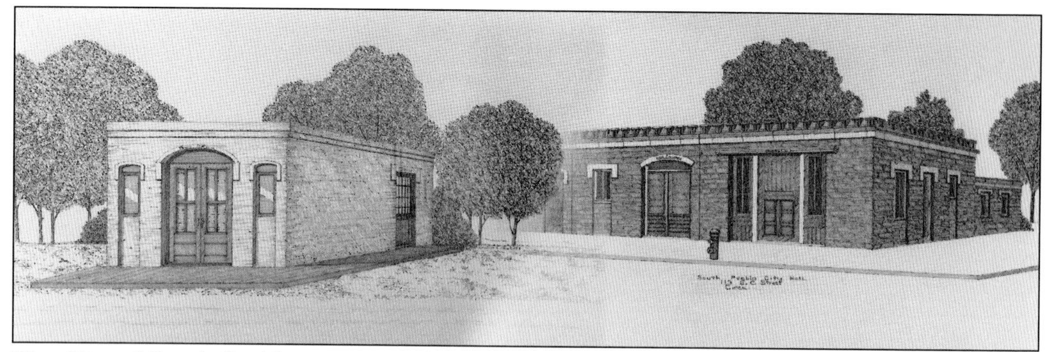

The City of South Pueblo constructed its first city hall (left) after incorporating in 1873. The modest one-story structure later housed a laundry and served other commercial functions. Central Pueblo City Hall (right) was constructed after the town incorporated in 1882. The building was addressed as 117 Central Main, putting it in the middle of the street just north of Memorial Hall. (Pueblo County Historical Society.)

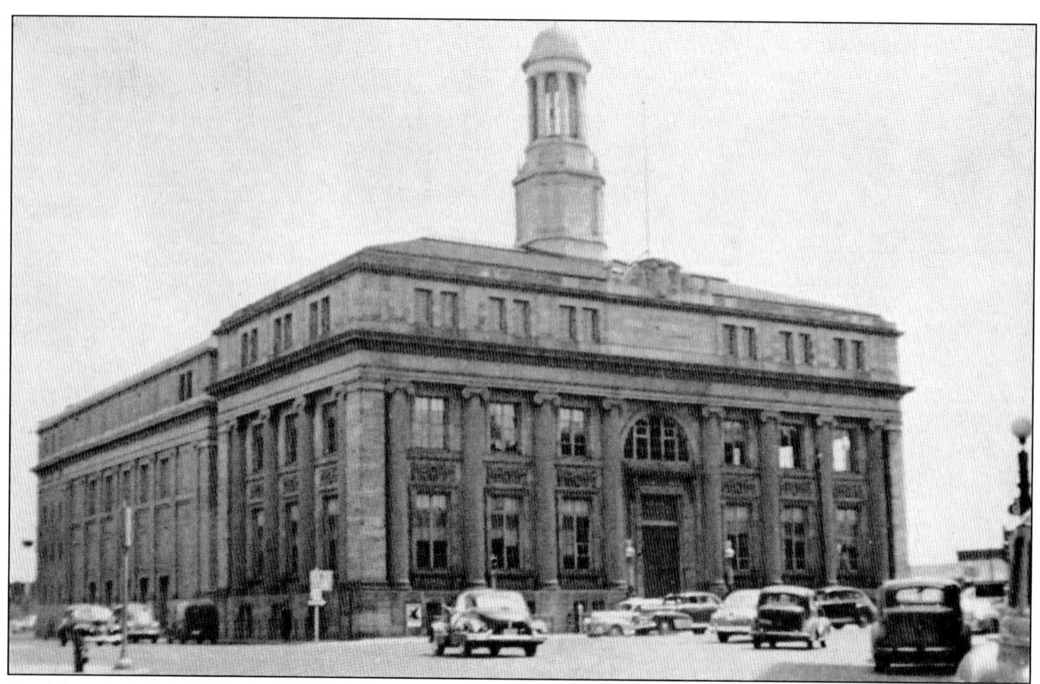

Pueblo City and Memorial Hall was designed by renowned architect William E. Stickney. It was aptly named in remembrance of all the soldiers and civilians who supported the war effort. It opened in 1917, but it was not dedicated until 1920 because of World War I. (PH-P-40-01-001.)

Six

Agriculture and Water

Water has always been a driving force in the history of Pueblo. With water available, agriculture became an economic pillar. Early settlers implemented irrigation practices by digging ditches to run water to their crops. After a fire in 1868 almost wiped out the city, it was determined that a public water system was in order, and a bond was passed in 1874. In that same year, construction began at the city's first waterworks.

Colorado's first water law granted use of the resource to agricultural landowners in 1876. The state engineer's office was established in 1879 in order to regulate and organize irrigation districts. The city of Pueblo, situated on the confluence of the Fountain and Arkansas Rivers, was particularly susceptible to the flooding of the Arkansas; however, no flood was as deadly, or had a bigger impact on the history of the city, than the flood of 1921. Although the citizens of Pueblo were warned, few believed that the flood would be as catastrophic as it turned out to be. It took years for the city to recover and rebuild. The tragic experience motivated residents of the area to begin thinking about ways to divert the river to protect the community from future flooding. On April 8, 1922, the Colorado State Legislature held a special session and passed a bill to create the Pueblo Conservancy District, which was responsible for the rechanneling of the Arkansas River and constructing a levee. Unfortunately, this plan did not include flood mitigation along Fountain Creek and a 1965 Flood covered 53 blocks with the heaviest damage on the Eastside of Pueblo.

A monumental water project began 40 years after the flood of 1921 when the Fryingpan-Arkansas Water Diversion Project received presidential authorization in August 1962. It was one of the projects designed to divert water to arid southeastern Colorado from the Fryingpan River west of the Continental Divide and control natural drainage. It took years to plan, but finally led the way to the building of a dam which was completed in 1975; the resulting reservoir was named Lake Pueblo.

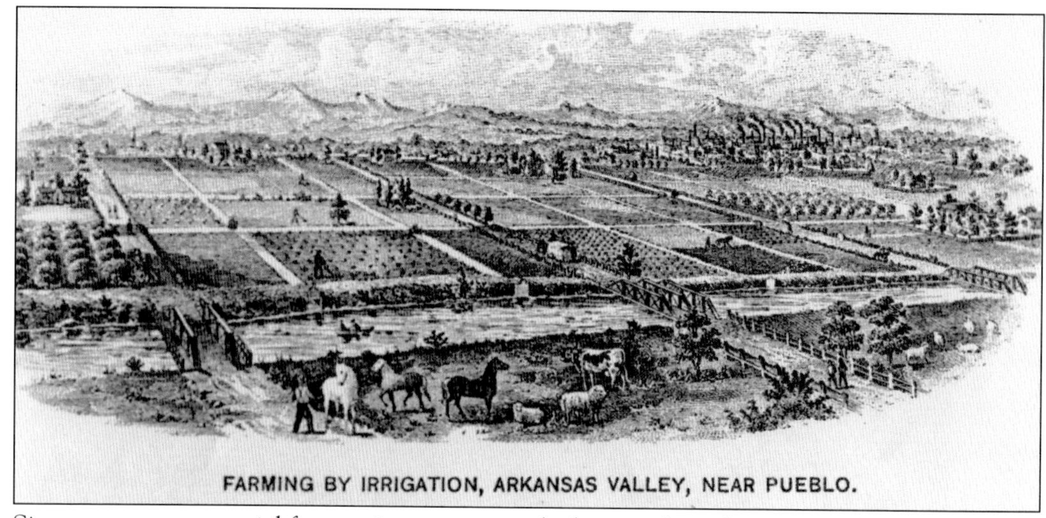

Since water was essential for growing crops, people dug canals to divert water from the streams. The oldest ditches in the state are recorded in the San Luis Valley. This sketch is representative of farming by irrigation in the Arkansas River valley just east of Pueblo. (PH-P-06-05-001.)

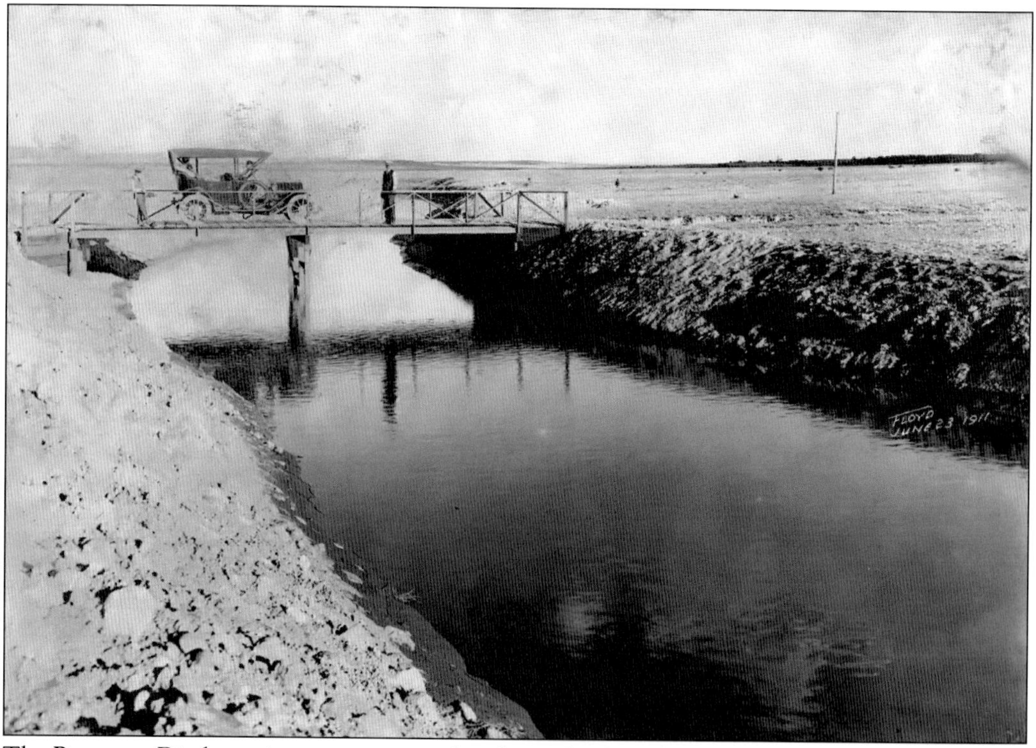

The Bessemer Ditch retains some water rights dating back to the 1860s but was not incorporated until 1888. Capital stock of the company was set at $200,000, with 20,000 shares at $10 per share. There was no set amount of water allocated to each stockholder, but the superintendent was charged with dividing an equal amount amongst shareholders (PH-P-718-02-001.)

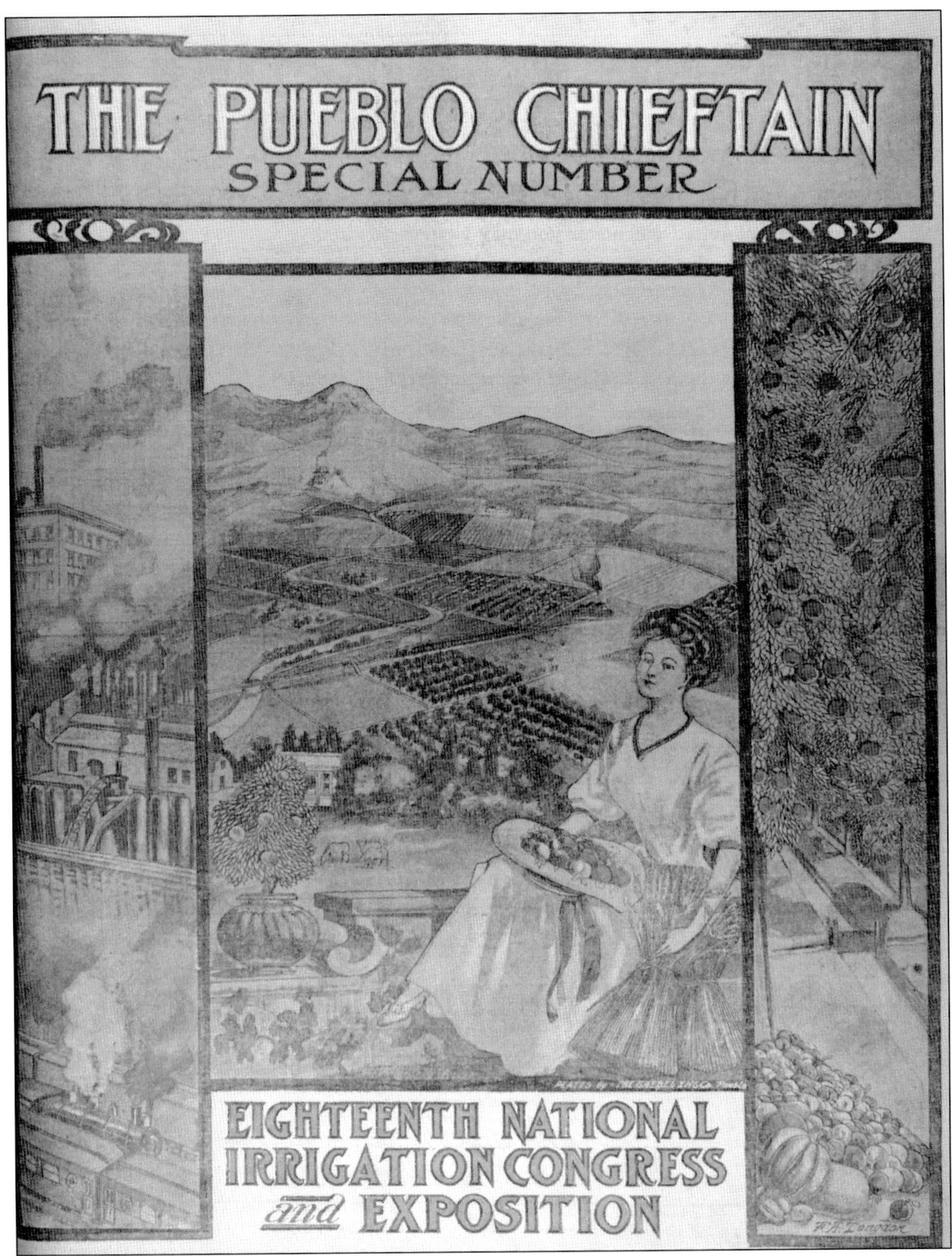

Pueblo was chosen as the site for the Eighteenth National Irrigation Congress September 26–30, 1910. It was such a monumental event in Pueblo that the name of the Grand Hotel was changed to the Congress Hotel. The *Pueblo Chieftain* newspaper devoted an entire edition to the Irrigation Congress held in Pueblo the last week of September 1910 and reported an estimated 10,000 visitors at the event dubbed "Irrigation Week." The gathering offered a platform for the federal government's plan to work toward reclamation projects in the arid West through massive irrigation ventures and provided a showcase for irrigators and their crops. Attendees acknowledged not only the agricultural but also the social benefits of irrigation and the farming it made possible, greatly impacting the city and county of Pueblo. (*Pueblo Chieftain.*)

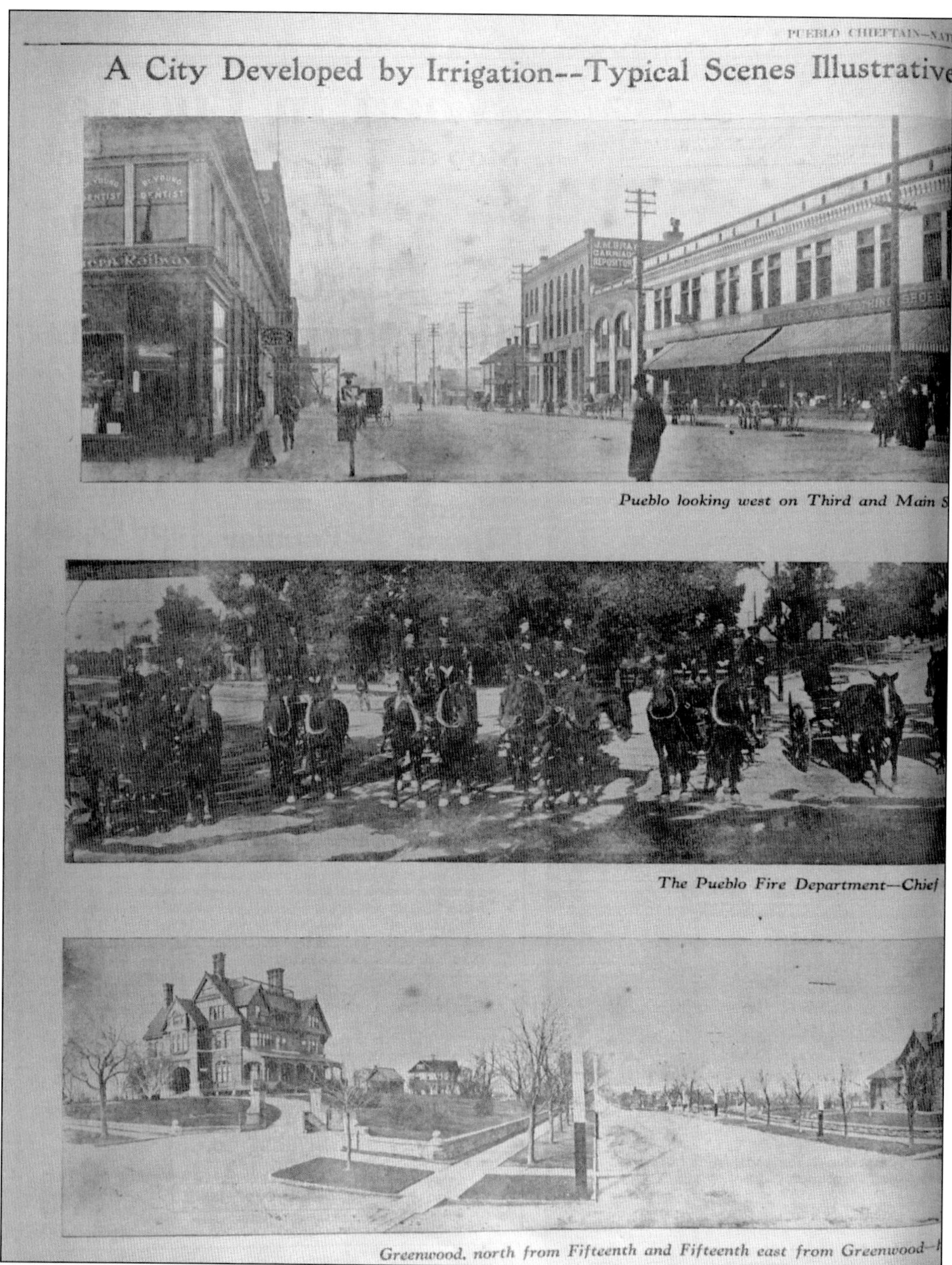

PUEBLO CHIEFTAIN—NAT

A City Developed by Irrigation--Typical Scenes Illustrativ

Pueblo looking west on Third and Main S

The Pueblo Fire Department—Chief

Greenwood, north from Fifteenth and Fifteenth east from Greenwood—

Several special-edition pages in the September 25, 1910, edition of the *Pueblo Chieftain* include information about how irrigation impacted city developments. These images show the center of Pueblo at the intersection of Third and Main Streets, the Pueblo Fire Department, and Mahlon Thatcher's Hillcrest estate, located at Fifteenth and Greenwood Streets. (*Pueblo Chieftain.*)

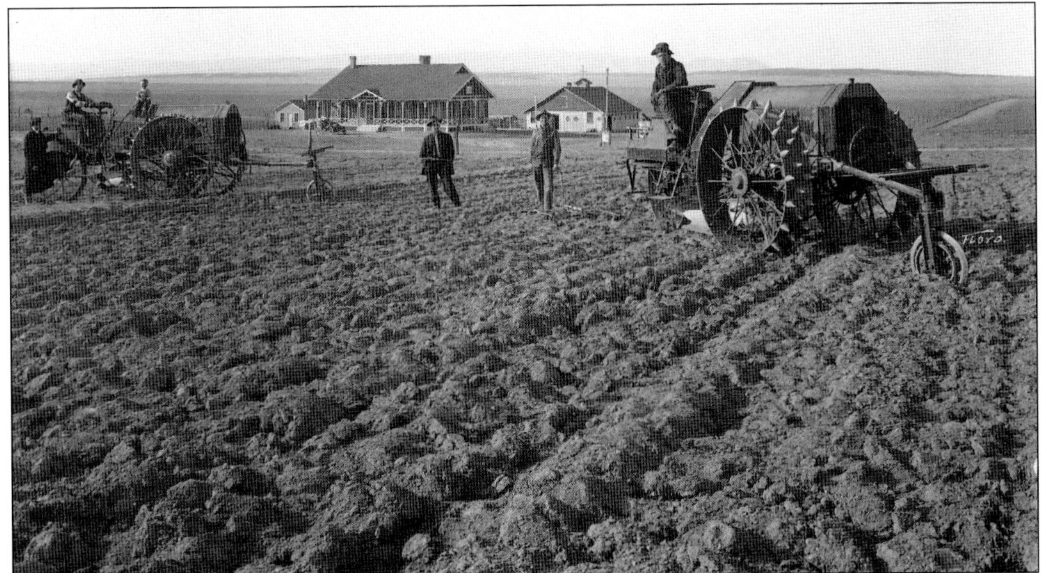

This image is representative of farms in Pueblo County. The tractors are being used to plow, and the rich soil is evident. Large farms remained feasible at the turn of the 20th century. The use of tractors, however, did not displace the ever-present migrant farmworkers. Laid-off steelworks employees also lent their backs to the harvest. (PH-P-06-06-001.)

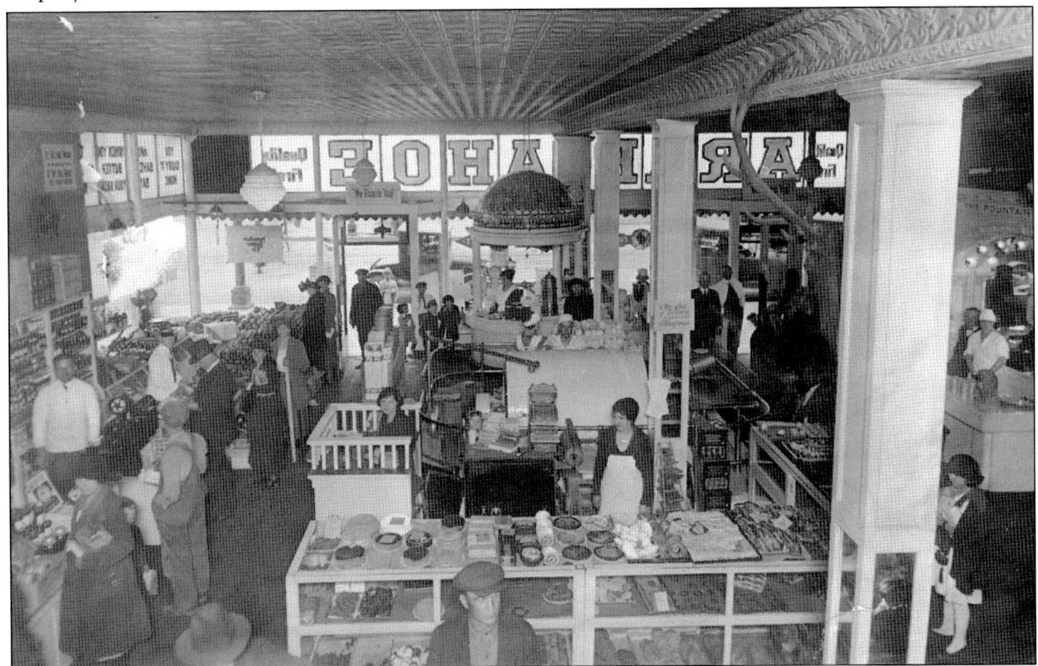

In the early 1900s, Pueblo boasted nearly 80 grocery stores. Depending on the location, these small stores served the neighborhoods of Pueblo with harvests meeting ethnic needs. For example, farmers raised fava beans for the Italian and Slovenian communities and *calabacitas* (zucchini) for the Mexican community. Pueblo Chile has become such a popular product it has developed its own brand and the popular Chile and Frijoles Festival is held every September with thousands of people attending. (PH-P-95-02.)

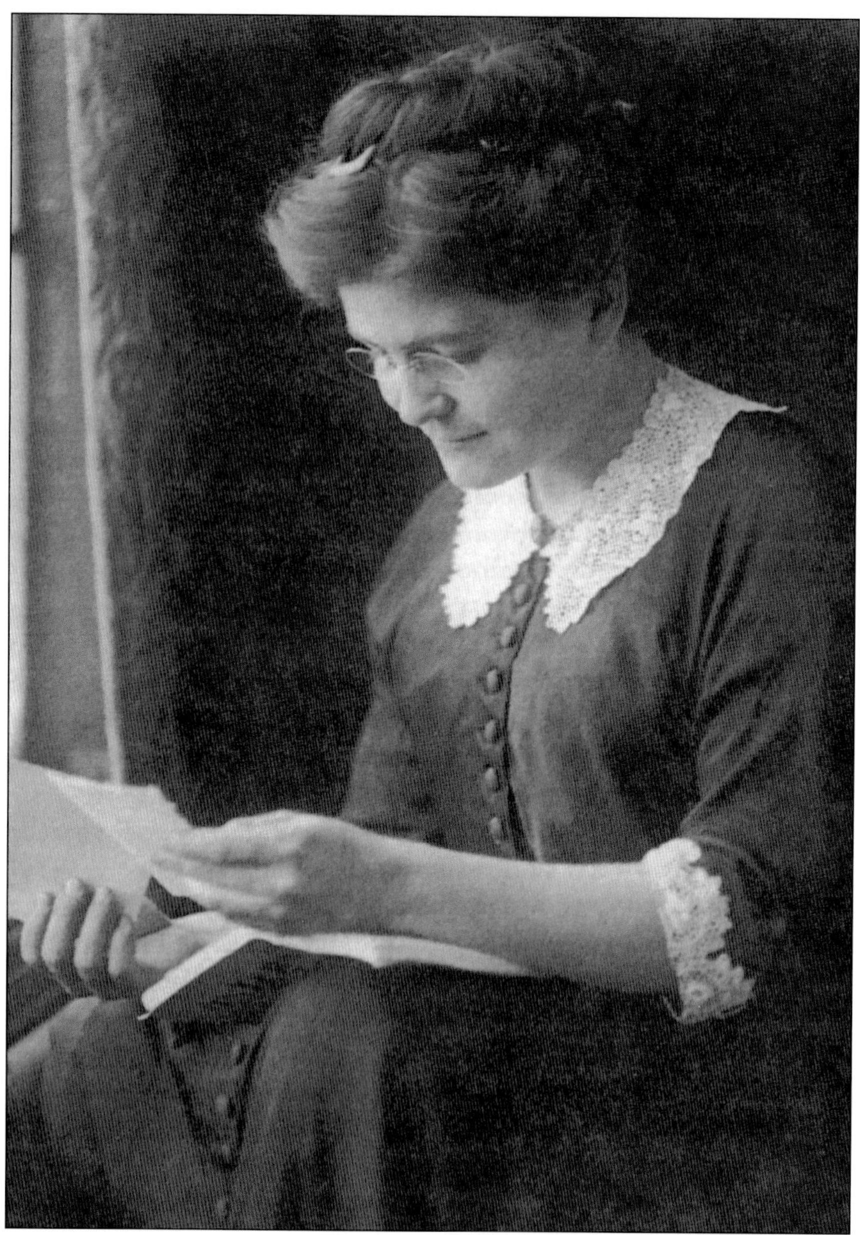

On June 2, 1921, operators in the telephone exchange building received the first warning of flooding along the Arkansas River upstream of Pueblo. Josephine Pryor, chief operator, refused to leave her post when relieved by night operator Grace Williams. Both began calling all operators not on duty to report at once for emergency work. In total, there were 39 operators who rushed into the Exchange Building to try to reach subscribers about the impending danger. Water soon encroached on the lower steps to the second floor, trapping the operators. One man who remained in the building, Byron Thady, did not mention the rising waters. At one point, a large barn swirled their way, missing them by a few inches. The tired operators and Byron were rescued by rowboat the following day and taken to higher ground. One year later, Byron received the Vail Gold Medal, and Josephine received the Vail Silver Medal, while the other women were also given awards. (PH-B-343-01_001.)

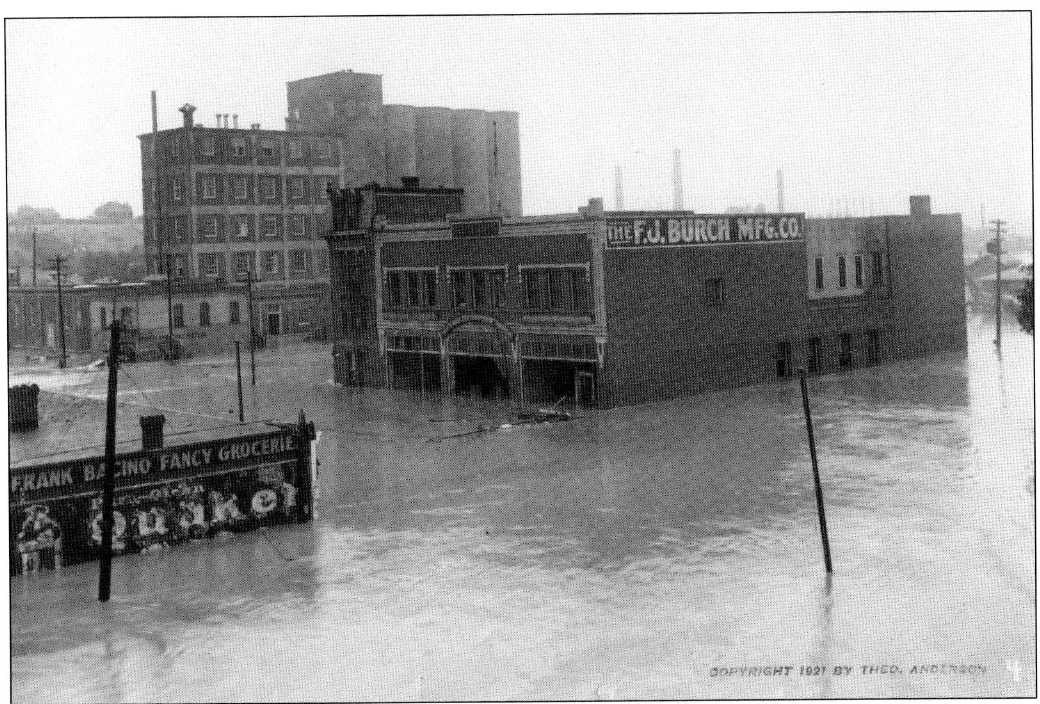

Floodwaters are 10 feet deep on First Street in this view looking southeast toward Santa Fe Avenue. The caption reads, "No place to pitch a tent." The death count was estimated at 1,500 people at the time, but modern estimates range from 98 to 250. Losses were estimated at $25 million for the period. (PH-P-284-01.)

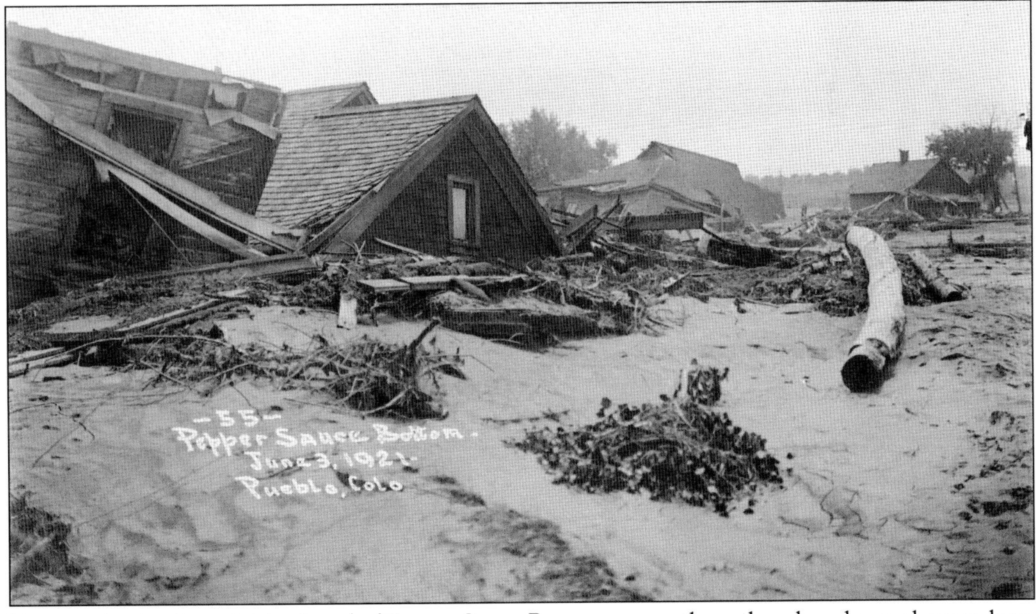

Devastation in the neighborhood of Pepper Sauce Bottoms, near the railroad yards, was horrendous. The neighborhood rested on low ground, some of the lowest in Pueblo, and was one of the first areas to become inundated with rising water, sweeping an unknown number of neighborhood residents to their deaths. The neighborhood remains prone to flooding to this day. (PH-P-289-02-001.)

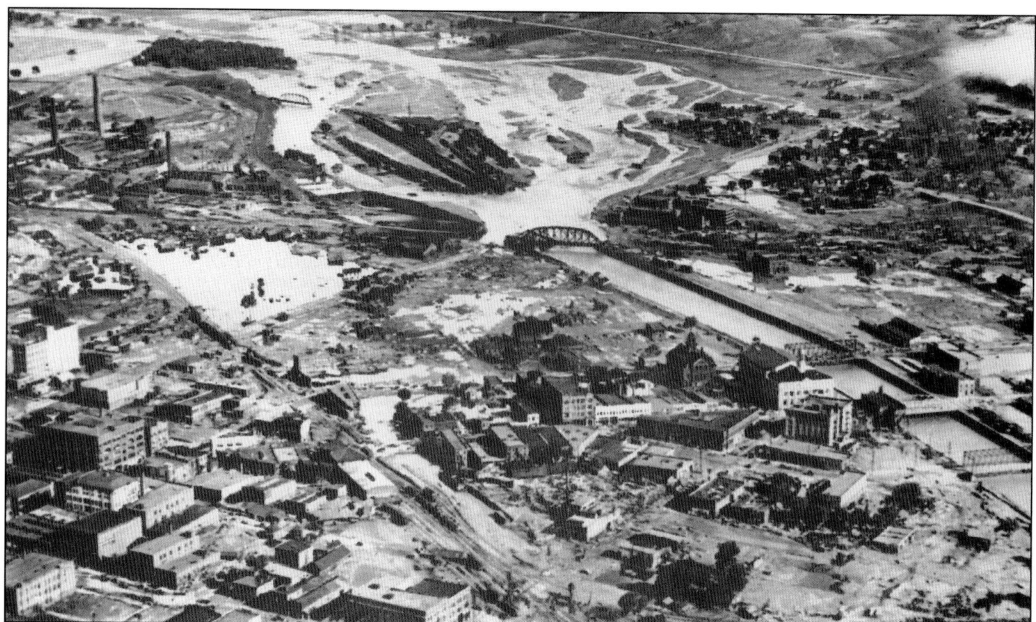

An aerial photograph of the devastation shows the disruption of bridges and roads in this view looking south. Remarkably, the floodwaters only destroyed the bridges over Fountain Creek, while the bridges over the Arkansas River remained standing. Water carried away over 600 homes. (PH-P-279-03_001.)

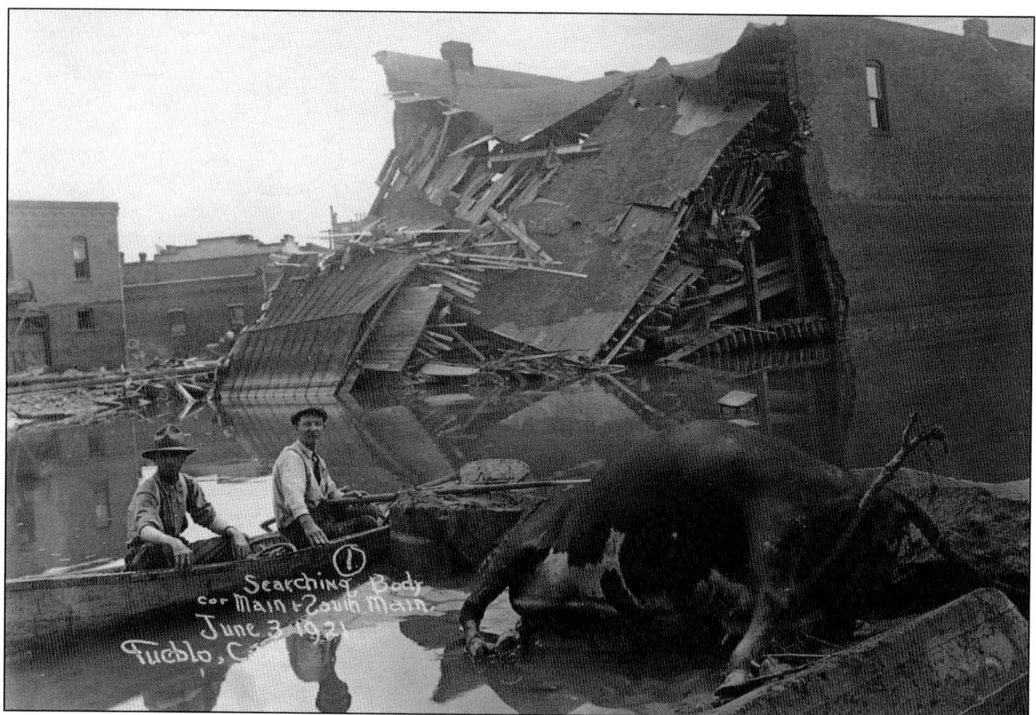

The caption on this photograph states, "Searching for bodies Main and South Main, June 3, 1921." Many horses and cattle died in the flood, and their bloated bodies could be seen all over the flood area. The rising water covered over 300 square miles. (PH-P-286-05-00.)

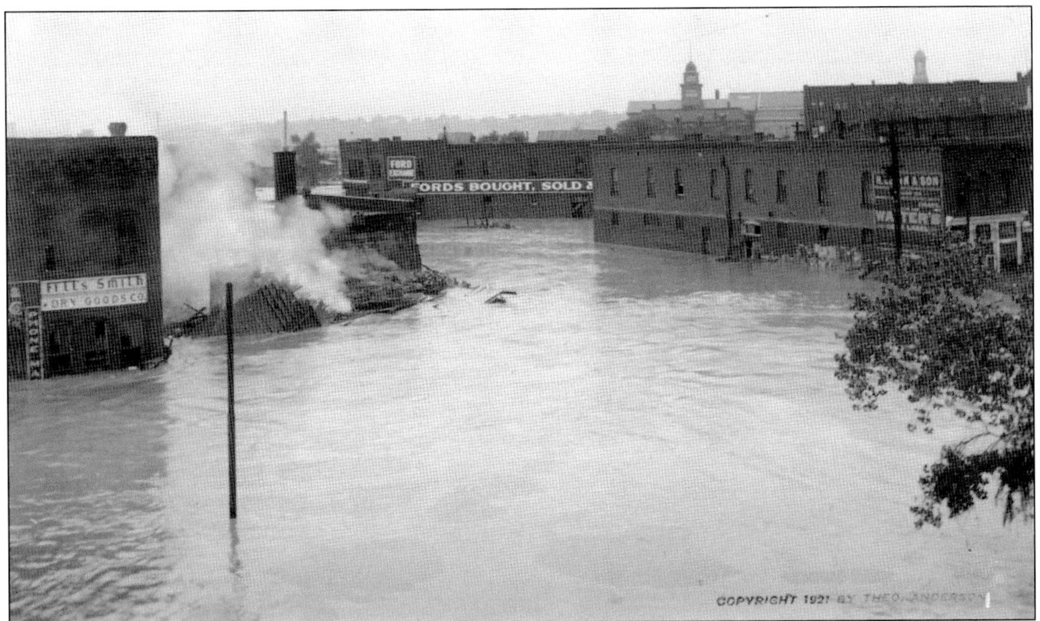

This image shows the depth of the flood at 1911 Central Main Street. A dry goods store is seen to the left and a "Fords Bought and Sold" advertisement is in the distance. The high-water mark was 9.8 feet at the Union Depot and 12.5 feet at the McCarthy Block, at the intersection of Union Avenue and Main Street. (PH-P-286-05-002.)

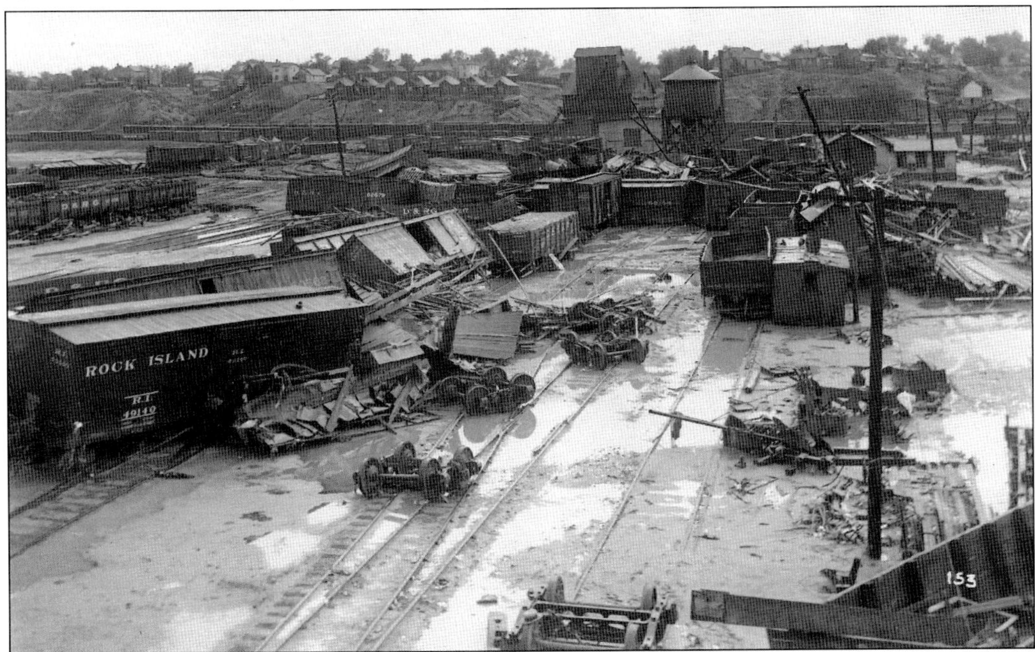

The loss to railroads was $4.5 million. Railroad cars were strewn across the downtown area. Federal assistance amounted to $100,000, appropriated by Congress to help the Army in cleaning up the debris. Most of the burden fell on property owners, businessmen, and the railroad companies. The telephone company inaugurated a new method of installing phone lines, triggered by the massive replacement needed to provide phone service after the flood. (PH-P-291-06.)

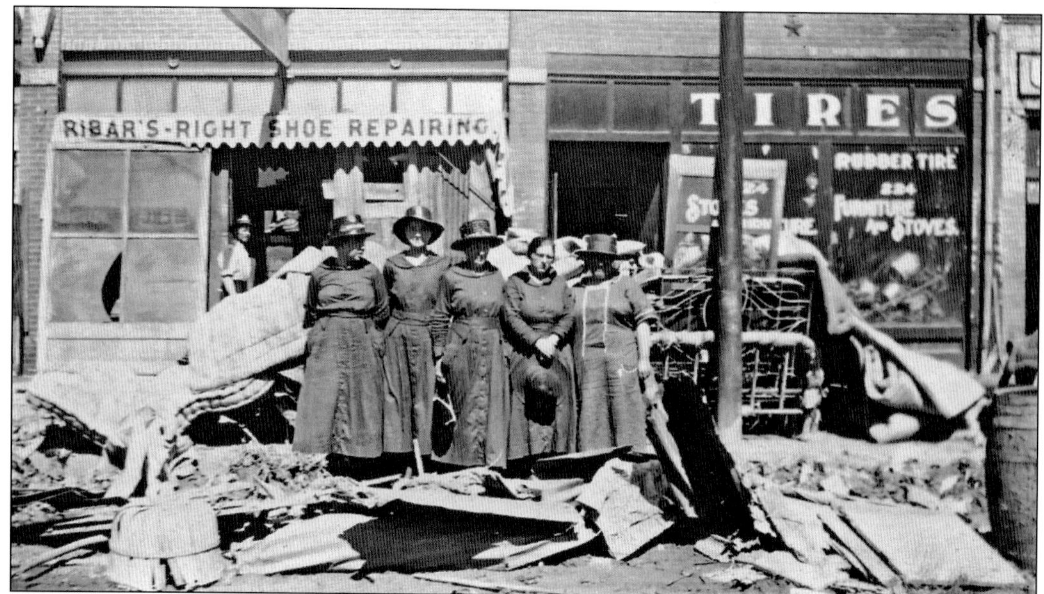

It seems like every able-bodied person in Pueblo took part in the recovery. Shown here are Salvation Army workers amid the flood destruction after the water had subsided. Naturally, a thorough cleanup effort took years to complete. (PH-P-292-03-001.)

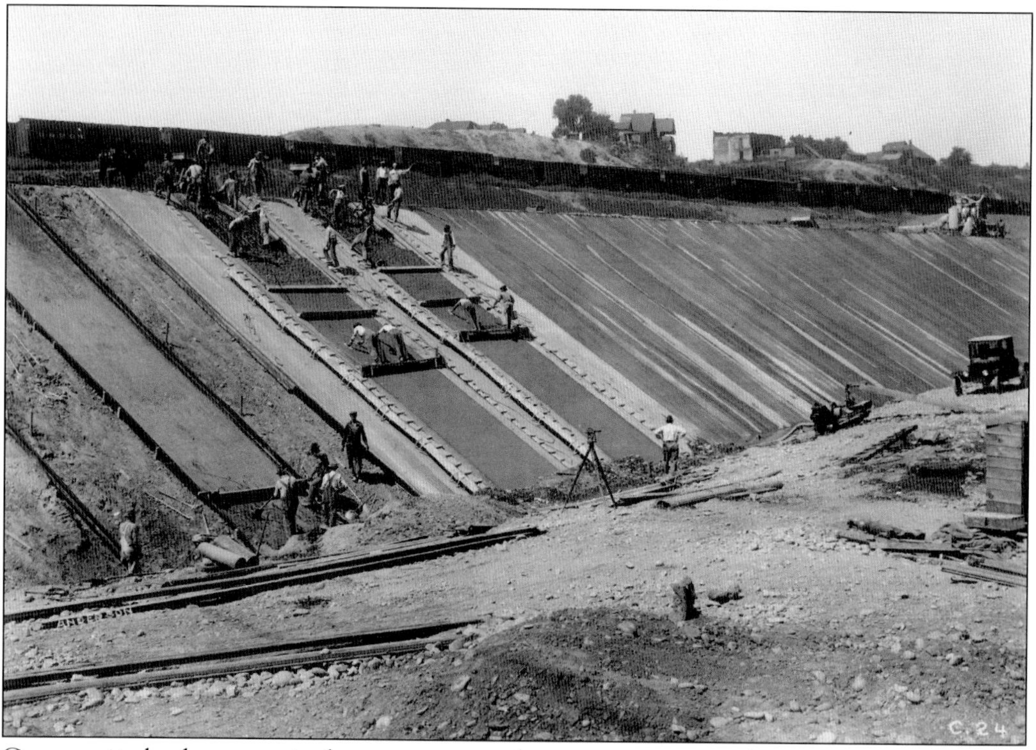

Community leaders organized a conservancy district to prevent a future catastrophe. Dikes were constructed, and the river was channeled southward. The largest flood mitigation project, the levee shown here was constructed in direct response to flooding in the downtown area. (PH-P-716-08-001.)

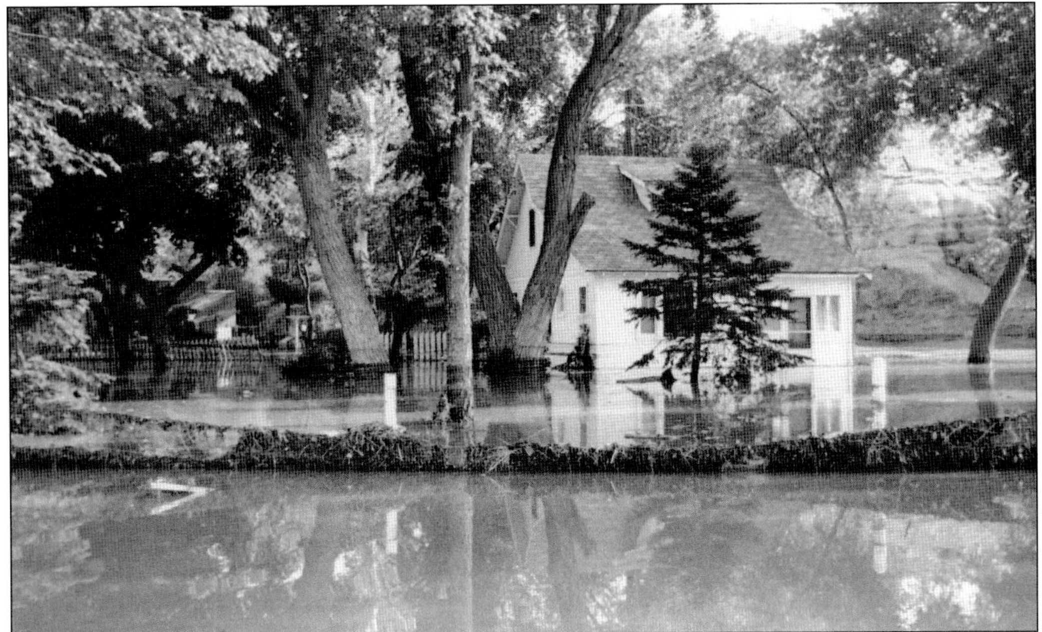

With water control projects only constructed to regulate Arkansas River flooding, there was nothing to stop the deluge of water careening down Fountain Creek in 1965. On June 17, gauges along the creek estimated a flow of 47,000 cubic feet per second. To this day, this is the highest such reading ever recorded in the city and well above the 34,000 cubic feet per second flow that occurred during the flood of 1921. (PH-P-298-01_003.)

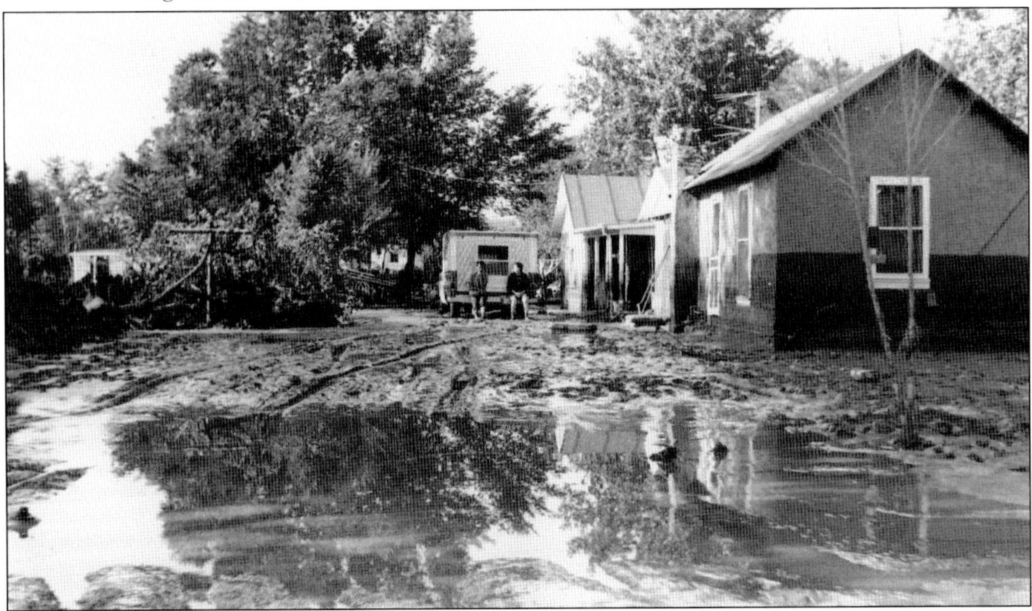

The 1965 flood covered approximately 53 city blocks with water up to eight feet deep. The water damaged 370 residences and 59 businesses. Metal buildings just north of the Fourth Street Bridge crashed into the bridge as floodwaters crested its eastern side. The bulk of this damage occurred in the Eastside neighborhood. The high-water mark is visible halfway up the side of this house. (PH-P-298-01-001.)

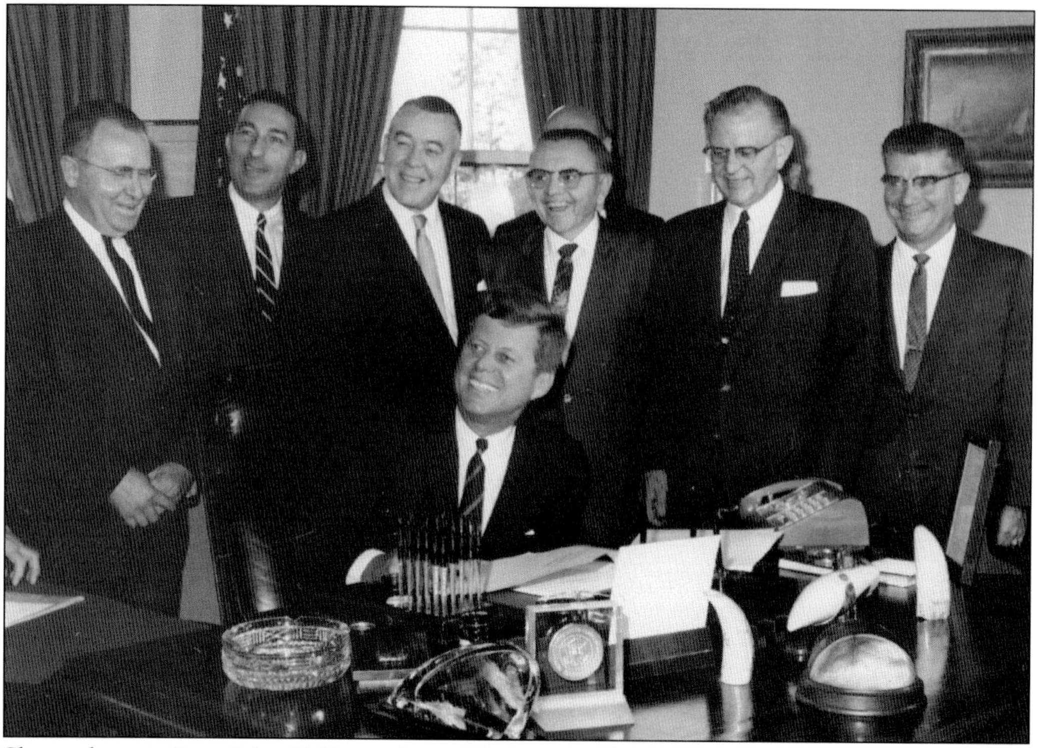

Shown here is Pres. John F. Kennedy in Washington, DC, on August 16, 1962, signing the legislation for the Fryingpan-Arkansas Trans-Mountain Diversion Project. This was done the day before Kennedy visited Pueblo. (PH-B-228-03-001.)

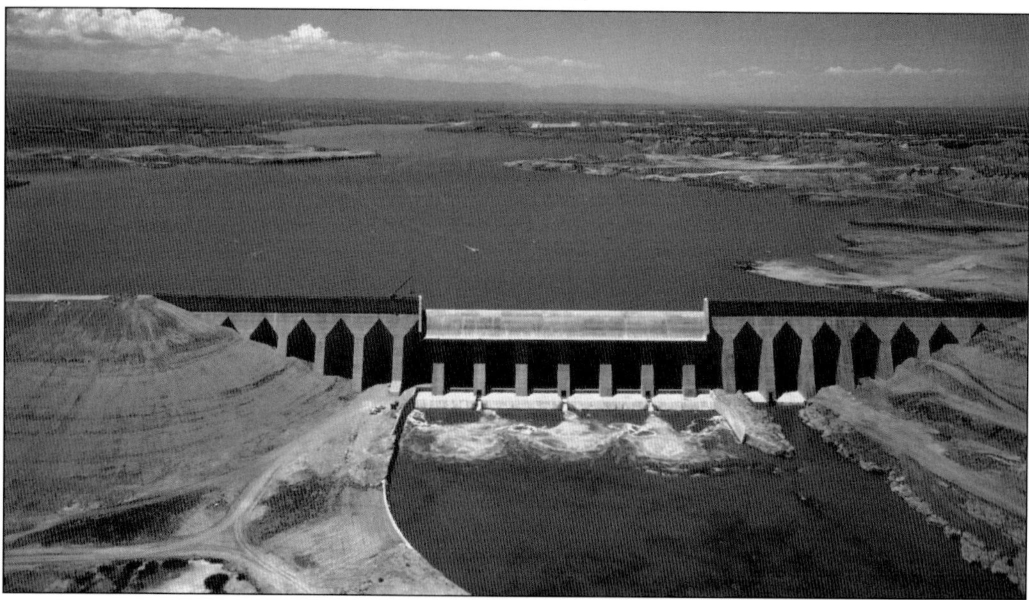

It took years to plan, but finally the Fryingpan-Arkansas Project paved the way for construction of a dam, which was completed in 1975 and formed Lake Pueblo. Total water capacity of the reservoir is 357,000 acre-feet, with 93,000 acre-feet reserved for flood control. Lake Pueblo has become a key economic and recreational asset to the city of Pueblo. (PH-P-728-03-004.)

Seven

Prohibition, the Great Depression, and Recovery

The 1920s and 1930s brought political changes, economic hardships, and natural disasters. In spite of the challenging times, Pueblo's residents have persevered.

The Eighteenth Amendment to the US Constitution, ratified on January 16, 1919, banned the sale of intoxicating liquors and ushered in Prohibition on January 16, 1920. Colorado had previously voted for prohibition in November 1914 with the goal of being completely dry by January 1, 1916. It made for an interesting time for bootleggers in Pueblo. Tunnels beneath Union and Santa Fe Avenues businesses connected buildings and allowed for easy escape should a speakeasy be raided. Prohibition proved hard to enforce and contributed to an increase in gang violence and other crimes. Finally, in 1933, the Twenty-First Amendment repealed the Eighteenth Amendment and Prohibition ended.

The stock market crash in October 1929 ushered in the era known as the Great Depression. Pueblo was especially affected, with thousands of losses in the manufacturing industry. President Roosevelt's New Deal programs buoyed Pueblo's economy with the Works Progress Administration, Civil Works Administration, and the Civilian Conservation Corps. The programs not only employed people but also created many projects that enhanced Pueblo's quality of life through the creation and construction of parks and infrastructure.

In addition to the challenges of the Great Depression, Puebloans and people in other southeastern Colorado counties found themselves in the middle of the Dust Bowl in the 1930s. Pueblo lies in the arid and semiarid West, which already suffered due to overgrazing and dryland farming techniques. Little rain fell during the drought, resulting in weak crop yields, which in turn meant no protection of the soil when the spring winds came. Direct relief to families in need came in the form of cash payments and food and goods allocations. These factors led to the Department of the Interior enacting new laws to establish grazing districts and to manage a grazing permit system.

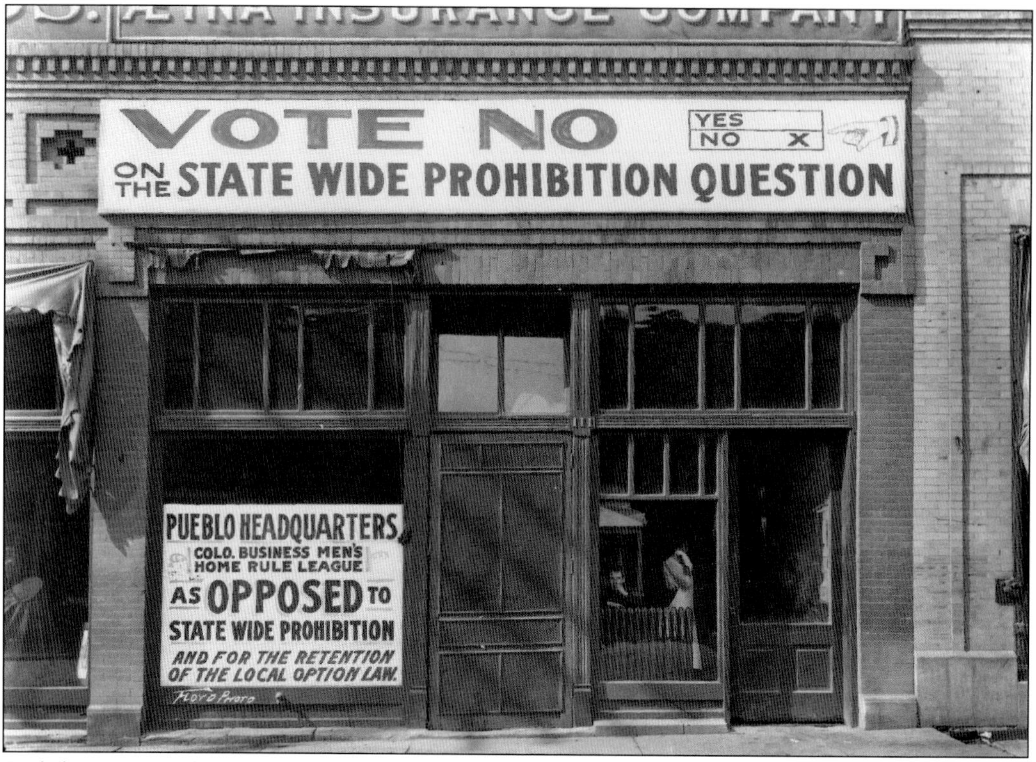

Prohibition was a hotly debated topic, and many businesses displayed their support or opposition. With Prohibition enacted, various rumrunners flourished in Pueblo, and speakeasies sprang up where residents could imbibe in secret. Prohibition also facilitated the introduction of organized crime in the city, and syndicates used Pueblo as a central location for communities south and east of the city as well. (PH-P-690-02_01.)

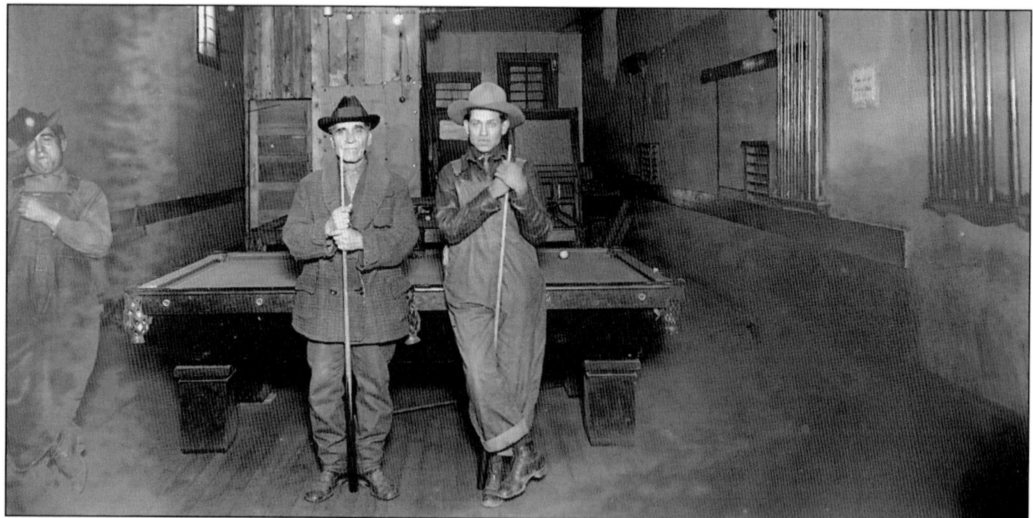

This is the interior of a tavern on Union Avenue during Prohibition, and it is obvious that no alcohol is being served. During the flood of 1921, liquor restrictions were lifted for 30 days as an emergency measure for combating the spread of disease in the flood area as reported in an article in the *Pueblo Chieftain* on June 9, 1921. (PH-P-700-05_001.)

The Great Depression ravaged the nation, and Pueblo was not spared. The Depression forced people in Pueblo to make do with what they had. Here, a Pueblo resident appears to have set up a roadside market, selling produce next to a vehicle body that serves as his home. (PH-P-307-03.)

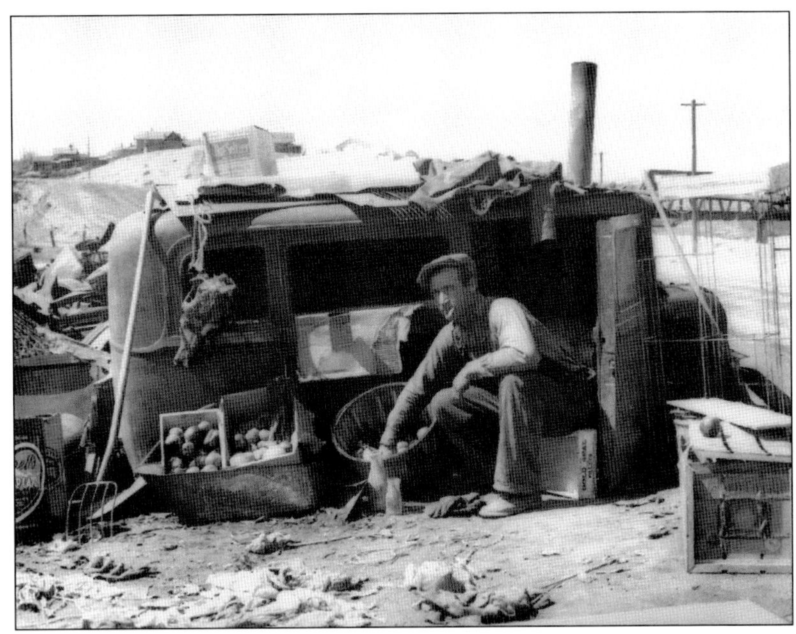

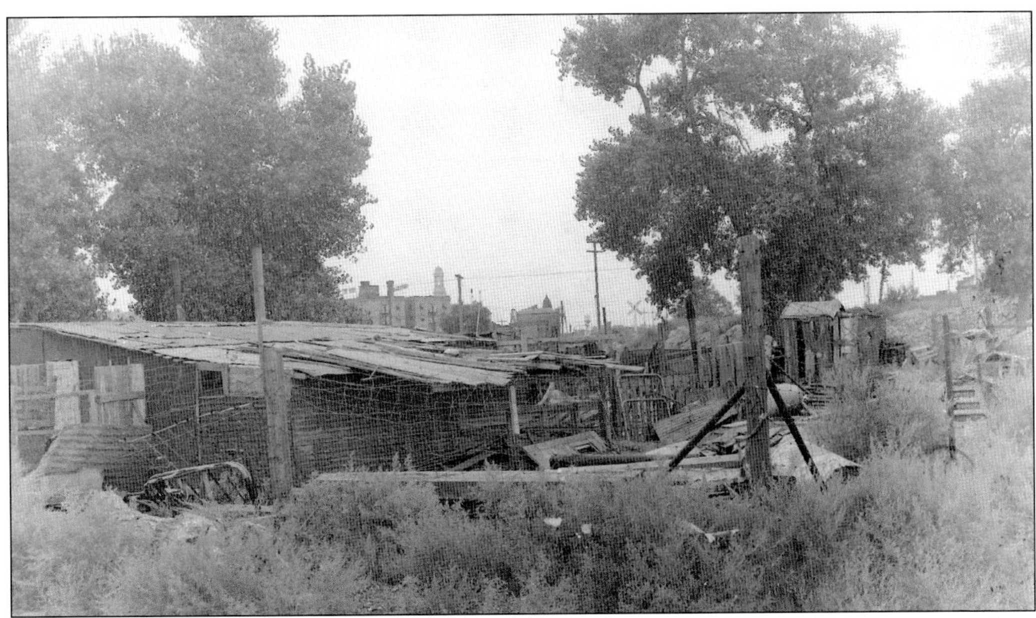

This is a photograph of a slum in Pueblo during the Great Depression. Shanty towns such as this cropped up throughout the city. It appears that nothing was wasted as residents became more resourceful reusing building materials that were no longer useful or had been thrown out. Memorial Hall can be seen in the background of this photograph. (PH-P-838-01.)

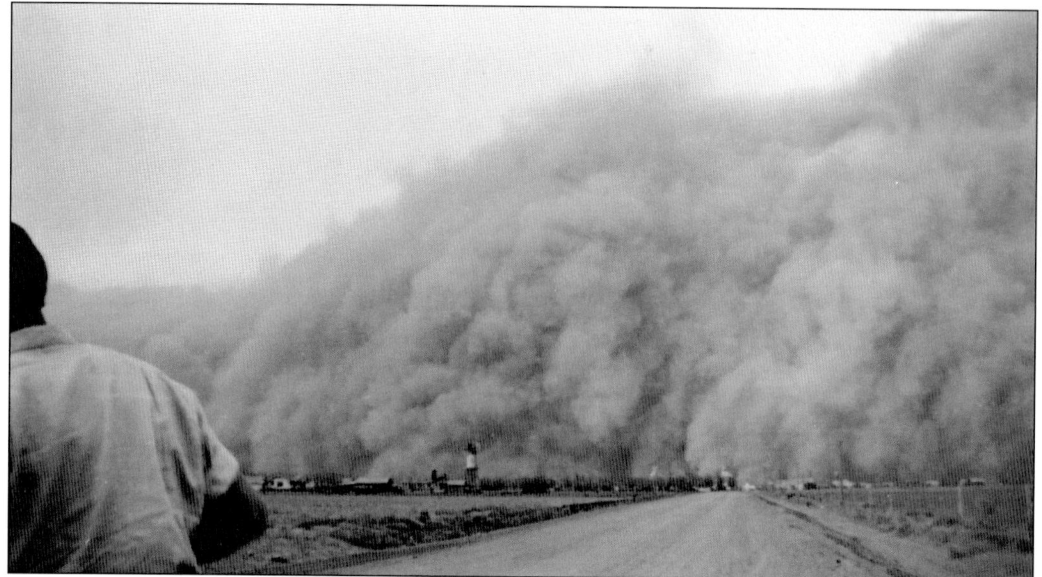

In 1933, the dust storms were so intense that they made everyday life almost impossible for both people and livestock. People were forced to eat meals under a tablecloth, and they wore goggles or masks of wet towels while outdoors. Piling as high as snowdrifts, dust covered roads, fences, and cars; rail traffic was stopped (PH-P-116-02.)

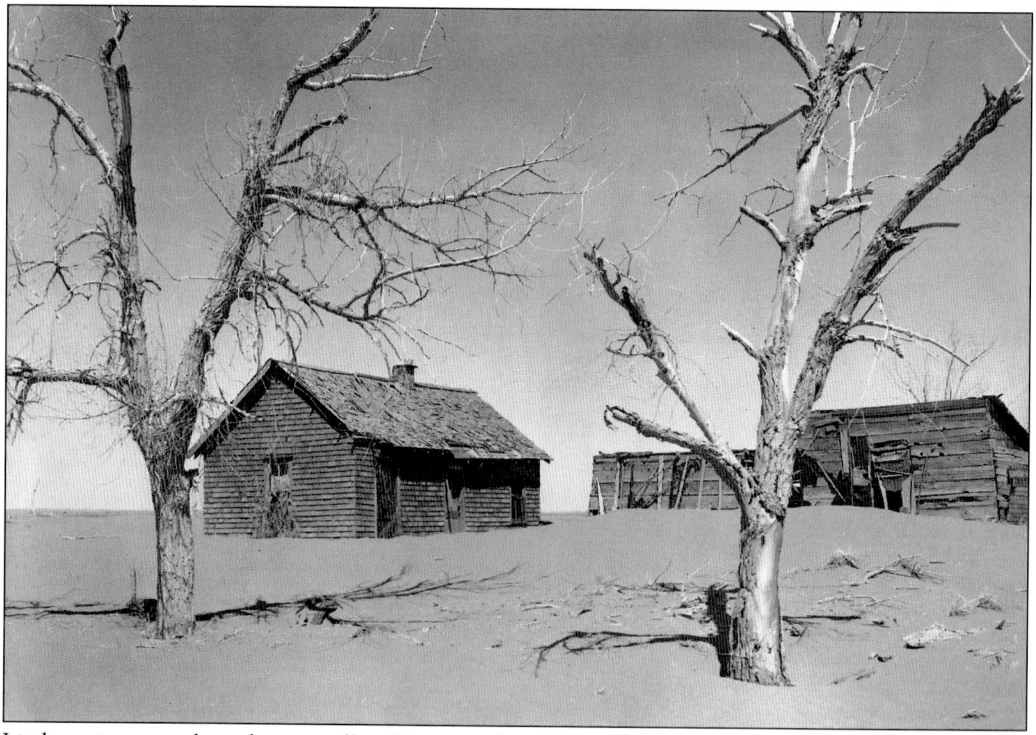

Little moisture and an almost endless blowing of soil created difficult living conditions for families. Direct relief to families came, but for some, it was not soon enough, as many rural residents had fled to cities. Farmers learned crop rotation techniques to conserve the soil when the moisture finally returned. The dark years of the Dust Bowl slipped into history. (PH-P-02-01-02.)

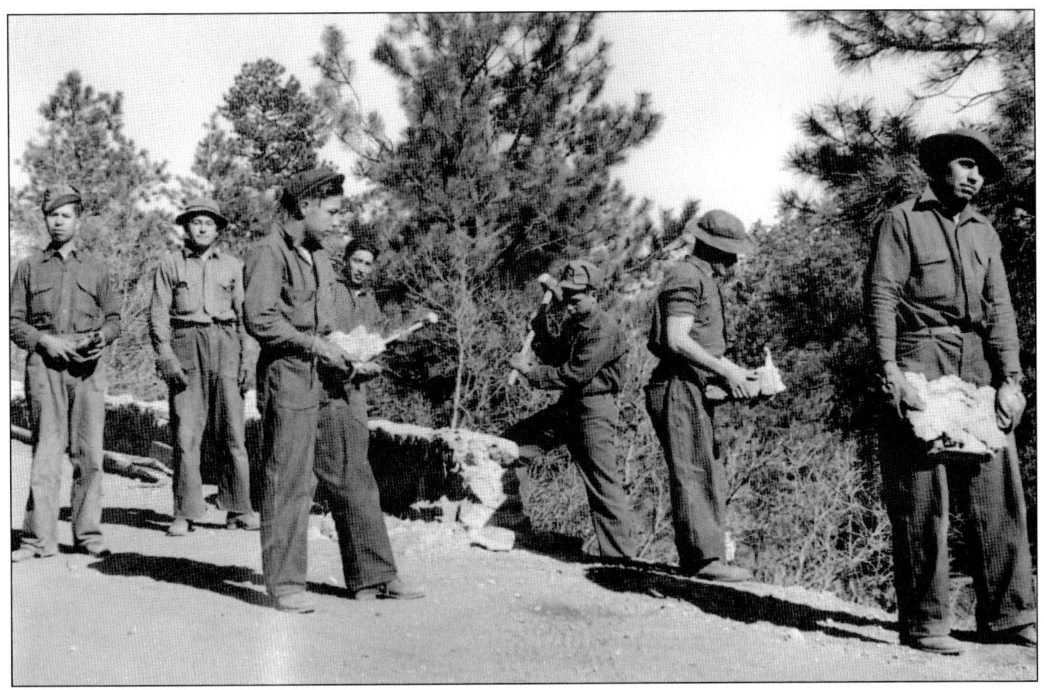

While combating the Great Depression, Works Progress Administration and Civil Works Administration workers contributed greatly to Pueblo as a community through their building projects. Here, workers are seen at one unidentified area park. One such project culminated in the construction of the band shell at Mineral Palace Park on the shores of Lake Clara. (PH-P-189-01.)

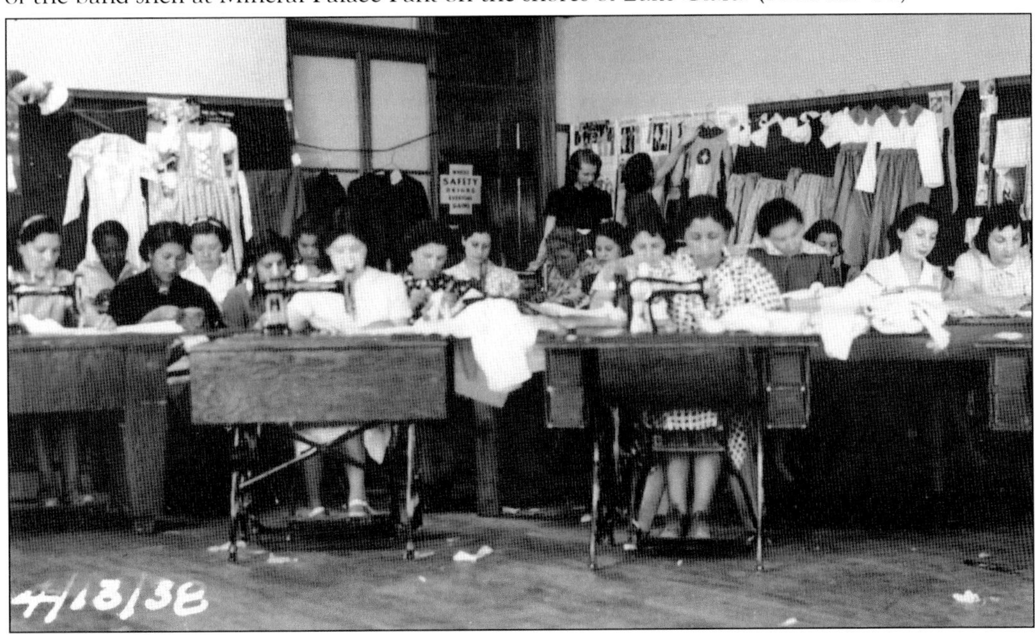

For some women, New Deal programs offered employment in sewing rooms. Women learned how to draw clothing patterns and sew garments on new Singer sewing machines. Nationally, 13.5 percent of Works Progress Administration employees were women and 7 percent of those sewed for a living. (PH-P-754-04.)

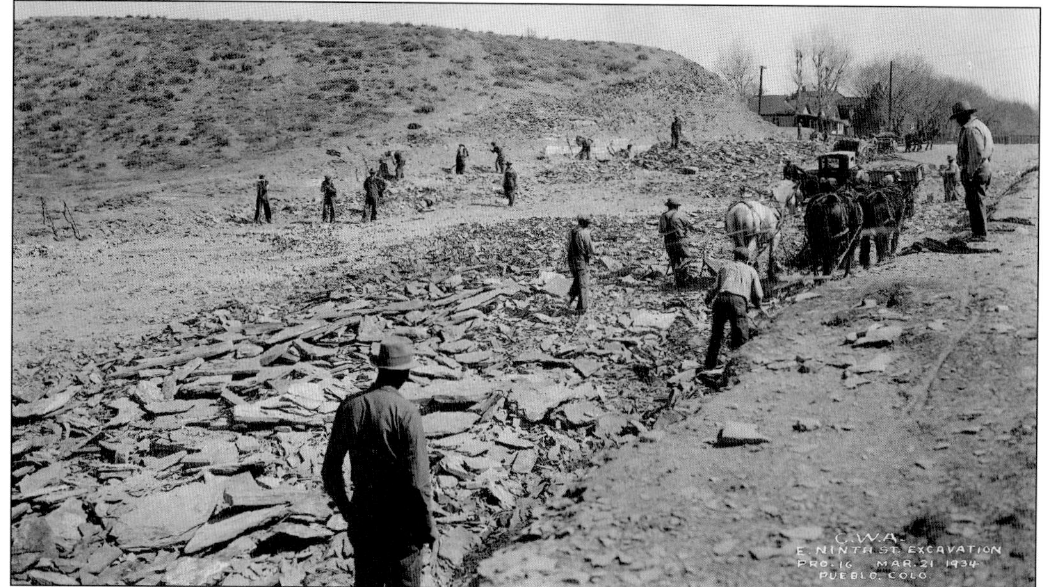

Workers in this photograph are excavating East Ninth Street in order to extend the thoroughfare eastward. Works Progress Administration projects often utilized materials created from one project in order to complete another. The limestone seen here could have easily been used elsewhere within the city. (PH-P-754-04_005.)

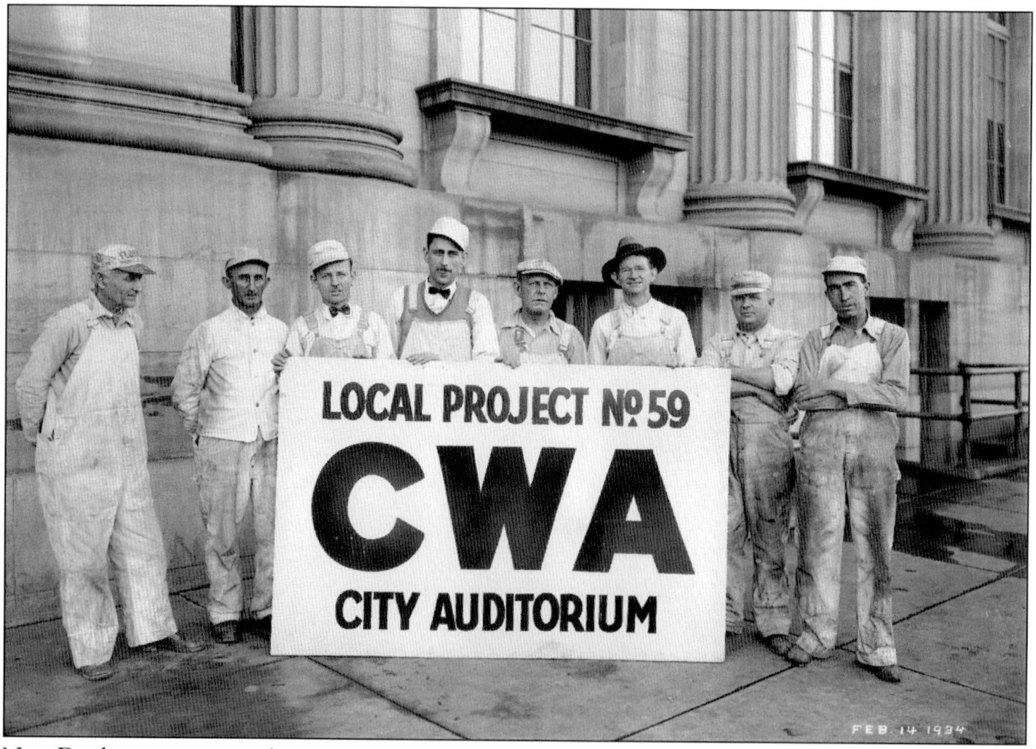

New Deal projects not only constructed facilities, they maintained them as well. The Civil Works Administration employees pictured here in 1934 performed several maintenance tasks at City and Memorial Hall on South Union Avenue. (PH-P-754-04_004.)

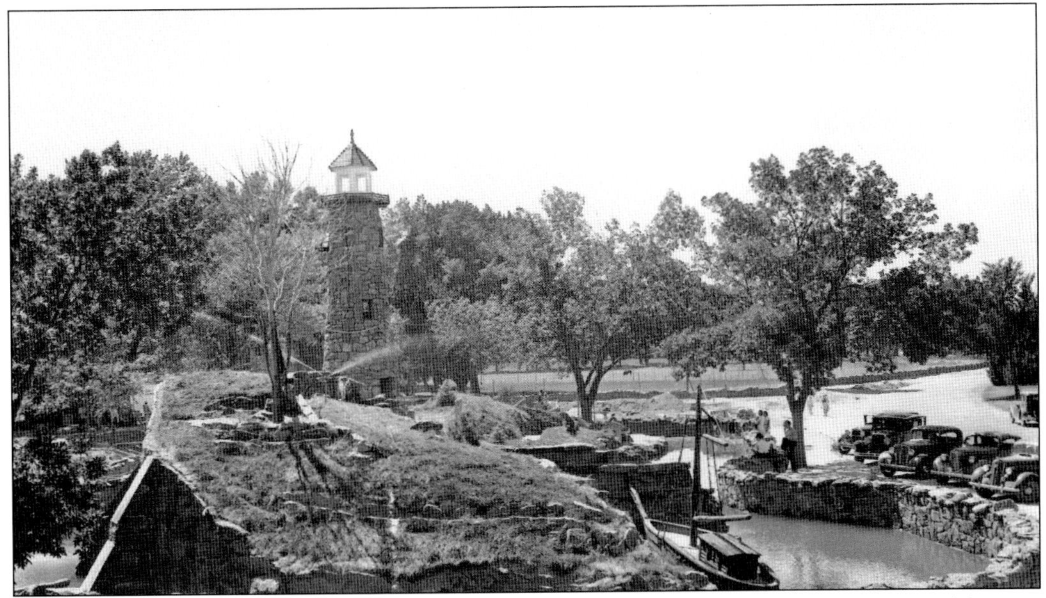

Employees of three New Deal agencies constructed six structures, two of which were buildings to form the Pueblo Zoo. Workers randomly placed rusticated sandstone rocks, quarried 25 miles west of Pueblo, to form the structures. Monkey Moat and Monkey Island are seen in this photograph when automobiles still traversed the zoo property. (PH-P-745-0_01.)

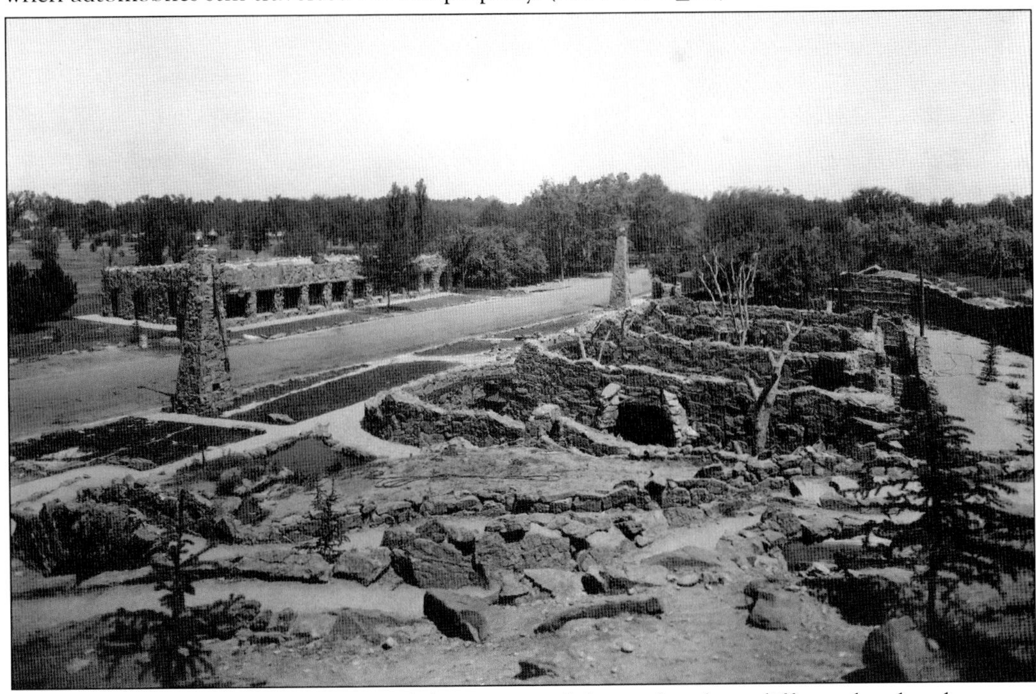

The Pueblo Zoo was created by consolidating animals housed at three different local parks to one 30-acre parcel within Pueblo City Park. The animals were moved to the new location, but they were housed in cages. The later years of the Great Depression brought substantial improvements to the zoo that allowed animals to roam in more natural settings without the extraneous use of bars. (PH-P-745-07_001.)

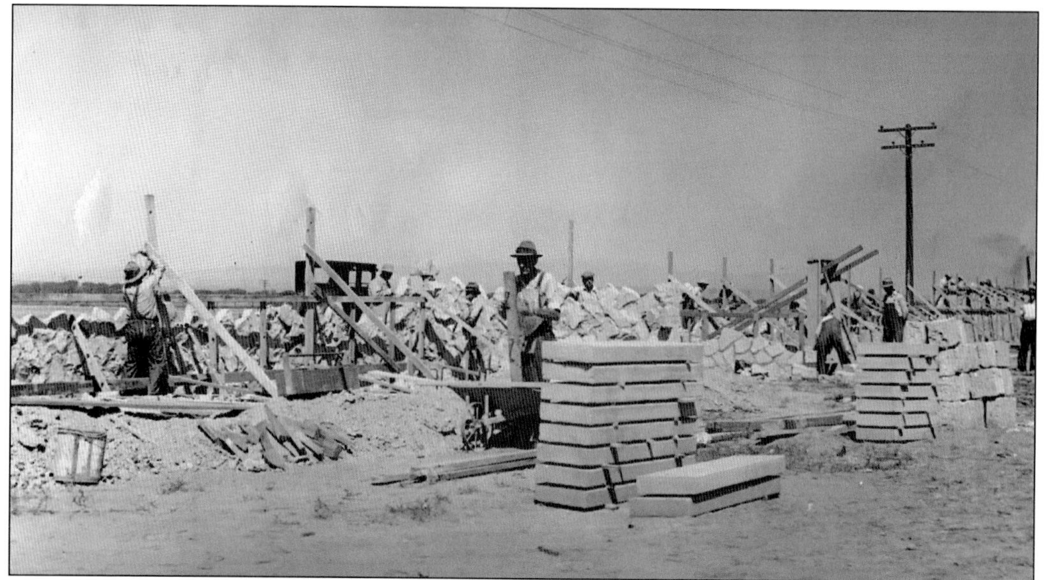

Buildings at the Colorado State Fairgrounds were another large project undertaken by New Deal agencies. The use of local rusticated stone, obtained for a nearby quarry, continued at the Fairgrounds. In this photograph, workers construct the horse arena and accompanying stalls. (PH-P-254-01.)

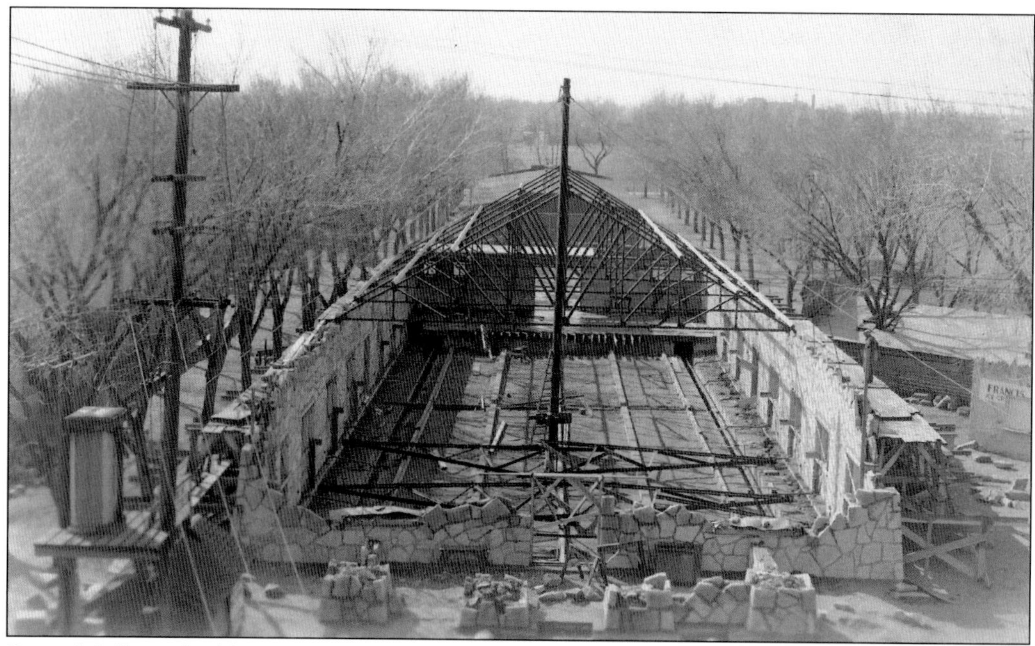

Several different buildings and structures within the Fairgrounds were constructed with New Deal labor at various times throughout the decade. Shown here is the 4-H Auditorium built in 1938. The city of Pueblo provided $3,396, and the Work Progress Administration provided $22,441 to build the auditorium. (PH-P-254-02.)

Eight

Nationalism and the Home of Heroes

Pueblo has always maintained a link to Washington, DC. Presidential visits seemed to occur regularly in the city, as did visits from presidential candidates. The presidents who visited Pueblo include: Theodore Roosevelt (1903), William Howard Taft (1909), Woodrow Wilson (1919), Herbert Hoover (1928), Franklin D. Roosevelt (1936 and 1938), Harry S. Truman (1952), Dwight D. Eisenhower (1957), John F. Kennedy (1962), William J. Clinton (1995), and Barack Obama (2012). George H.W. Bush visited the city while campaigning for president.

The availability of federal programs under different administrations strengthened the link to Washington. For example, the Pueblo Ordnance Depot brought thousands of jobs into Pueblo during the 1940s. Additionally, the federal government turned over the land of the Pueblo Army Air Base to the city in 1948 to use as a municipal airport. This replaced the airport on Prairie Avenue across from the State Fairgrounds.

Pueblo citizens have served in every war since the Civil War, beginning with the formation of the Colorado Volunteers in 1862. They have fought with honor in the Spanish-American War, World War I, World War II, Korean War, Vietnam War, and currently in the Middle East. Several monuments located throughout Pueblo honor veterans.

On July 12, 1993, the Congressional Record recognized Pueblo as the "Home of Heroes," because more living Medal of Honor recipients called the city home than any other city in the United States. The Pueblo City Council then adopted this moniker for Pueblo. A memorial was placed outside of the Pueblo Convention center for the four living recipients William J. Crawford, Carl L. Sitter, Raymond G. "Jerry" Murphy, and Drew D. Dix. Civilians also provided essential domestic support to war efforts. Women and organizations such as the Red Cross and the Salvation Army were essential to the war efforts and also deserve recognition. Women filled the shortage of employees at CF&I, worked as volunteers, or found a most unique way of contributing; for example, Mary Babnik Brown donated her hair.

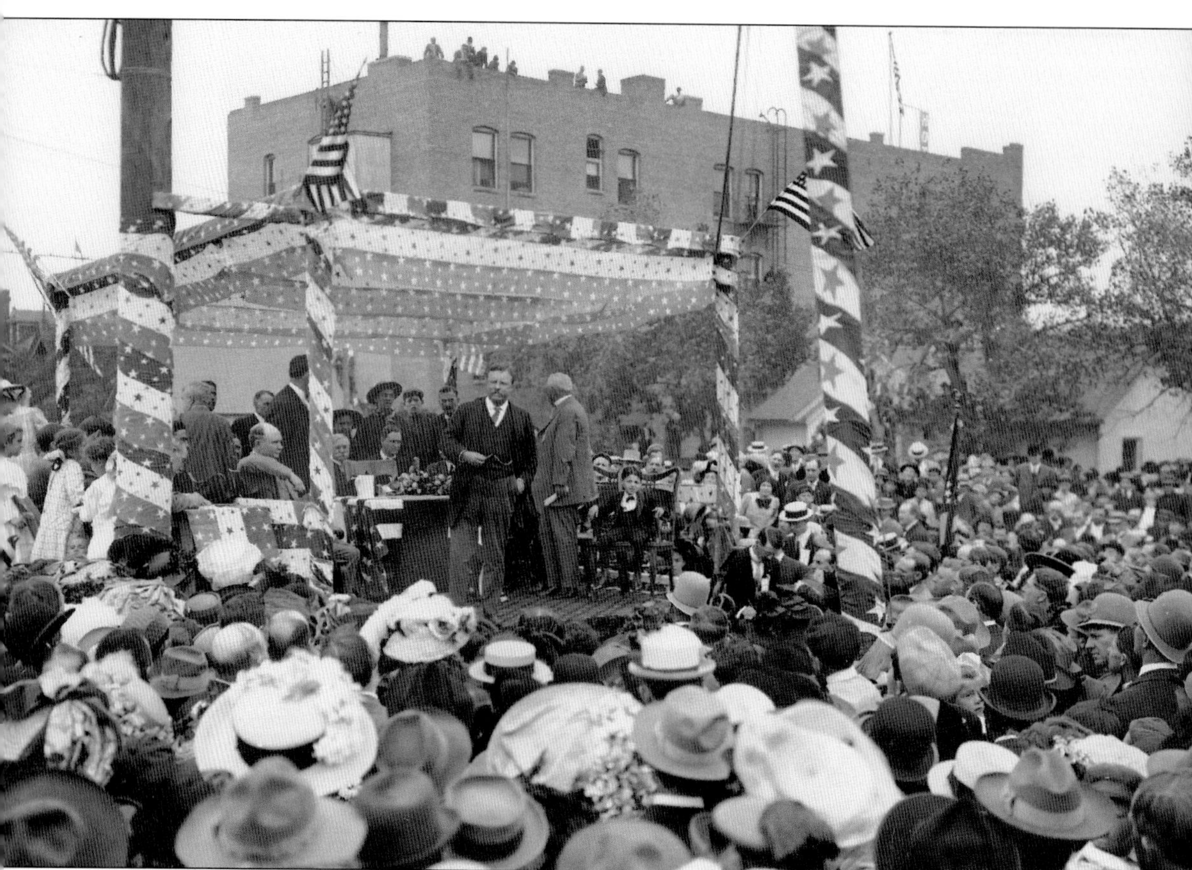

Pres. Theodore Roosevelt visited Pueblo three times. In 1903, as president, Roosevelt was greeted by one of the largest parades Pueblo had ever seen. The *Pueblo Chieftain* headline read, "All is in readiness to extend a rousing reception to nation's Chief Executive—Entire City is eagerly awaiting." In September 1910, Roosevelt (shown here) returned after his two terms in office ended to dedicate the cornerstone of the new YMCA, and he returned to the city once again in September 1912 when he campaigned for president as a member of the Progressive Bull Moose Party. (PH-P-381-03.)

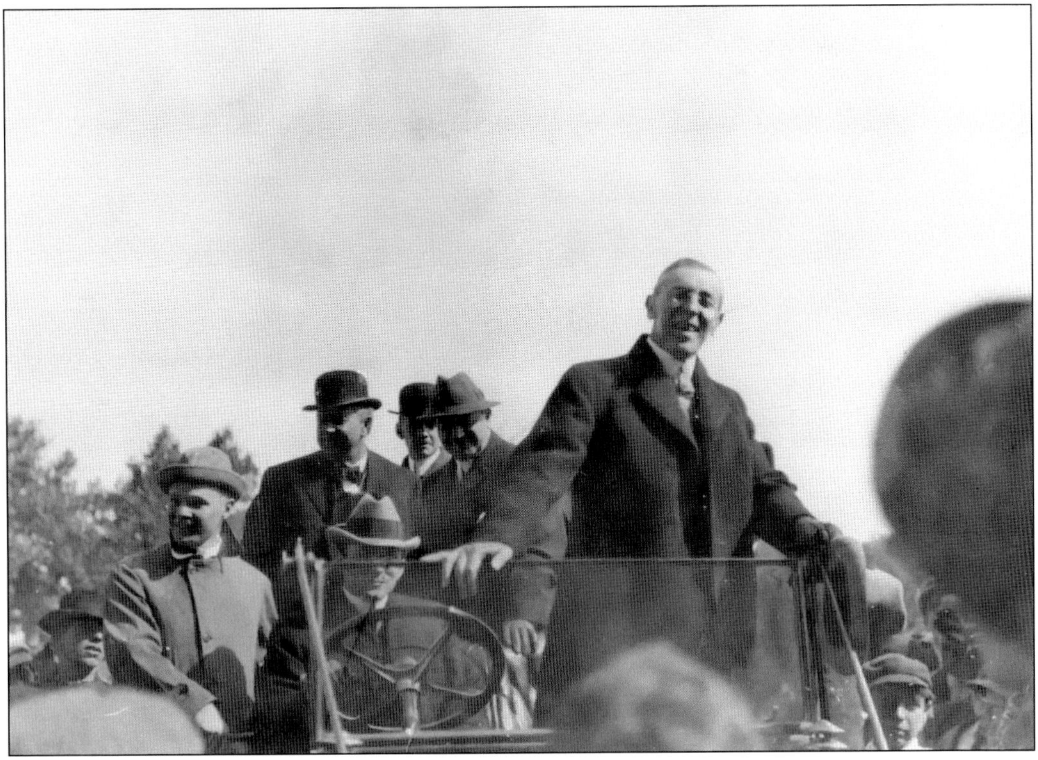

On September 25, 1919, Pres. Woodrow Wilson made his last public address at the Pueblo Memorial Hall while on a national tour promoting the League of Nations. Wilson was not feeling well earlier in the day and when he spoke at Memorial Hall, his condition worsened. He suffered a stroke shortly after the speech and served the remainder of his term in poor health. (PH-P-469-01.)

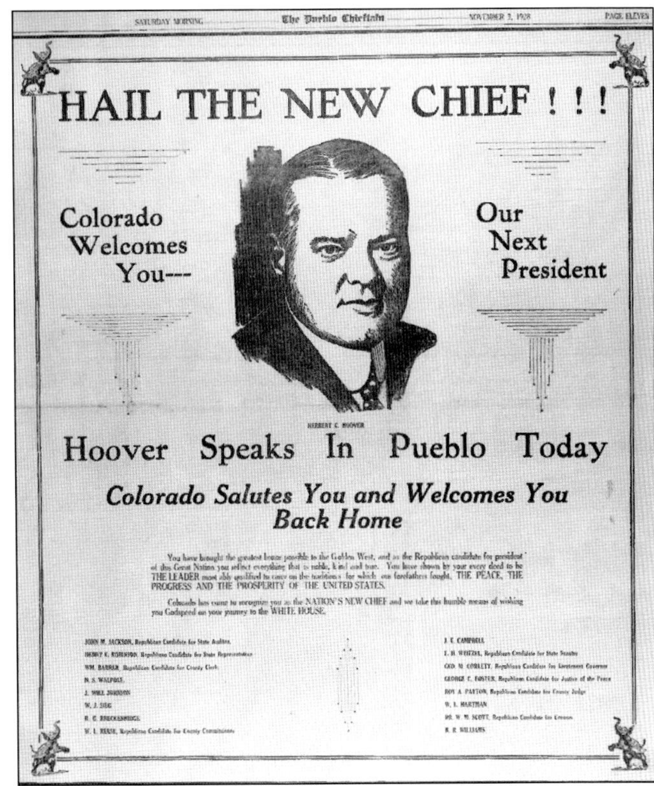

SATURDAY MORNING — The Pueblo Chieftain — NOVEMBER 3, 1928 — PAGE ELEVEN

HAIL THE NEW CHIEF ! ! !

Colorado Welcomes You---

Our Next President

HERBERT C. HOOVER

Hoover Speaks In Pueblo Today

Colorado Salutes You and Welcomes You Back Home

You have brought the greatest honor possible to the Golden West, and as the Republican candidate for president of this Great Nation you reflect everything that is noble, kind and true. You have shown by your every deed to be THE LEADER most ably qualified to carry on the traditions for which our forefathers fought, THE PEACE, THE PROGRESS AND THE PROSPERITY OF THE UNITED STATES.

Colorado has come to recognize you as the NATION'S NEW CHIEF and we take this humble means of wishing you Godspeed on your journey to the WHITE HOUSE.

JOHN M. JACKSON, Republican Candidate for State Auditor.
HENRY E. ROBINSON, Republican Candidate for State Representative
WM. BARBER, Republican Candidate for County Clerk.
N. S. WALPOLE.
J. WILL JOHNSON
W. J. SIEG
R. C. BRECKENRIDGE.
W. L. REESE, Republican Candidate for County Commissioner.

J. E. CAMPBELL
E. H. WEITZEL, Republican Candidate for State Senator
GEO. M. CORLETT, Republican Candidate for Lieutenant Governor
GEORGE C. FOSTER, Republican Candidate for Justice of the Peace
ROY A. PAYTON, Republican Candidate for County Judge
W. L. HARTMAN
DR. W. M. SCOTT, Republican Candidate for Coroner
R. R. WILLIAMS

Although the advertisement headline states, "Hail The New Chief!!!," Herbert C. Hoover was not yet president when he campaigned in Colorado and stopped in Pueblo on November 3, 1928, only three days before the election. Hoover returned to the city in November 1932 for a short speech in front of the Union Depot while traveling to his home in California. (*Pueblo Chieftain*.)

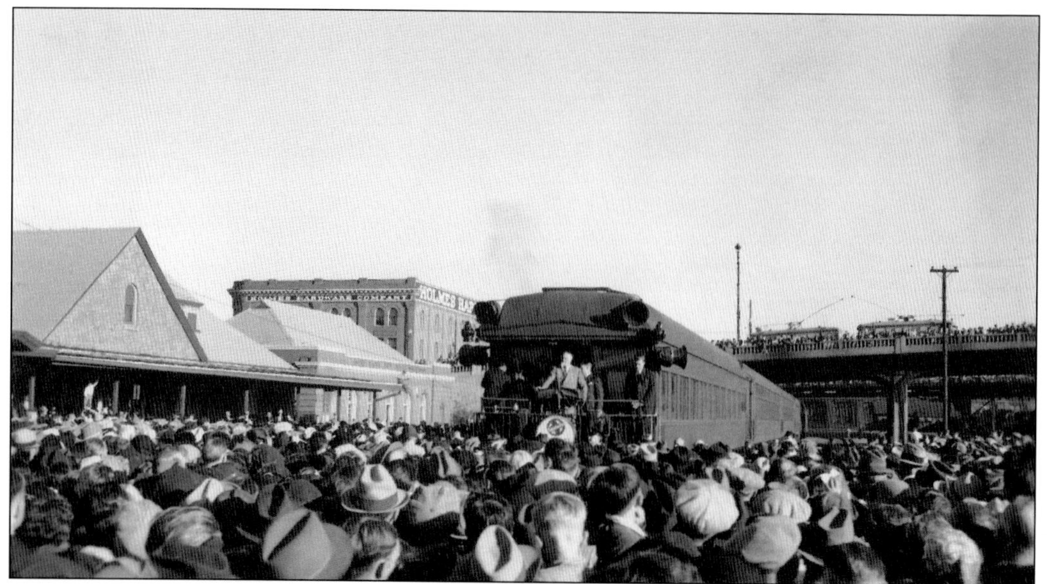

Pres. Franklin D. Roosevelt became known for his whistle-stop speeches. Roosevelt campaigned for reelection in this manner on July 12, 1938, at the Pueblo Union Depot. He also visited Pueblo in 1936. (PH-P-380-02_001.)

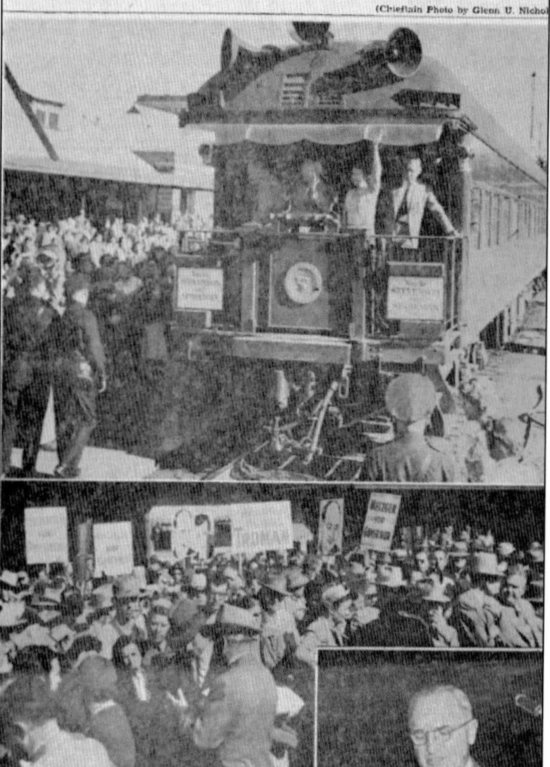

Crowds Greet President Here Tuesday

President Truman had a cheery wave for more than 6,000 Puebloans as his 18-car speci
train pulled out of Union Station Tuesday after a 20-minute whistlestop here. Beside hin
his daughter Margaret, who was greeted with enthusiastic applause when her father in
troduced her. In bottom photo, a portion of the crowd as they awaited the president's ap
pearance on the rear platform of his whistlestop special. And in inset, Truman delivers
mildly bitter attack on Republican presidential nominee Dwight D. Eisenhower during hi
seven-minute talk.

(Chieftain Photo by Glenn U. Nichol

Pres. Harry S. Truman's whistle-stop tour arrived in Pueblo on October 7, 1952. The Pueblo speech lasted only seven minutes, and the stop lasted only 20 minutes, but the crowd was estimated at more than 6,000 people. (*Pueblo Chieftain*.)

Dwight D. Eisenhower, as military man and president, often visited Colorado in the 1950s because the family of his wife, Mamie, lived in the state. Here, he is wearing a so-called ten-gallon felt hat, the John B. Stetson product that was the trademark of the West. The hat was presented to him by Lewis Rhodes, president of the Pueblo Chamber of Commerce. (PH-P-133-01.)

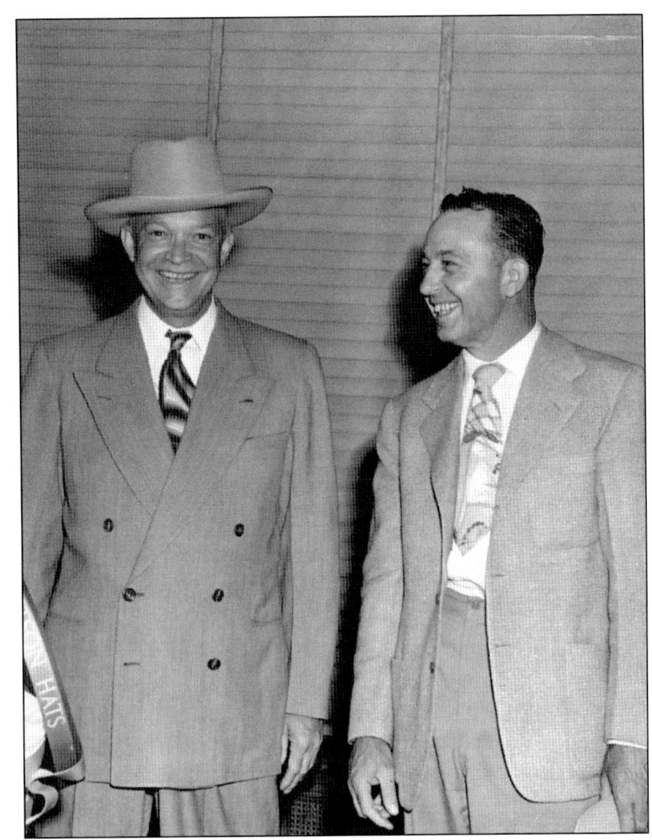

President Kennedy visited Pueblo on August 17, 1962, the day after he signed the legislation to create the Fryingpan-Arkansas Project. A large ceremony with approximately 12,000 attendees was held at Pueblo Community College. A parade that started at the airport went through the east side of Pueblo, continued downtown, and reached its destination at Dutch Clark Stadium, where President Kennedy addressed the crowd. (PH-P-B-228-03_002.)

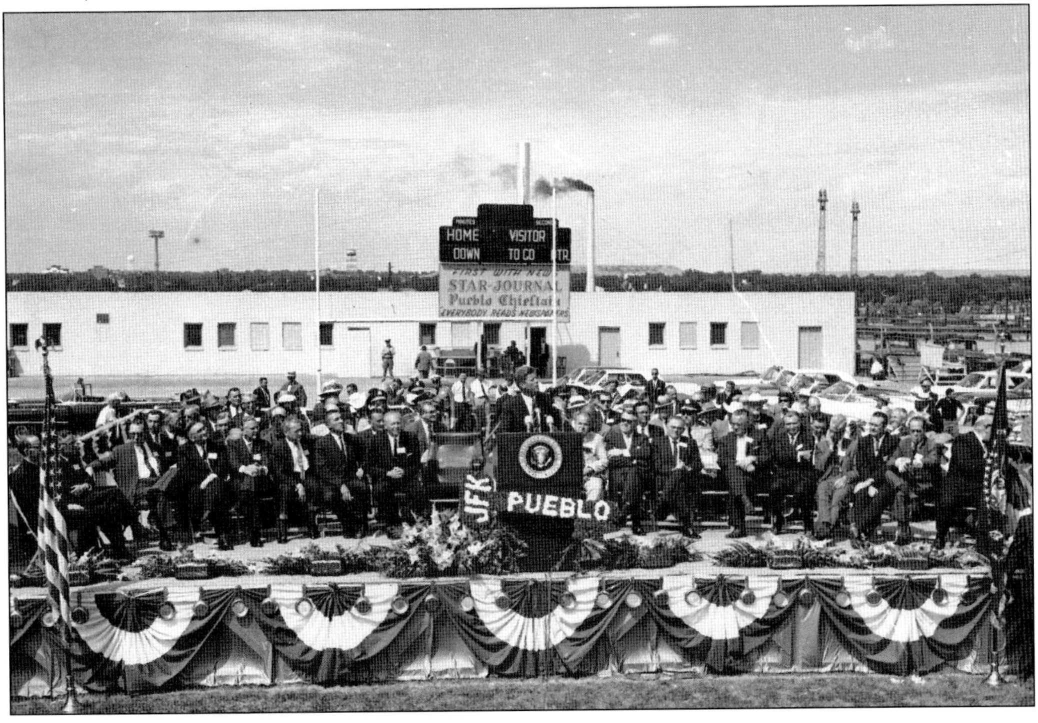

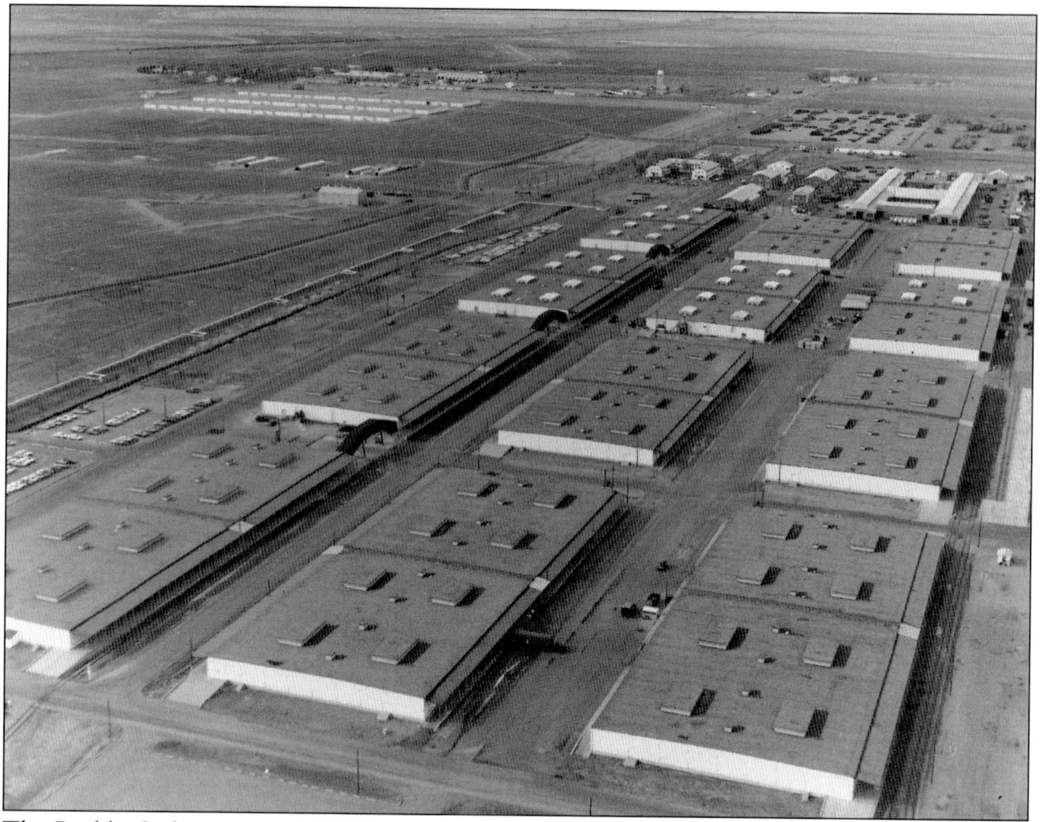

The Pueblo Ordnance Depot was built in 1942 on approximately 23,000 acres east of the city. The land was acquired under the first War Powers Act of 1941 and Executive Order 9001. The Depot received the first load of ammunition for storage on August 1942. During the Korean War, the depot employed nearly 8,000 civilians. (PH-P-372-02_003.)

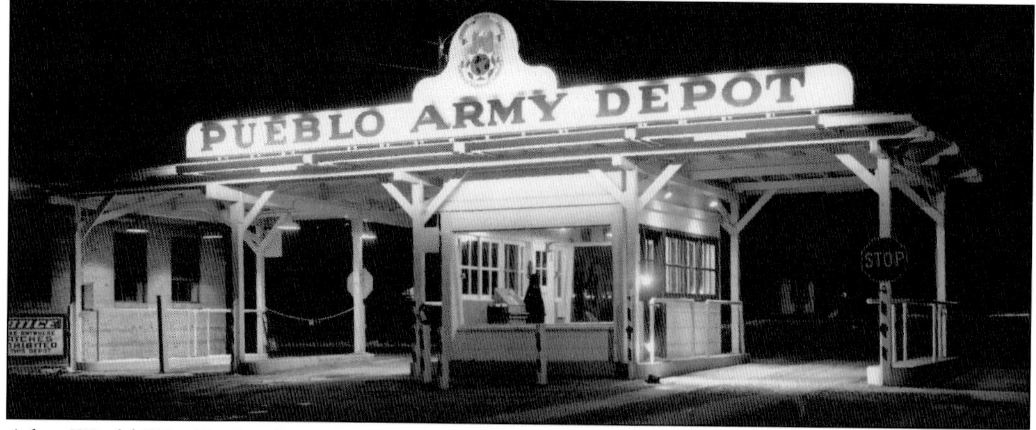

After World War II, the depot served as an ammunition distribution center for six states. It was renamed the Pueblo Army Depot in 1962, and once housed Nazi art, including some of the German art collection of Adolf Hitler, confiscated during World War II for United States Army historical properties. The present Pueblo Chemical Depot houses eight percent of the nation's original chemical stockpile. The process of destroying and disposing of the stockpile started in 2016 and will continue until completion. (PH-P-372-05-009.)

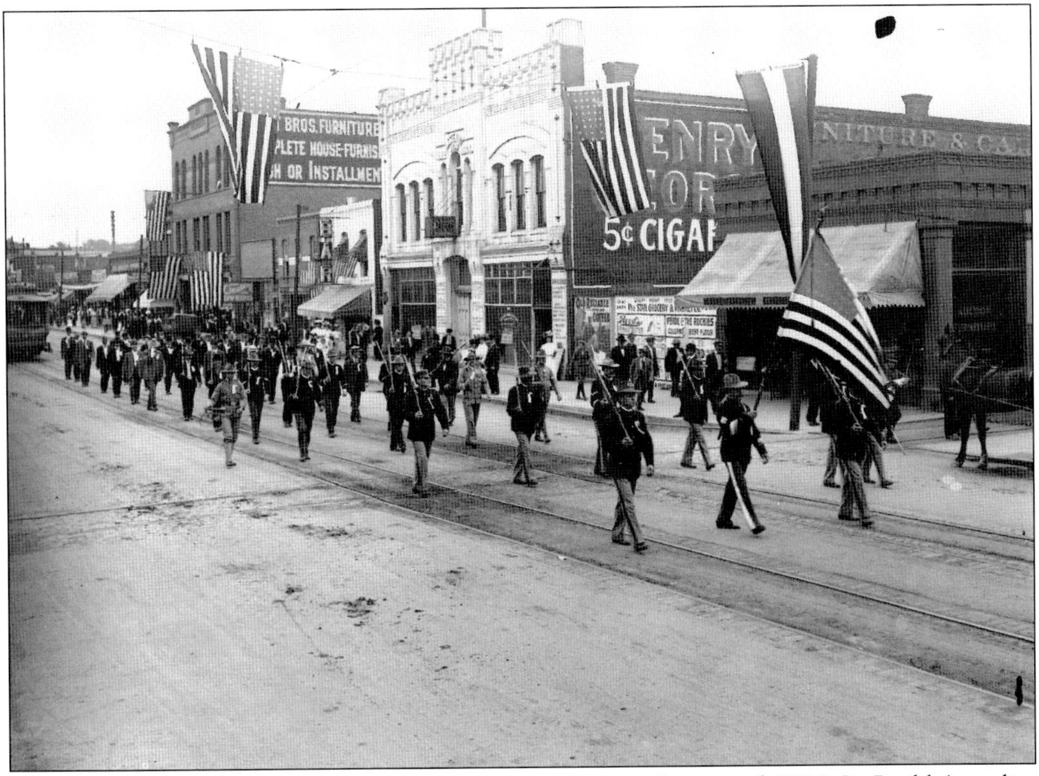

This image shows a Spanish-American War veterans parade around 1900. In Pueblo's earlier years, all parades formed at the Union Depot, marched north on Union Avenue to Main Street, and then northward to the courthouse. These Spanish-American War veterans are marching past the original Armory Building, which stood on the west side of Union Avenue between D and E Streets. (PH-P-333-02.)

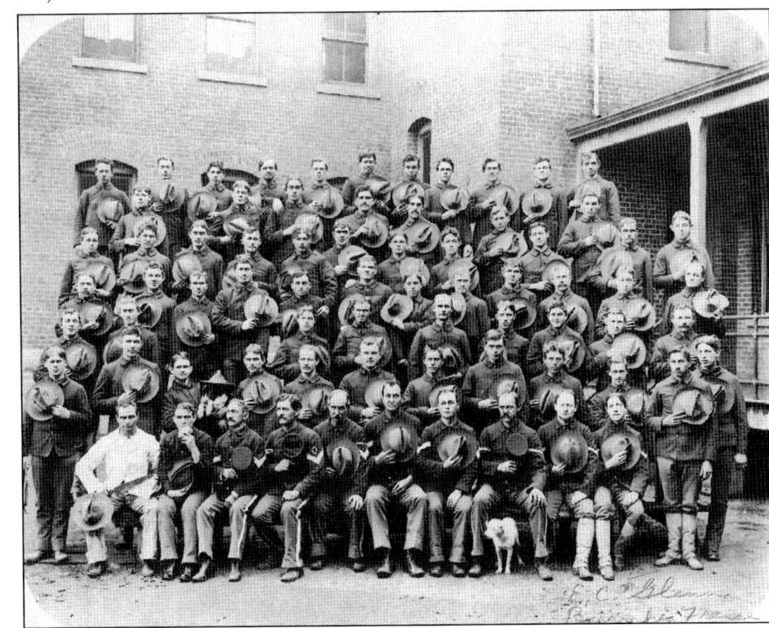

While waiting for a train to take them to Camp Crawford in Missouri, a group of soldiers from Pueblo gathered for this c. 1918 photograph. They were later deployed to France. (PH-P-741_001.)

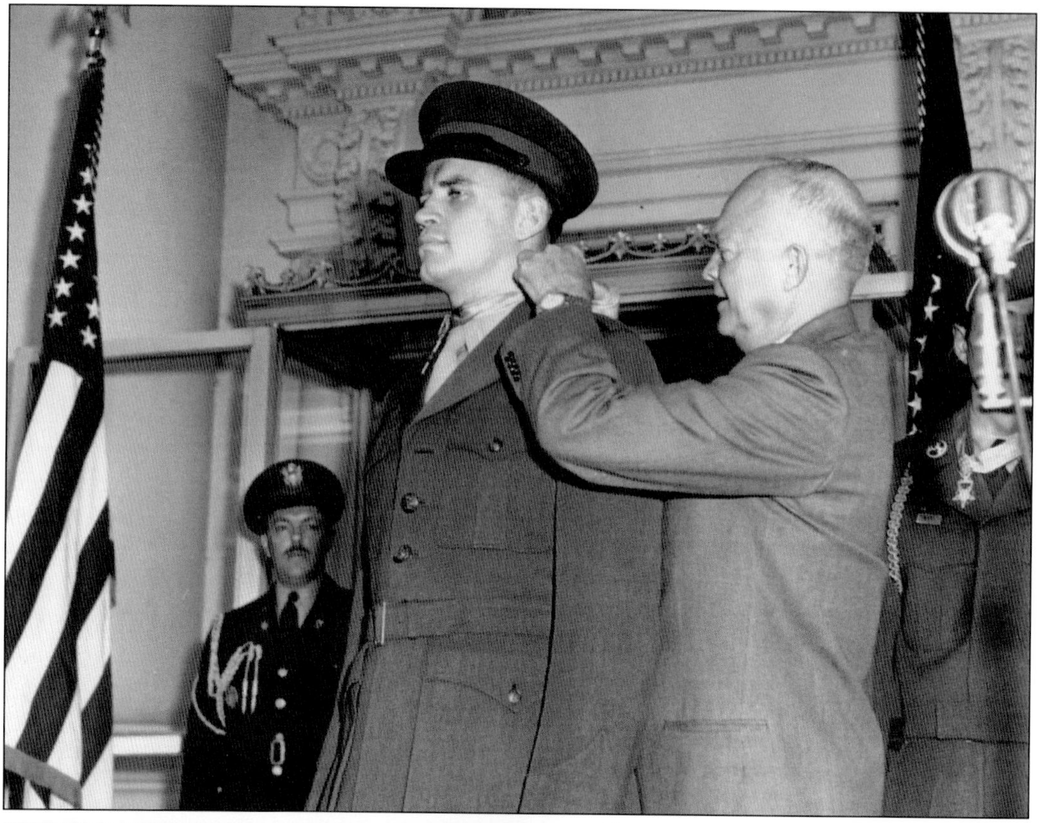

Upon presenting Raymond G. "Jerry" Murphy (Marines) with his Medal of Honor, Pres. Dwight D. Eisenhower stated, "What is it . . . something in the water out there in Pueblo? All you guys turn out to be heroes!" In Korea, Murphy organized a rescue effort following a failed raid in February 1953 that accounted for all of his fellow Marines and refused treatment of his injuries until all others had been treated. (PH-P-309-01-001.)

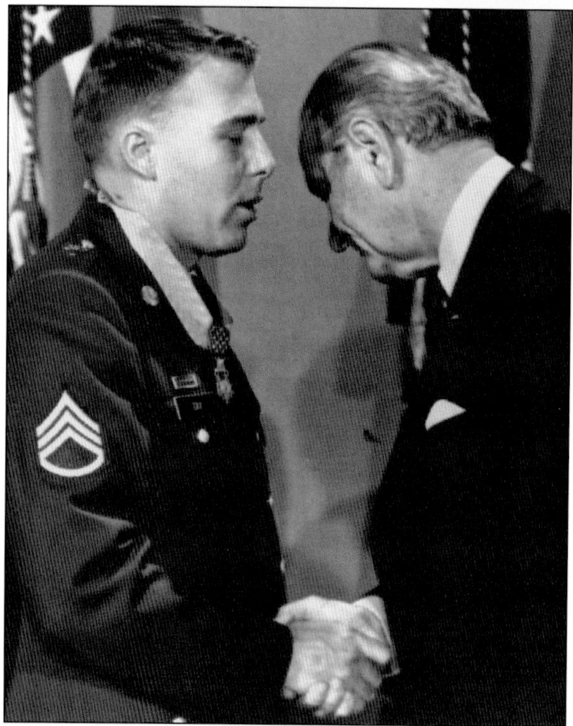

Drew D. Dix (Army) is presented his Congressional Medal of Honor by Pres. Lyndon B. Johnson. Dix was the first Green Beret to receive the Medal of Honor. His actions saved the lives of numerous South Vietnamese forces and civilians. Dix retired with the rank of major after 20 years in the Army. (PH-PH-B-124-01-001.)

William J. Crawford (Army) earned the Medal of Honor for his actions in 1943 during World War II. He single-handedly demolished three hidden German machine gun locations while working as a company scout. Crawford served 19 months as a prisoner of war, during which time his father was presented with the Medal of Honor posthumously in Crawford's stead. Still very much alive, Crawford returned to Colorado at the end of the war and was personally presented his medal in 1985 by Pres. Ronald Reagan. The bronze sculpture was created by David Dirrim. (Tammi Moe.)

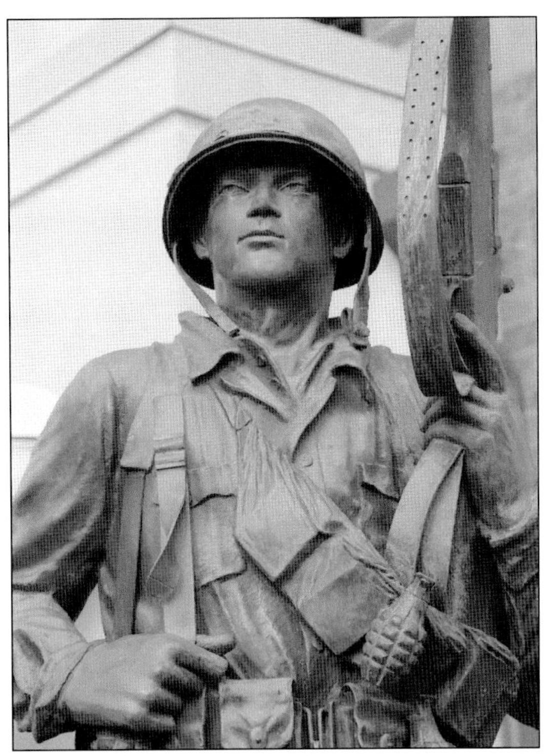

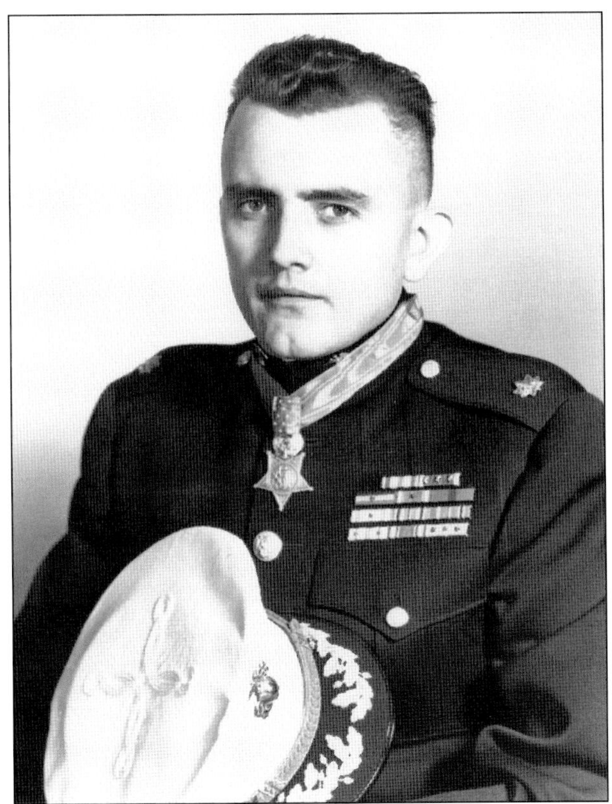

While being outnumbered more than 20 to 1, Carl L. Sitter (Marines) and his fellow soldiers fought Chinese troops in mainly hand-to-hand combat for three nights in temperatures reaching 60 degrees below zero during the winter of 1950 in Korea. Sitter retired as a Marine colonel. He died one month before receiving a bachelor's degree at age 77. (PH-P-B-399-01-001.)

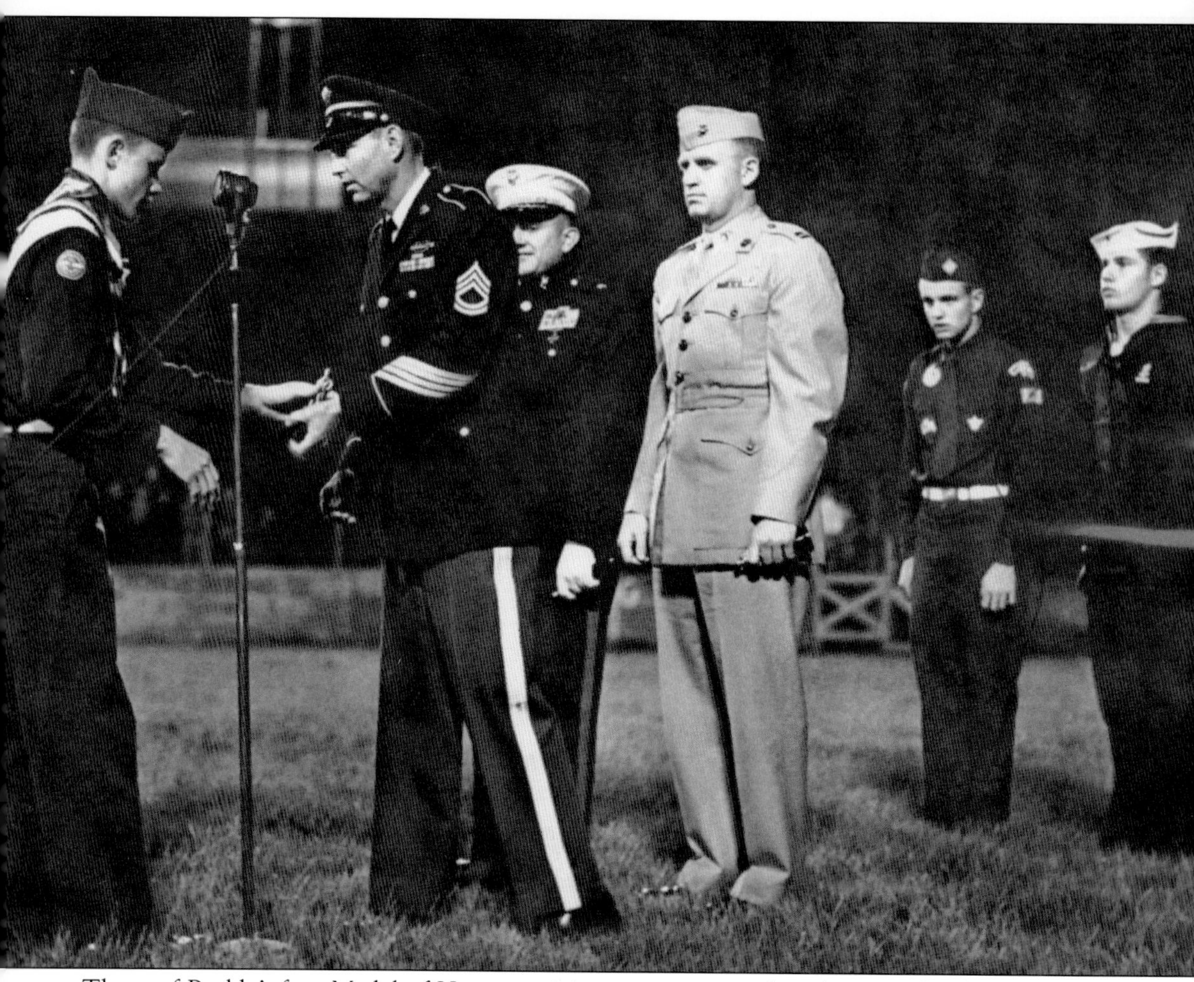

Three of Pueblo's four Medal of Honor recipients are seen in this photograph of a Boy Scout ceremony. William J. Crawford, the first Medal of Honor recipient to hail from Pueblo, is pictured receiving an award from a local Scout. Carl L. Sitter (third from left) and Raymond G. "Jerry" Murphy (fourth from left) are also identified. (PH-P-255-03.)

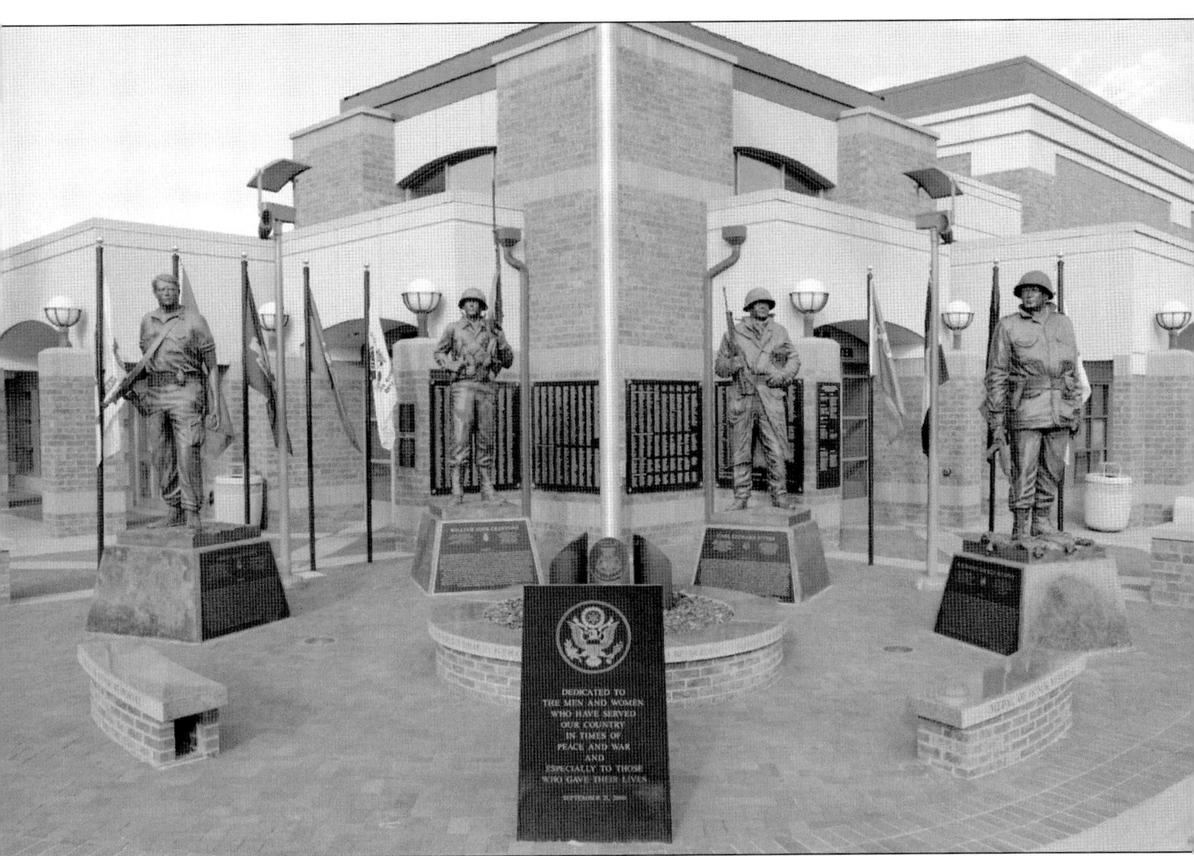

The Pueblo Medal of Honor Memorial was unveiled in September 2000 during the Congressional Medal of Honor National Convention. Colorado artists David Dirrim (bronze) and William Yates (granite) began the memorial in 1998. All four native Pueblo medal recipients are depicted in bronze, and the memorial also lists the names of all other medal recipients and the locations where they were earned. Pueblo also has countless other military memorials throughout the city. Other memorials include Veterans Memorial Bridge (all wars) at the Pueblo Riverwalk; Vietnam War memorials at City Park, Colorado State University–Pueblo, and along North Elizabeth Street; the Korean War Memorial at the Pueblo County Courthouse; the USS *Pueblo* Memorial at the Pueblo Convention Center; and artillery pieces at Mineral Palace Park. (Tammi Moe.)

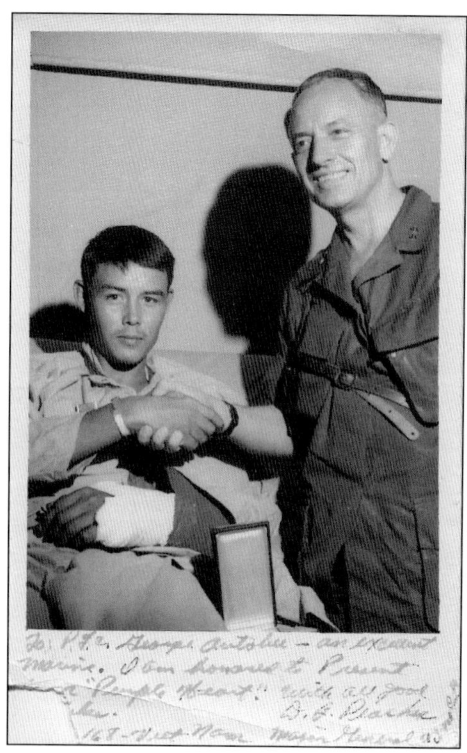

Pvt. 1st Class George Autobee (left) is seen here with Maj. Gen. D.J. Preacher in 1968 at Da Nang Naval Hospital, Vietnam. Autobee was wounded twice in combat, after having served 16 months in the Marine Corps. He was commissioned to the rank of captain and served in the Army Reserves 10th Mountain Division and the 406th Combat Support Hospital from 1980 to 1988. George is the great-great-great-grandson of Charles Autobees, who is discussed in chapter 1. (George Autobee.)

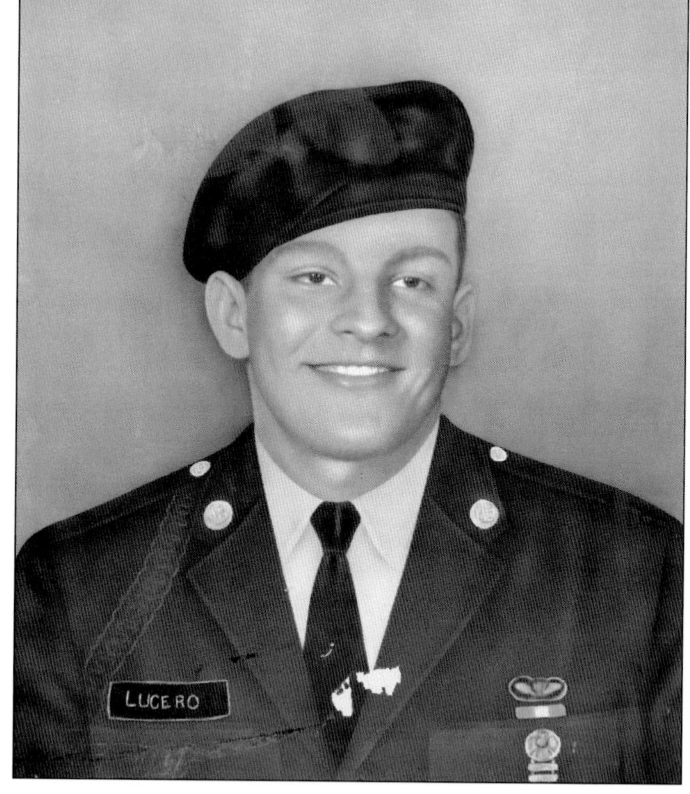

Pueblo's Eastside library was named after Patrick Arnold Lucero, a 19-year-old soldier who died in Vietnam in 1968. Pueblo City Council noted Lucero's life as "symbolic of values emblematic to Pueblo's community connections to veterans." Lucero was awarded a Bronze Star with an Oak Leaf Cluster for valor. A library in Vietnam also bears Lucero's name and was organized under the auspices of Peace Trees Vietnam. (William R. Lucero, PDJ [Patrick's brother].)

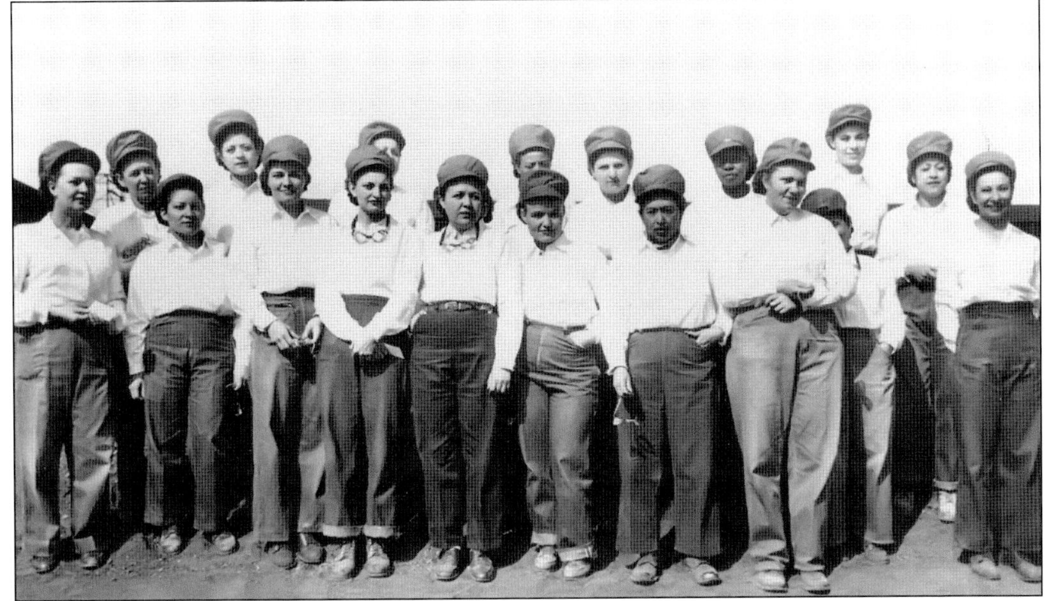

With many men deployed during World War II, women filled the traditional male roles in industry. The women of Pueblo were no exception, especially with increased steel production at CF&I. Pictured here are 18 of the hundreds of women who worked in manufacturing. To help the war effort, CF&I workers also produced ordnance during the war. (PH-P-225-11-001.)

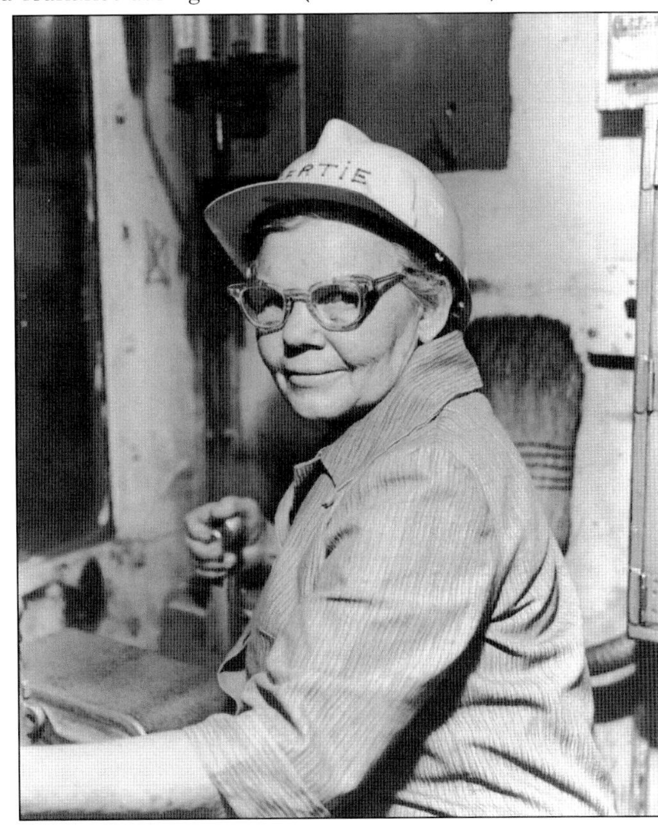

Gertrude "Gertie" Lipich Jordan worked for CF&I for more than 30 years. Her career at the steelworks began in 1943 during World War II. She remained in the CF&I work force after the war and retired in 1974. (PH-P-225-00.)

THE WHITE HOUSE

WASHINGTON

November 6, 1987

Dear Mrs. Brown:

I was pleased to learn of your strong love for our nation, of how you donated your hair to the war effort during World War II and of its use as crosshairs in the Norden bombsight, helping our bombadiers sight enemy ground targets in Europe and the Pacific. You can be very proud of a selfless act that set a splendid example during wartime. Your story has touched me deeply.

When I hear of such patriotism, I am reminded of what an honor it is to be called to serve as President of the United States.

Nancy joins me in sending our warm best wishes for a very Happy 80th Birthday.

Sincerely,

Ronald Reagan

Mrs. Mary Babnik Brown
303 Spring Street
Pueblo, Colorado 81003

Thirty-five-year-old Mary Babnik's 34-inch-long golden hair was her favorite feature. In 1943, however, she cut it off and donated it in response to a government contractor asking for blonde, untreated hair measuring more than 22 inches in length. Babnik's donation was never publicized until 1987, when an article in the Pueblo Chieftain declared her hair was used in the development of the Norden bombsight. That same year, Pres. Ronald Reagan sent a letter to the now 80-year-old Babnik thanking her for her patriotism. In 1991, it was revealed that the use of Babnik's hair for the Norden bombsight had never been verified and that it may have only been used for testing a bombsight. The actual fate of Babnik's hair remains unknown, but her act made her a hometown hero. (*Pueblo Lore, Journal of the Pueblo County Historical Society*, June 2001.)

Nine

Recreation, Culture, and Art

Recreation, culture, and art have played a significant role in Pueblo's history. Pueblo has been home to the Colorado State Fair since its inception in 1872, when the Southern Colorado and Industrial Association held its first exposition. In 1901, fair administrators purchased land that would become the permanent fairgrounds location. The annual fair is a celebration of Colorado's agricultural wealth that features rodeos, carnivals, and exhibits. Under the leadership of Henry Reyes and George Sandoval, Fiesta Day was added in 1967 to showcase the state's Hispanic heritage.

Sports such as football, softball, basketball, and hockey have been an important part of Pueblo's leisure activities. Baseball has a long history of being a popular sport in Pueblo, from professional teams like the Pueblo Dodgers to local youth clubs such as the Old Timers. Competitions between high schools have been taking place for over 100 years. Pueblo's Parks and Recreation Department offers many citywide recreational opportunities. City Park has a small amusement park, and visitors to the amusement park can ride the beautifully preserved historic carousel.

Cultural opportunities abound in the city, as do several venues for arts and cultural festivals. Probably the most visible of Pueblo's artistry were murals painted on the Arkansas River levee. Pueblo's vibrant arts community includes thriving art galleries; the Sangre de Cristo Arts and Conference Center; and citywide murals depicting history, people, and social issues. Pueblo has been home to several theaters. Since the first performances in Memorial Hall in 1923, Puebloans have flocked to see both local and national performers. Memorial Hall was renovated in 2013 and brought back to its former splendor and hosts a variety of performances annually. The Historic Arkansas Riverwalk has been developed into a beautiful addition to Pueblo's downtown. *Song of Pueblo,* a compilation of 15 songs composed by Daniel Valdez, tells the history of Pueblo through song.

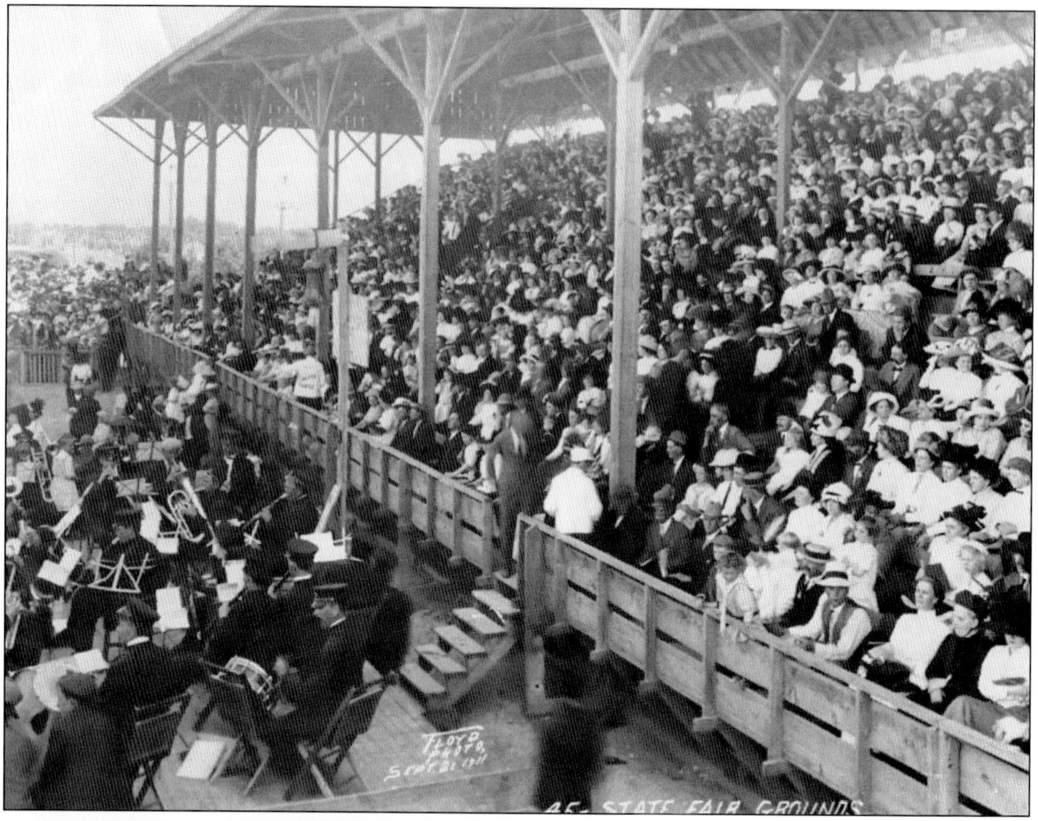

The Southern Colorado Agricultural and Industrial Association held its first exposition on October 9, 1872, on the outskirts of Pueblo. The fair evolved and grew to a statewide exposition, and organizers procured a new site at the northwest end of Abriendo Avenue. The state legislature designated Pueblo as the fair's permanent home in 1888. The fair moved again in 1890, to a site on the western shore of Lake Minnequa, and moved to its current location in 1901. (PH-P-240-03_001.)

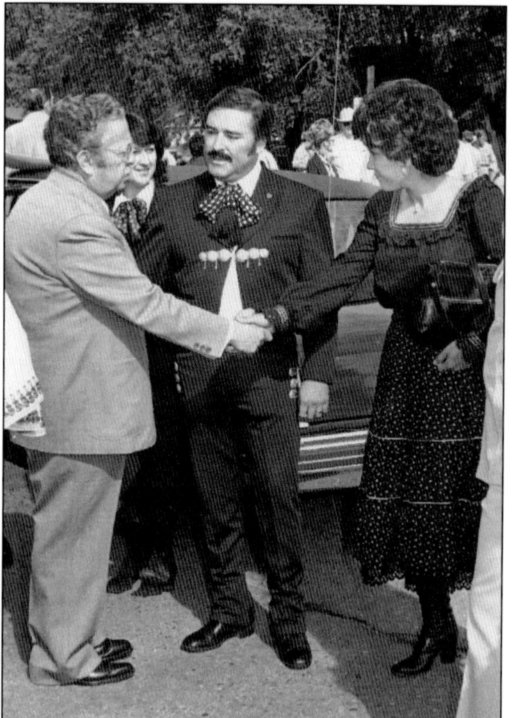

The Puebla/Pueblo Sister City Program began in 1970, when Henry Reyes brought the proposal to city council and received unanimous approval. Shown in this 1977 photograph are an unidentified delegate from the municipal precinct of Puebla, Mexico; Henry Reyes (center); and Laura DeHerrera (right), a Denver state representative. In 1972, the city of Pueblo constructed the Puebla-Pueblo Plaza on Union Avenue near El Pueblo Museum. Today, Pueblo has many sister cities. (PH-B-537-01_001.)

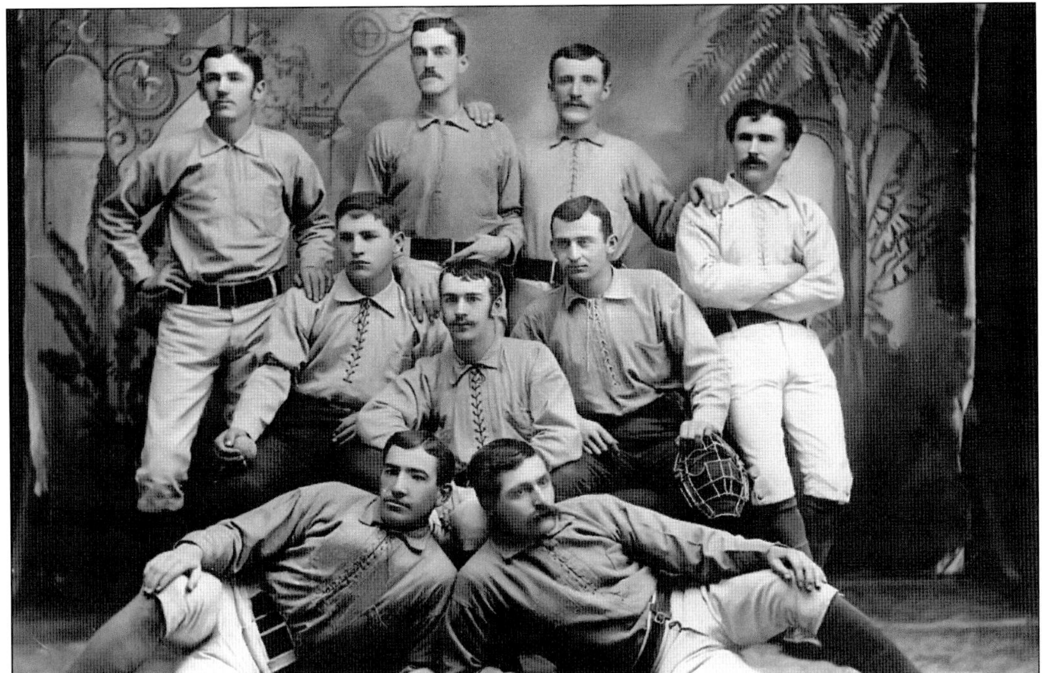

Baseball in Pueblo can trace its roots to the Pueblo Baseball Club, founded on May 23, 1871. Interest in keeping a professional team in town waxed and waned throughout the 1800s, though the town kept an on-again, off-again relationship with several different semiprofessional teams and leagues into the 21st century. This photograph of a Pueblo baseball team was taken in 1880. The players, who are all firemen, are posing in a studio. (PH-P-585-07_001.)

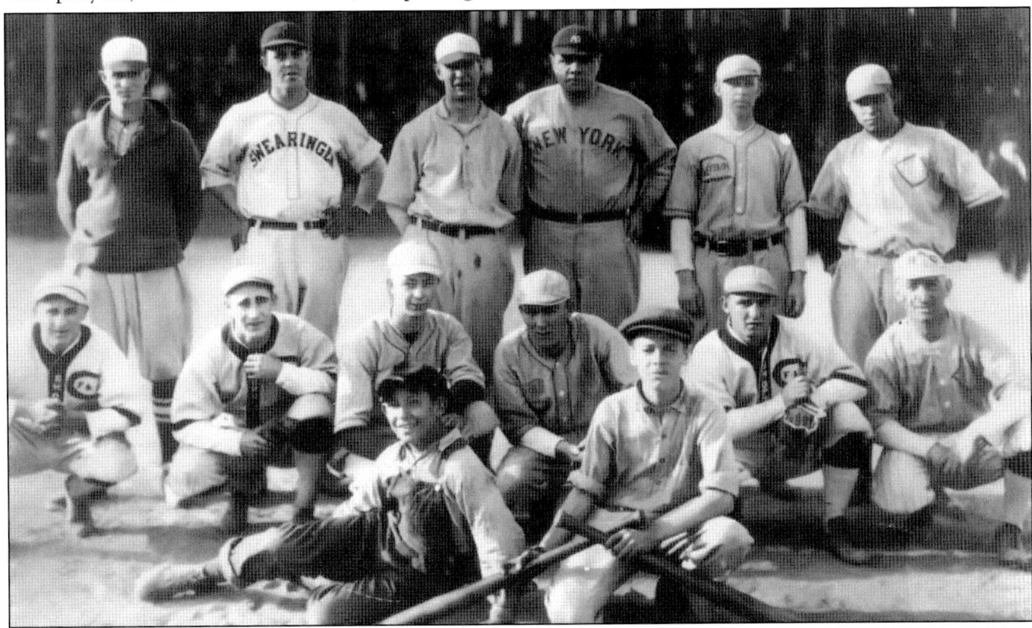

Pueblo fielded a minor-league baseball club, the Pueblo Dodgers—an affiliate of the Brooklyn Dodgers—from 1947 to 1957. Babe Ruth (pictured fourth from left in the second row) visited the city multiple times. (PH-P-585-09_003.)

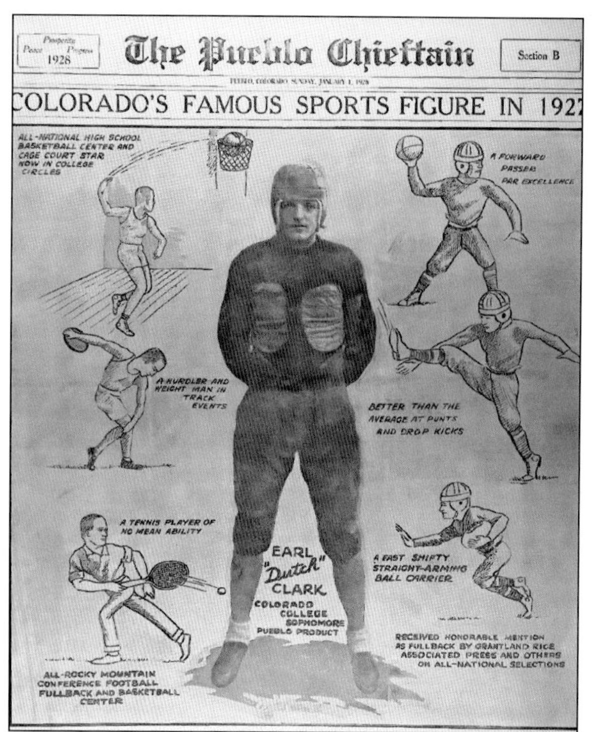

Peace Prosperity Progress 1928

The Pueblo Chieftain

Section B

PUEBLO, COLORADO, SUNDAY, JANUARY 1, 1928

COLORADO'S FAMOUS SPORTS FIGURE IN 192

ALL-NATIONAL HIGH SCHOOL BASKETBALL CENTER AND CAGE COURT STAR NOW IN COLLEGE CIRCLES

A FORWARD PASSER PAR EXCELLENCE

A HURDLER AND WEIGHT MAN IN TRACK EVENTS

BETTER THAN THE AVERAGE AT PUNTS AND DROP KICKS

A TENNIS PLAYER OF NO MEAN ABILITY

EARL "Dutch" CLARK

COLORADO COLLEGE SOPHOMORE PUEBLO PRODUCT

A FAST SHIFTY STRAIGHT-ARMING BALL CARRIER

RECEIVED HONORABLE MENTION AS FULLBACK BY GRANTLAND RICE ASSOCIATED PRESS AND OTHERS ON ALL-NATIONAL SELECTIONS

ALL-ROCKY MOUNTAIN CONFERENCE FOOTBALL FULLBACK AND BASKETBALL CENTER

Earl "Dutch" Clark was born in Fowler, Colorado, just east of Pueblo, and played quarterback and tailback—as well as coached—the Detroit Lions. In 1963, he became the first man from Colorado to be inducted into the NFL Hall of Fame. The primary football stadium in Pueblo was named after Clark. The Bell Game between Central and Centennial High Schools started in 1892, is the longest-running high school football rivalry west of the Mississippi River, and routinely sells out the 10,000-seat capacity Dutch Clark Stadium. Every autumn, each school vies to keep or retake the bell for that year. The Cannon Game competition between South and East High Schools also takes place each fall—an annual tradition that began in 1959. The winning team gets to paint the cannon and bell with its school colors. (Left, DO-415-1928-01-01-B1; below, P-H-B-101-02-002.)

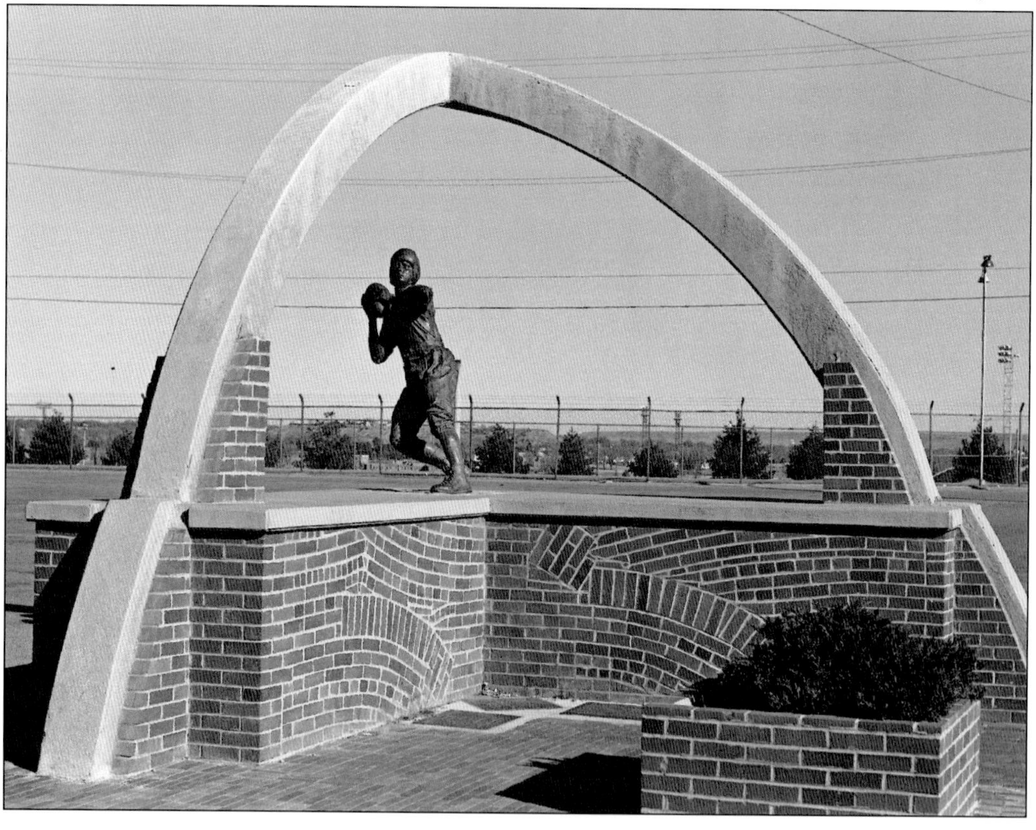

In 1911, the C.W. Parker Company of Abilene, Kansas, manufactured its No. 72 carousel, dubbed the "Carry Us All Three Abreast Carousel." The City of Pueblo purchased the carousel in 1914 and installed it at Lake Minnequa. When the amusement park closed around 1940, the carousel was moved to its present location at Pueblo's City Park. In 1983, the carousel was listed in the National Register of Historic Places. The carousel celebrated its 105th anniversary in May 2016. This carousel is considered one of Pueblo's gems. (Tammi Moe.)

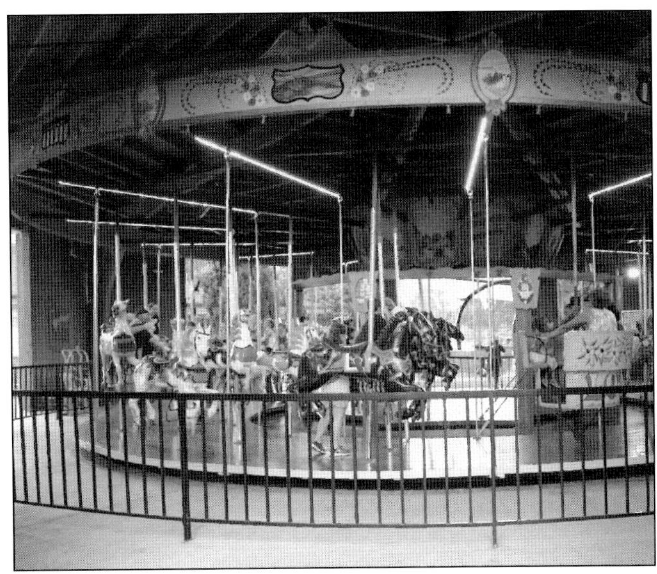

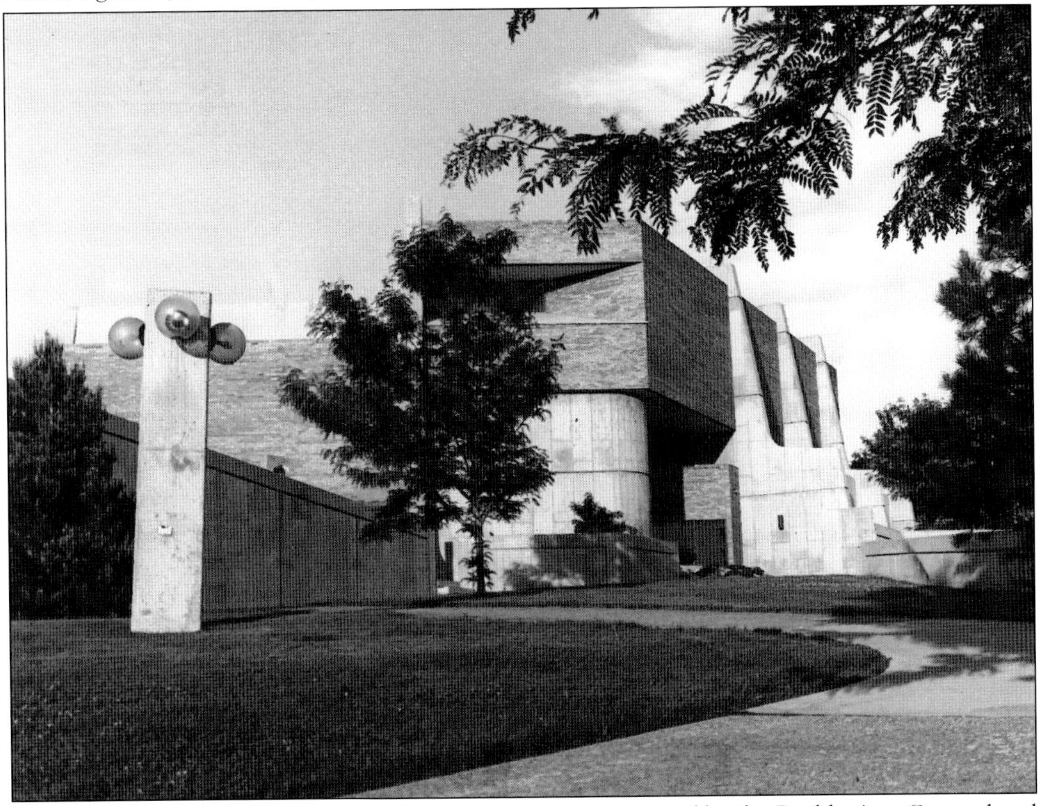

The Sangre de Cristo Arts and Conference Center was proposed by the Pueblo Arts Council and funded by the Pueblo County Commissioners and the US Economic Development Administration. It opened in 1972 and is the epicenter of arts and culture in Pueblo. It is well known for having the Western collection of Francis E. King. The complex houses a large conference facility, a theater, four art galleries, studio and classroom space, a dance studio, and the Buell Children's Museum. (PH-P-498-03_001.)

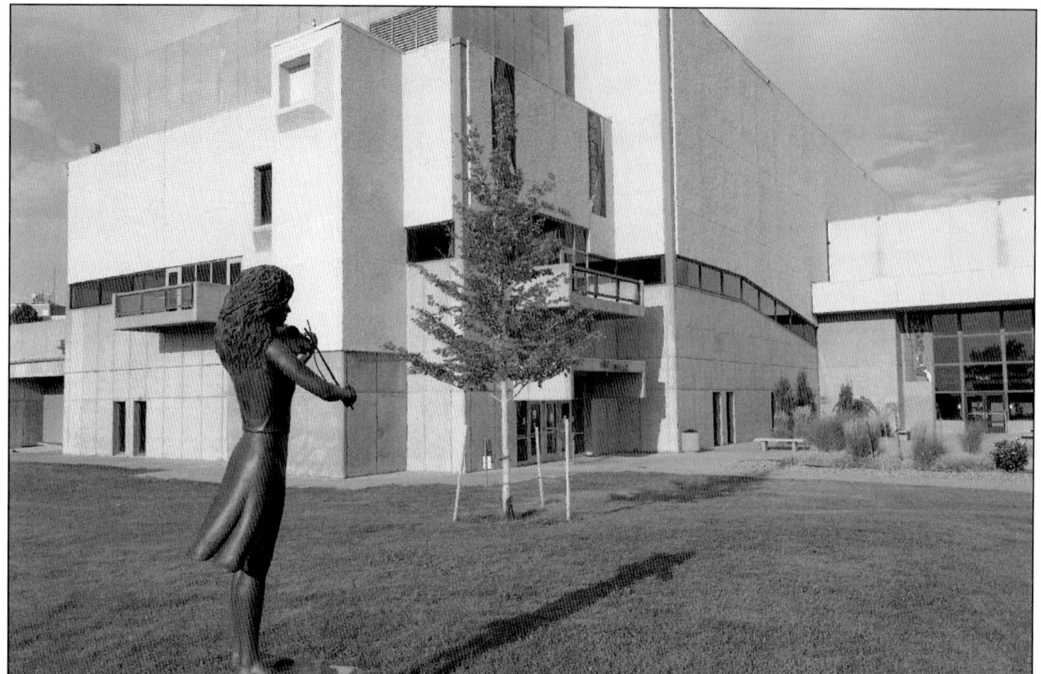

Colorado State University–Pueblo, which started out as Pueblo Junior College in 1933, has gone through several name changes, including the one to its current name in 2003. CSU–Pueblo features a wide variety of art on the campus. The Fine Art Gallery in Hoag Hall inside the Capps Capozzolo Academic Center exhibits both students work and that of renowned artists from all over the world. Annual events include international exhibitions and panel discussions by scholars and noted art historians. (Tammi Moe.)

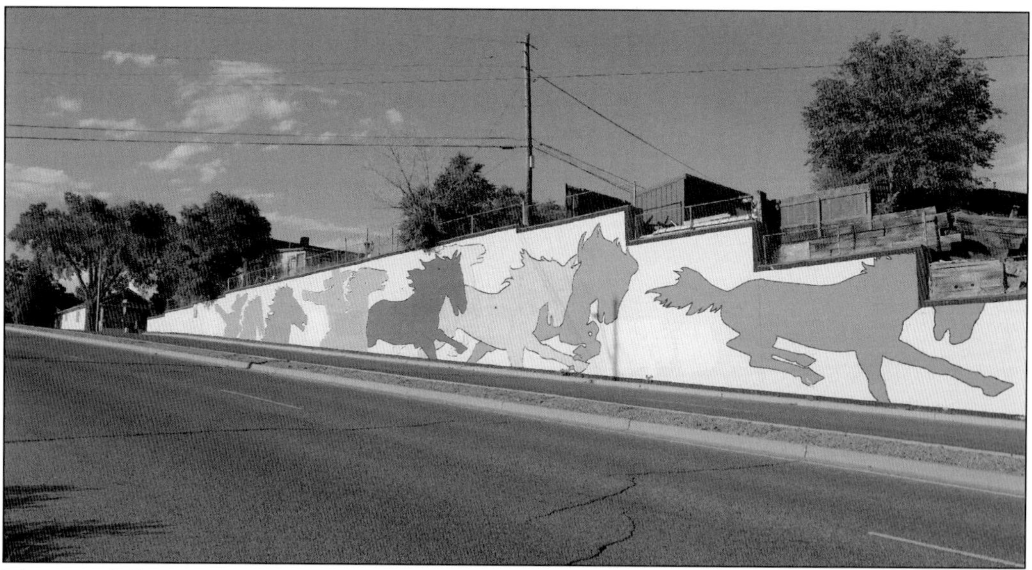

The mural *El Vaquero*, pictured here, was painted on a retaining wall on Joplin Avenue between East Third and Fourth Streets. The artist is Manual Casaus, a local, who painted the mural in 1996 with the help of Risley Middle School students. The mural is one example of the many murals painted throughout the city. (Tammi Moe.)

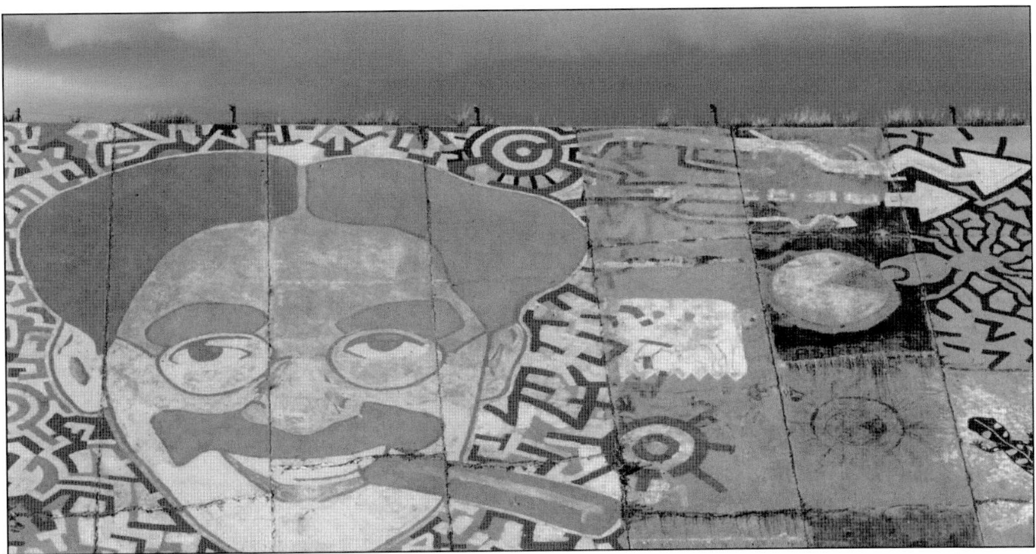

The Arkansas River levee was built to protect downtown Pueblo in direct response to the 1921 flood that destroyed most of the downtown area. Unbeknownst to the engineers who designed the levee, artists would see it as Pueblo's largest canvas. In the 1970s, a painting of a fish appeared, and other paintings soon followed. For years, artists refrained from signing their names and playfully signed their artwork with the words "Tee Hee." In 1997, the artwork along the Arkansas River was certified by the *Guinness Book of World Records* as the world's largest mural, standing at 60 feet high and approximately three miles long. The Pueblo Conservancy District began repairs to the levee in 2015, a process that lopped 12 feet off the top of the levee and replaced the aging concrete. The repairs destroyed much of the mural, but artists have pledged to replace it. (Above, Library of Congress; below, Edward Simms.)

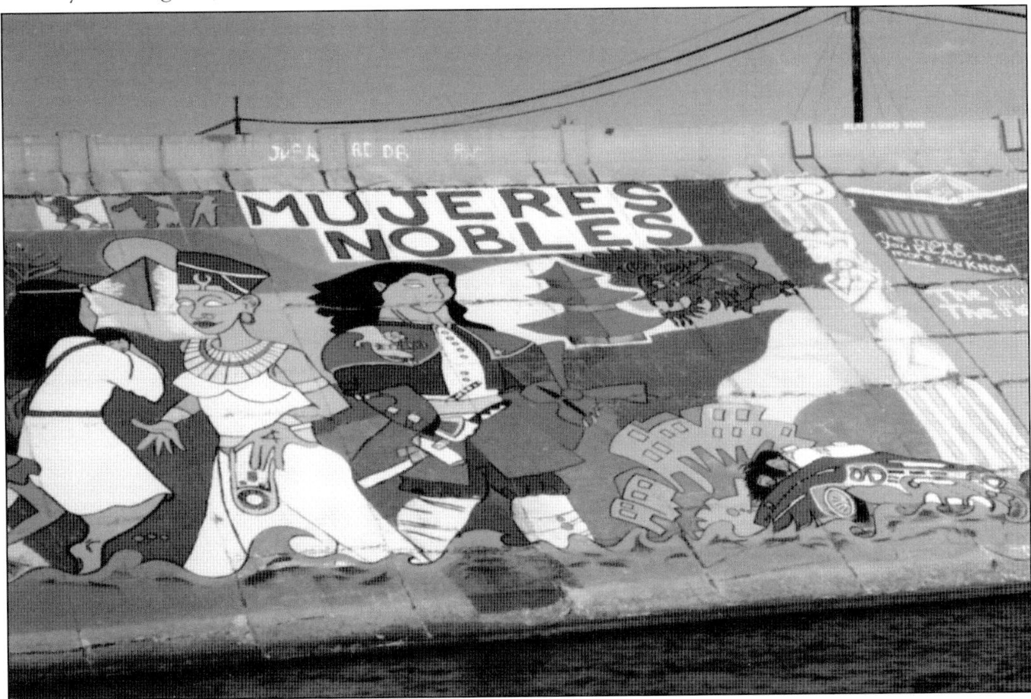

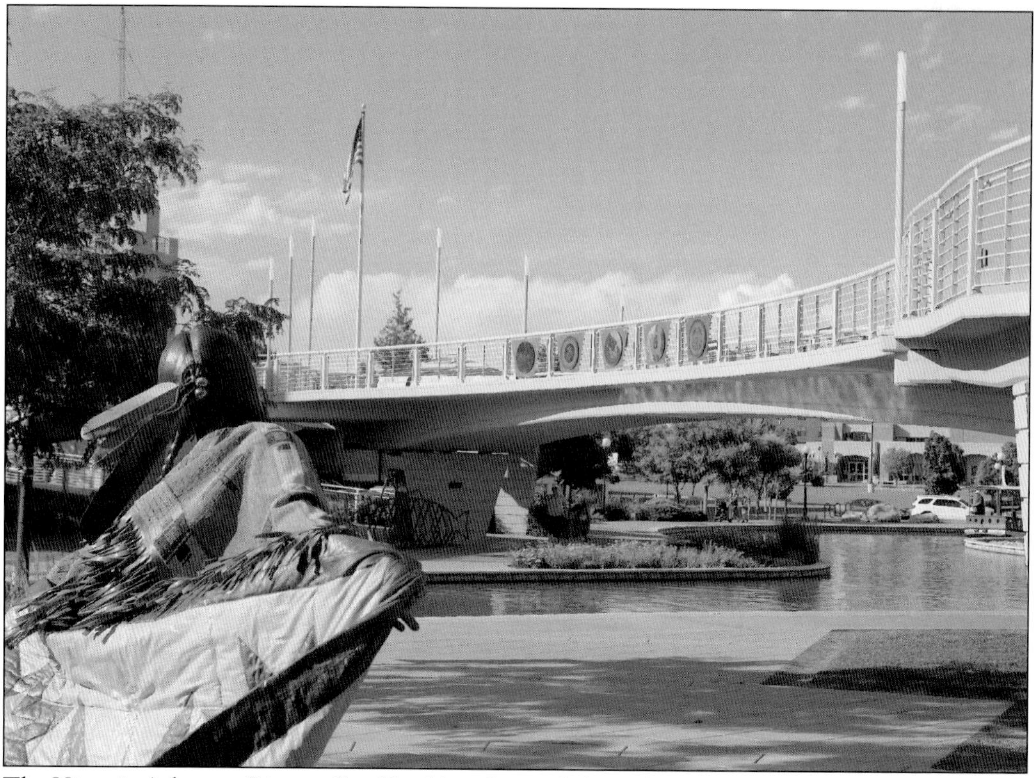

The Historic Arkansas Riverwalk of Pueblo is located along the original channel of the Arkansas River, dating from before the flood of 1921 that rechanneled the river to the south along the bluffs. The Riverwalk commemorates the history of Pueblo with displays along its entirety. Pedestrians will notice the former international border between the United States and Mexico, native animal sculptures, nature displays, a wall displaying the effects of the flood of 1921, gondola rides, an amphitheater, and even seasonal lighting displays. As Pueblo's history and prehistory began at the confluence of the Arkansas River and Fountain Creek, it is only appropriate that the city memorializes the importance of the location through the Riverwalk and brings its history to the forefront. The above image shows the Veterans Bridge, which is a tribute to all veterans. The below photograph depicts a sculpture of a Lakota woman and her quilt. It is called *Walking Among the Stars*, and the sculptor was John McGary. (Both, Tammi Moe.)

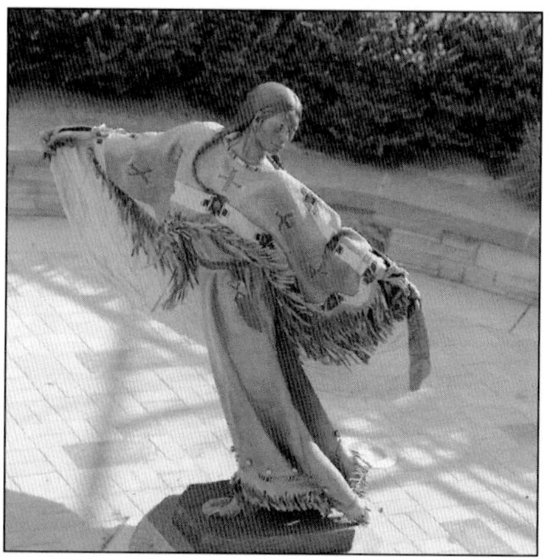

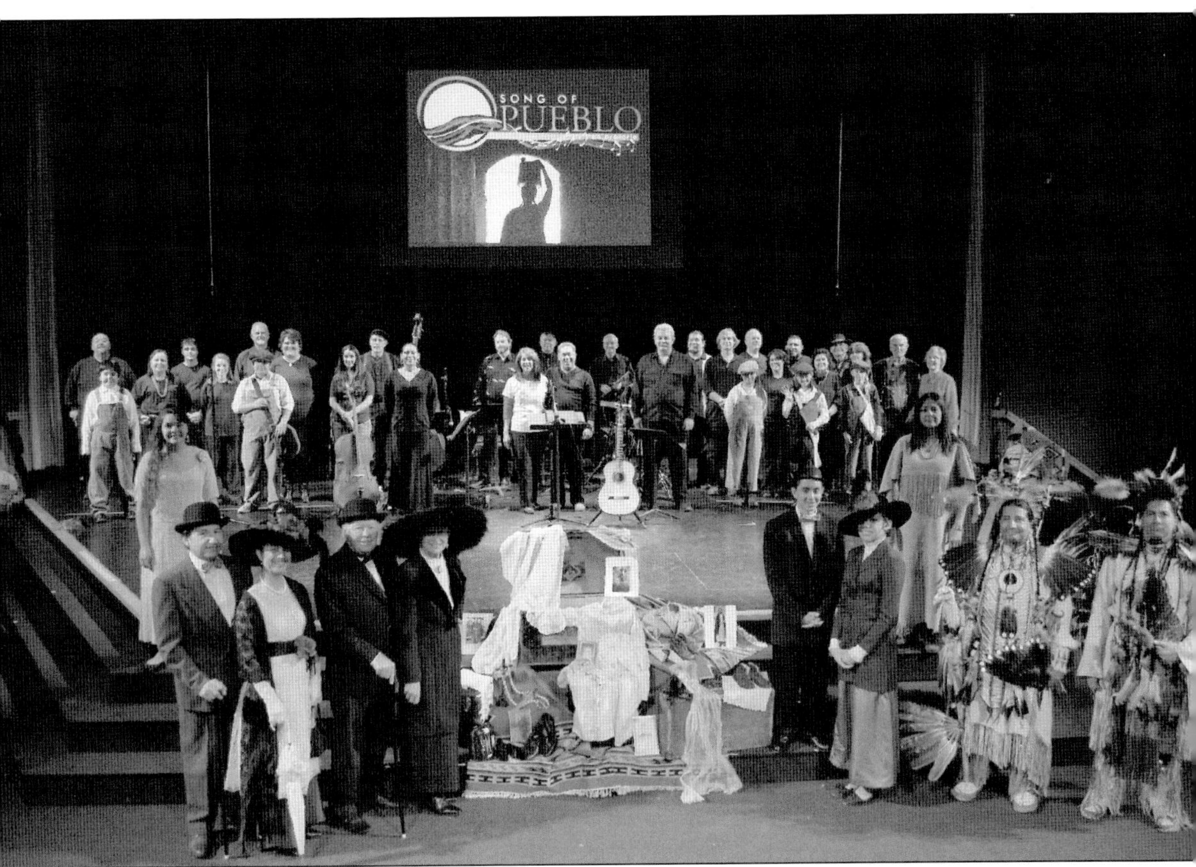

In 2008, Daniel Valdez, a Californian actor and singer, composed 15 original songs that capture the soul of Pueblo's regional stories and history for an oratorio called *Song of Pueblo,* and performances continue today. One of the program brochures states: "Like the Arkansas River itself, the stories flow from era to era, the Native Americans, French and Spanish, the trading post, the founding of Pueblo smelters, foundries and steel mills, coal mining and strikes, immigration, the flood and ethnic neighborhoods." The first performance featured Valdez himself, who in addition to being the composer and lyricist was also a vocalist. Shown here in this picture is the full cast of musicians, vocalists, and dancers who performed in the first shows. The following lyrics are most appropriate for a book on Pueblo: "Sing, we sing, tonight we bring, the Song of Pueblo, the People's town. In this place that history shaped we are a Pueblo, the People's Town." (Juan Espinosa, Songofpueblo.org.)

About the Special Collections Department of the Pueblo City-County Library District

The Special Collections and Museum Services Department of the Pueblo City-County Library District has been collecting and preserving materials of local historical interest since the late 1800s. Housed on the third floor of the Robert Hoag Rawlings Library at 100 East Abriendo Avenue, in Pueblo, Colorado, the department provides reference materials and online information resources to assist with historical research.

The Western Research Room houses a specialized noncirculating collection of rare materials related to the history of Colorado, the Rocky Mountain West, and Northern New Mexico, with emphasis on Pueblo and the Arkansas River valley. These resources include archival and photograph collections, newspaper clippings, yearbooks, oral interviews, local history videos, rare history books, maps and drawings, the Pueblo Water Collection, the Works Progress Administration Collection, the Colorado State Fair Collection, city directories, telephone directories, regional newspaper microfilm, and aerial historical and regional maps. The department also makes accessible the microfilm of the *Pueblo Chieftain* newspaper from 1868 to the present.

The department houses a vast genealogy collection comprised of resources from across the United States, including local family histories, and has an extensive New Mexico collection. The department also provides learning aids and guides to conducting genealogical research and access to several research databases. The department keeps and updates an extensive obituary index for deaths in Pueblo County. Periodicals, newspapers, manuscripts, and an extensive Civil War reference collection are available.

The Digital Collections Program is dedicated to broadening access to unique historical materials contained within the Pueblo City-County Library District's Special Collections Department through the acquisition/creation, maintenance, and preservation of these unique materials in digital format. The library's digital collection program is a long-term project, and new collections are added as they become available. Access to the digital collection is available at the library's website, www.pueblolibrary.org.

Bibliography

Acosta, Heraldo. *General William Jackson Palmer's Spanish Streets of Pueblo 1872*. Pueblo, CO: Pueblo Celebration of Cultural Diversity, 2008.

Buckles, William G. *The Search for El Pueblo: Through Pueblo to El Pueblo, An Archaeological Summary*. Denver: Colorado Historical Society, 2006.

Cragin, Francis W. Collection of 28 notebooks and other information. Pioneers' Museum, Colorado Springs.

Dodds, Joann West. *Pueblo a Pictorial History*. Norfolk: Donning Company Publishers, 1982.

———. *They All Came to Pueblo, A Social History*. Virginia Beach: Donning Company Publishers, 1994.

Fry, Eleanor. *Smelters of Pueblo*. Pueblo, CO: Pueblo County Historical Society, 2000.

Fry, Eleanor and Ione Miller. *Pueblo, An Illustrated History*. Carlsbad, CA: Heritage Media Corp., 2001.

Hall, Frank, *History of the State of Colorado*. Chicago: Blakely Printing Company, 1889.

History of the Arkansas Valley, Colorado. Chicago: O.L. Baskin & Co., 1881.

Lecompte, Janet. *Pueblo, Hardscrabble, Greenhorn*. Norman: University of Oklahoma Press, 1978.

Martinez, Wilfred O. *Anza and Cuerno Verde: Decisive Battle*. Pueblo, CO: El Escritorio Publishing, 2001.

Sandoval, David A. *Spanish/Mexican Legacy of Latinos in Pueblo County*. Pueblo, CO: Pueblo City-County Library District, 2012.

Scamehorn, H. Lee. *Pioneer Steelmaker in the West: The Colorado Fuel and Iron Company, 1872–1903*. Boulder, CO: Pruett Publishing, 1976.

Smiley, Jerome C., Frank C. Goudy, Fred P. Johnson, L.E. Leinen, W.F.R. Mills, Robert S. Morrison, Walter H. Olin, and Wilber F. Stone. *Semi-Centennial History of the State of Colorado*. Vol. 2. Chicago: Lewis Publishing, 1913.

Thomas, Alfred Barnaby. *Forgotten Frontiers: A Study of the Spanish Indian Policy of Don Juan Bautista de Anza, Governor of New Mexico 1777–1787*. Norman: University of Oklahoma Press, 1932.

Van Ness, John R. and Christine, eds. *Spanish and Mexican Land Grants in New Mexico and Colorado*. Manhattan, KS: Sunflower University Press, 1980.

Other resources are from the Special Collections Department at Robert Hoag Rawlings Library, including newspaper clippings; photograph collections; archival boxes; oral histories; the *Pueblo Chieftain* newspaper articles; the National Register of Historic Places; and the *Pueblo Lore*, a journal published by the Pueblo County Historical Society.